MODERN BRITISH PLAYWRITING: THE 1990s

VOICES, DOCUMENTS, NEW INTERPRETATIONS

Aleks Sierz FRSA is Visiting Professor at Rose Bruford College, and author of *In-Yer-Face Theatre: British Drama Today* (Faber, 2001), *The Theatre of Martin Crimp* (Methuen Drama, 2006), *John Osborne's Look Back in Anger* (Continuum, 2008) and most recently *Rewriting the Nation: British Theatre Today* (Methuen Drama, 2011). He also works as a journalist, broadcaster, lecturer and theatre critic.

D0144874

in the same series from Methuen Drama:

MODERN BRITISH PLAYWRITING: THE 1950s
by David Pattie
Includes detailed studies of works by T. S. Eliot, Terence Rattigan, John Osborne and Arnold Wesker

MODERN BRITISH PLAYWRITING: THE 1960s
by Steve Nicholson
Includes detailed studies of works by John Arden, Edward Bond, Harold Pinter and Alan Ayckbourn

MODERN BRITISH PLAYWRITING: THE 1970s
by Chris Megson
Includes detailed studies of works by Caryl Churchill, David Hare, Howard Brenton and David Edgar

MODERN BRITISH PLAYWRITING: THE 1980s
by Jane Milling
Includes detailed studies of works by Howard Barker, Jim Cartwright, Sarah Daniels and Timberlake Wertenbaker

MODERN BRITISH PLAYWRITING: 2000–2009
by Dan Rebellato
Includes detailed studies of works by David Greig, Simon Stephens, debbie tucker green, Tim Crouch and Roy Williams

MODERN BRITISH PLAYWRITING: THE 1990s

VOICES, DOCUMENTS, NEW INTERPRETATIONS

Aleks Sierz

Series Editors: Richard Boon and Philip Roberts

Methuen Drama

Methuen Drama

1 3 5 7 9 10 8 6 4 2

First published in Great Britain in 2012 by Methuen Drama

Methuen Drama, an imprint of Bloomsbury Publishing Plc

Methuen Drama
Bloomsbury Publishing Plc
50 Bedford Square
London WC1B 3DP
www.methuendrama.com

Copyright © 2012 by Aleks Sierz

General Preface copyright © 2012 Richard Boon and Philip Roberts
'Sarah Kane' copyright © 2012 Catherine Rees
'Anthony Neilson' copyright © 2012 Trish Reid
'Mark Ravenhill' copyright © 2012 Graham Saunders
Vesper copyright © 2012 Philip Ridley
'A Tear in the Fabric' copyright © 2004, 2012 by Mark Ravenhill

The rights of the author and contributors to be identified as the authors of this work have
been asserted by them in accordance with the Copyright, Design and Patents Act, 1988

Paperback ISBN: 978 1 408 12926 5
Hardback ISBN: 978 1 408 18133 1

A CIP catalogue record for this book is available from the British Library

Available in the USA from Bloomsbury Academic & Professional, 175 Fifth Avenue /3rd
Floor, New York, NY 10010. www.BloomsburyAcademicUSA.com

Typeset by Mark Heslington Ltd, Scarborough, North Yorkshire
Printed and bound in the UK by MPG Books Ltd, Bodmin, Cornwall

Caution
This book is sold subject to the condition that it shall not, by way of trade or
otherwise, be lent, resold, hired out, or otherwise circulated in any form of binding
or cover other than that in which it is published and without a similar condition,
including this condition, being imposed on the subsequent purchaser.

All rights reserved. No part of this publication may be reproduced in any form or by
any means – graphic, electronic or mechanical, including photocopying, recording,
taping or information storage and retrieval systems – without the written permission
of Bloomsbury Publishing Plc.

This book is produced using paper that is made from wood grown in managed,
sustainable forests. It is natural, renewable and recyclable. The logging and manufacturing
processes conform to the environmental standards of the country of origin.

CONTENTS

GENERAL PREFACE

This book is one of a series of six volumes which seek to characterise the nature of modern British playwriting from the 1950s to the end of the first decade of this new century. The work of these six decades is comparable in its range, experimentation and achievement only to the drama of the Elizabethan and Jacobean dramatists. The series chronicles its flowering and development.

Each volume addresses the work of four representative dramatists (five in the *2000–2009* volume) by focusing on key works and by placing that work in a detailed contextual account of the theatrical, social, political and cultural climate of the era.

The series revisits each decade from the perspective of the twenty-first century. We recognise that there is an inevitable danger of imposing a spurious neatness on its subject. So while each book focuses squarely on the particular decade and its representative authors, we have been careful to ensure that some account is given of relevant material from earlier years and, where relevant, of subsequent developments. And while the intentions and organisation of each volume are essentially the same, we have also allowed for flexibility, the better to allow both for the particular demands of the subject and the particular approach of our author/editors.

It is also the case, of course, that differences of historical perspective across the series influence the nature of the books. For student readers, the difference at its most extreme is between a present they daily inhabit and feel they know intimately and a decade (the 1950s) in which their parents or even grandparents might have been born; between a time of seemingly unlimited consumer choice and one which began with post-war food rationing still in place. Further, a playwright who began work in the late 1960s (David Hare, say) has a far bigger body of work and associated scholarship than one whose emergence has come within the last decade or so (debbie tucker green, for example). A glance at the Bibliographies for the earliest and latest volumes quickly reveals huge differences in the range of secondary material available to our authors and to our readers. This inevitably means that the later volumes allow a greater space to their contributing essayists for original research and scholarship, but we have also actively encouraged revisionist perspectives – new looks – on the 'older guard' in earlier books.

So while each book can and does stand alone, the series as a whole offers as coherent and comprehensive a view of the whole era as possible.

Throughout, we have had in mind two chief objectives. We have made accessible information and ideas that will enable today's students of theatre to acquaint themselves with the nature of the world inhabited by the playwrights of the last sixty years; and we offer new, original and often surprising perspectives on both established and developing dramatists.

Richard Boon and Philip Roberts
Series Editors
September 2011

Richard Boon is Professor of Drama and Director of Research at the University of Hull

Philip Roberts is Emeritus Professor of Drama and Theatre Studies at the University of Leeds

ACKNOWLEDGEMENTS

My main thanks goes to my partner Lia Ghilardi, who helped me at every stage of this book. I would also like to thank the series editors, Richard Boon and Philip Roberts, for their original vision, professional guidance and excellent advice. Likewise, I am extremely grateful for all kinds of help to my publisher Mark Dudgeon at Methuen Drama, and to the members of his staff: especially Ross Fulton, Charlotte Loveridge, Helen Flood, Chris Parker and Neil Dowden. My guest contributors – Catherine Rees, Trish Reid and Graham Saunders – delivered their superb chapters on time, and responded to my editorial suggestions with unfailing good humour. Especially helpful in assembling the Documents section was my fellow series author Dan Rebellato, and grateful thanks should also go to Simon Kane, Mel Kenyon, Anthony Neilson, Mark Ravenhill and Philip Ridley. I am also indebted to Cath Badham, Michael Blyth, Keith Bruce, David Greig, Sarah Jane Marr and Simon Trussler. Thanks guys!

Aleks Sierz, London, July 2011

INTRODUCTION: LIVING IN THE 1990s

Nastasja One day. I'll tell you the story of my life. I'll write it for a play and they'll make it into a worldwide film.
— David Greig, *The Cosmonaut's Last Message to the Woman He Once Loved in the Former Soviet Union*, 1999

Background

At the start of Jonathan Coe's novel *The Rotters' Club*, two young people, Sophie and Patrick, meet in a restaurant, and she asks him to imagine how different the past is. For her, Britain in the 1970s was:

> Completely different. Just think of it! A world without mobiles or videos or Playstations or even faxes. A world that had never heard of Princess Diana or Tony Blair, never thought for a moment of going to war in Kosovo or Afghanistan. There were only three television channels in those days Patrick. Three! And the unions were so powerful that, if they wanted to, they could close one of them down for a whole night. Sometimes people even had to do without electricity. Imagine![1]

Although it is easier to imagine the 1990s than the 1970s, today's Sophies and Patricks might also find it strange to imagine a world without the iPhone, iPod, Facebook, Twitter, Skype, Wikipedia, Kindle, Nintendo DS, audio downloads or MacBook Air laptop. At the very start of the decade, the digital revolution was nowhere to be seen, the driving forces behind Britpop (Noel Gallagher or Damon Albarn) were unknown teenagers and British theatre was seen as in crisis. In global terms, the terrible genocides in Rwanda and Bosnia hadn't yet happened, China was not yet a major economic player and Saddam Hussein seemed containable; very few people had heard of Osama bin Laden. In British politics, John Major was prime minister, Tony Blair was a minor politician and New Labour hadn't been invented yet. David Cameron was still working as a junior researcher in the Conservative Research Department after leaving Oxford University. Other, less privileged, students didn't have to pay tuition fees. So the 1990s are already something of a foreign country, whose inhabitants did things differently.

1. Everyday life[2]

Family life
The traditional family is dead, killed off by cohabitation and divorce.

- In 1999, only about 200,000 first marriages take place in the UK, with average age at first marriage twenty-eight for women and thirty for men. Cohabitation increases, with 1.5 million or 15 per cent of all couples cohabiting. Unmarried motherhood rockets, with the highest rate in Europe of children born outside marriage.
- 73 per cent of households are composed of heterosexual couples (1996).
- 9 per cent of households with children are headed by lone parents (1996).
- Britain has the highest divorce rate in Europe.
- The life expectancy of children born in 1999 is seventy-five years for boys and eighty years for girls.
- There are 4,400 Britons more than 100 years old (1991).
- The UK has the highest rate of teenage pregnancies in Europe.
- The average man or woman has sex once a week.

Housing: governments promote private home ownership, but few new homes are built. Repossessions of homes, due to failure to keep up mortgage payments in the economic recession, reach peaks of 75,500 and 68,500 in 1991–2.

More than 80 per cent of homes have central heating, fridges, freezers, washing machines and telephones.

Car ownership reaches 70 per cent.

Most common cause of death: cancer and heart disease.

Work life

The average weekly wage is £400 (1999).

The most striking trend is the decline of the traditional family model of male breadwinner and dependent wife, with the rise of the two-earner family. Part-time work is more common, with about two-fifths of mothers in part-time jobs.

In 1992, unemployment reaches 2.6 million.

In 1994, 53 per cent of women are economically active.

Work

Work is a curse, but the alternative is purgatorial. In the 1990s, there is a polarisation between work-rich and work-poor households, between those with two earners and others with none. There's a rapid rise in inequality and poverty: in the early 1990s, about one Briton in six lives in poverty. Child poverty grows, with 4.4 million children – one-third – living in poor households in the late 1990s. The number of low-income workers peaks at 20 per cent of the workforce in 1992. For about one in ten couples with children, neither parent is employed, and these families are a sharp contrast to two-earner couples. Only half of single mothers are employed. Many rely on social security benefits.

North–South divide: Londoners earn 50 per cent more than equivalent workers in the North East. The South East has the highest proportion of people earning £50,000 or more.

In 1995, the Joseph Rowntree Foundation report on income and wealth shows that inequality in Britain is worse than it has been for fifty years, and the gap between rich and poor is growing faster than in any other Western country.

By 1999, just over half the population describe themselves as middle class, and about 40 per cent as working class.

Women average 75 per cent of men's earnings.

We need employment, which requires more capital stock and higher investment, which will be the most effective instrument for the social objective of bringing the marginalised back into the fold. And that in turn will involve the redistribution of income.

– Will Hutton, *The State We're In*
(London: Vintage, 1996, rev. edn), p. 24

Things we bought
Braun alarm clock, Dyson hoover, IKEA furniture, Bondi Blue iMac personal computer, red AIDS ribbon, Sony Playstation, bottle of Evian water, thong, combat trousers, Cazal sunglasses, paperback of Philip Pullman's *Northern Lights*, Aeron office chair, Ecstasy pills, Jimmy Choo shoes, Wonder bra, Nokia mobile phone, poppers, Nintendo Gameboy, *Big Issue* magazine, cyclist anti-smog mask, Poundland bargain, Agent Provocateur lingerie, ethical knitted hat, Reebok pumps, plastic cartoon lunchbox, rollerblades.

Things we said
As if, bad hair day, bitch, chill out, don't go there, eat my shorts, get over it, mother of all, not!, OMG, so, talk to the hand, wassup?, whatever, wicked, wig out, yo.

Words we made up
Afro-Saxons, bling, booze-cruise, chick-flick, crib, cyber, diss, dotcom, email, fairtrade, feminazis, Futon Man, gastro-pub, himbo, homeboy, hottie, job seeker, metrosexual, minger, mockney, morph, on-message, phat, pimping, regime change, slacker, Y2K.

What things cost
Cappuccino in Costa coffee shop (London, 1998)	£1
First-class postage stamp (1999)	26p
The Times newspaper (1999)	35p
Pint of beer (1999)	£1.73

Pint of milk (1999)	26p
Dozen eggs (London, 1999)	£1.57
Average West End theatre ticket (1995)	£28
Average price of a new house (1992)	about £70,000
Average price of a new house (1999)	about £112,000

Society

Dysfunctional family: although Princess Diana, wife of Prince Charles (heir to the throne), is an international superstar celebrity, all is not well with the Royal Family. At the end of 1992, Queen Elizabeth II laments that she has had an *annus horribilis*. You can see Her Maj's point. Look at the marriage problems of her kids: in March, her son Prince Andrew separates from his wife Sarah, known as 'Fergie'. In April, the Queen's daughter Princess Anne divorces her husband Mark Phillips. In June, Andrew Morton's startlingly frank *Diana: Her True Story* is published. In November, Windsor Castle, a royal residence, is damaged by fire. In December, Charles and Diana separate. In 1996, they divorce, as do Andrew and Fergie. When Princess Diana dies in a car crash on 31 August 1997, the Queen's perceived indifference causes a crisis in public support for the monarchy.

Bad cops: on 22 April 1993, black teenager Stephen Lawrence is stabbed to death by a gang of white racists. The police fail to secure evidence for a conviction despite the arrest of five suspects. A public inquiry in 1999, headed by Sir William Macpherson, concludes that the Metropolitan Police Force is 'institutionally racist'. The phrase haunts race relations.

Child murder: on 12 February 1993, two ten-year-old boys, Robert Thompson and Jon Venables, abduct and murder the toddler Jamie Bulger in Liverpool. The grainy CCTV footage of the boys taking their victim from a shopping centre becomes a symbol of social anomie, and the allegation that the two boys had watched a horror movie video, *Child's Play 3* (1991), sparks a debate about violence in film. The most notorious murder of the decade.

Devilish problem: on 27 February 1991, nine children suspected of being sexually abused by their families are removed by social services on the remote island of South Ronaldsay in Orkney. The suspicion is that a satanic abuse paedophile ring is involved, but no evidence is ever discovered, and the children eventually return to their families. But fear of abuse pervades society.

Because I got high: on 16 November 1995, Leah Betts, a schoolgirl from Essex, dies after taking an Ecstasy pill. Although her death is due to drinking too much water, it kick starts a moral panic about drugs. A poster campaign uses her photograph, with the headline 'Sorted: Just One Ecstasy Tablet Took Leah Betts'. In 1998, a European Commission report says that a higher proportion of teenagers and adults take drugs in the UK than in other EU countries. Drug references permeate culture.

Crime and punishment: under the Conservative government, in 1993, Home Secretary Michael Howard announces that 'prison works' and favours a tough approach: the prison population rises to 50,000. Tony Blair, opposition Home Secretary in 1992, prefers a more nuanced approach encapsulated in the soundbite: 'tough on crime, tough on the causes of crime'. But the prison population continues to rise under New Labour. Because of an improving economy, crime falls by 10 per cent in 1995–9. Despite this, popular culture remains fascinated by criminals.

Terror old and new: in 1991, the Guildford Four, the Maguire Seven and the Birmingham Six – convicted as IRA terrorists in the 1970s – all have their sentences quashed by the High Court after it emerges that police tampered with evidence in the original trials. Although most people in the UK are preoccupied with acts of violence by the IRA, a new terrorist enemy arrives: in 1993, the World Trade Center in New York is hit by an Islamic terrorist, Ramzi Yousef, with a truck bomb that kills six people; in 1998, the bombing of US embassies in Dar es Salaam (Tanzania) and Nairobi (Kenya) by Al-Qaeda results in 300 deaths.

Money never sleeps: in 1994, Lloyd's – the world's largest insurance broker – faces heavy loses following court rulings in the USA which makes it liable for payouts for asbestosis sufferers whose claims go back for decades. The Lloyd's Names – private individuals who agreed to take on insurance risk liabilities in return for profits from premiums – go bankrupt. Lloyd's itself is almost destroyed by the payouts.

Gay life: in 1991, actor Sir Ian McKellen visits Downing Street to discuss laws about gays. In 1994, the age of consent for gay men is reduced from twenty-one to eighteen (the age for heterosexuals remains sixteen). During the decade, there is an increasing acceptance of people living a gay lifestyle. Certainly, there is a much greater visibility for gays (including lesbians), with 'gay villages' in areas such as Soho, London, and many more representations of gays in the media, especially on television.

Race and religion: Britain is mainly white and mainly secular. In 1994, ethnic-minority groups make up 5.5 per cent of the UK population and 20 per cent of London's population. Half of the ethnic-minority population is UK born. In 1992, 6.4 million people attend a Christian church (Anglican, Roman Catholic, Presbyterian, etc.), 15 per cent of the total population, the lowest attendance in Europe; there are 500,000 Muslims, 270,000 Sikhs and 140,000 Hindus.

Domestication of porn: the growth of the internet makes pornography widely available. Likewise, television channels, such as Channel 4 and the new Channel 5, screen more programmes about porn. Channel 5 in particular becomes notorious for broadcasting programmes such as *UK Raw*, *Compromising Situations* and *Sex and Shopping*.

Careless community: in 1990, the Conservative government institutes a system of 'Community Care' for mental patients. The policy is meant to enable them to stay in their own homes. Without adequate supervision, however, many become increasingly vulnerable, a danger to themselves and to others. For example, in December 1992,

7

Jonathan Zito is killed by Christopher Clunis, a paranoid schizo-phrenic, at Finsbury Park underground station.

Trauma and survival: bad news dominates the media. The Bosnian civil war introduces the horrific concept of ethnic cleansing (geno-cide), and the experience of post-traumatic stress disorder becomes more familiar. Although this condition usually refers to soldiers who have survived battle, it is also applied to domestic abuse victims.

Help yourself: self-help books, which offer suggestions for various ways of improving your life, become increasingly popular. They aim to boost self-esteem and make you feel better. Examples include Paul Wilson's *The Little Book of Calm* (1999), Rachel Swift's *Women's Pleasure: or How to Have an Orgasm as Often as You Want* (1994) and John Gray's *Men are from Mars, Women are from Venus* (1992). Such bestsellers are part of a trend towards a more therapy-oriented society, and suggest an acceptance of New Age philosophy, a yearning for spir-itual meaning. For those with a more immediate need to counter the blues, there is always Prozac.

2. Education[3]

Evidence shows the UK lagging behind other countries. To improve basic skills, such as literacy and numeracy, the standardised National Curriculum in secondary schools is further developed, and New Labour introduces literacy and numeracy hours in primary schools to help raise standards. Secondary schooling is compulsory until the age of sixteen, but compared to other European countries fewer pupils stay on after that age. For students, 1998 is the decisive date: New Labour introduces tuition fees payable by students as a way of raising money for expanding higher education. Scottish students at Scottish universities are exempt. In universities, postmodernism and poststructuralism remain the most important academic systems of thought and analysis.

Education, education, education.
– Tony Blair's three top priorities, 1996

3. Media[4]

Television

The decade's new sitcoms follow the 1980s trend of more anarchic and eccentric ideas, notable examples being *Absolutely Fabulous, Men Behaving Badly, The Royle Family, Drop the Dead Donkey, The Vicar of Dibley, Father Ted, Knowing Me, Knowing You with Alan Partridge, One Foot in the Grave* and *The League of Gentlemen*. From the USA come *Friends, Frasier, Seinfeld, The Simpsons* and *South Park*.

The most popular television dramas are nostalgic frock-flicks: for example, the BBC adaptation of Jane Austen's *Pride and Prejudice* (1995) features Colin Firth as Mr Darcy in a famous wet-shirt moment. Epic series about society, such as Peter Flannery's *Our Friends in the North* (BBC2, 1996), are also popular, as well as docudramas such as *Hillsborough* (ITV, 1996) and political thrillers like *House of Cards* (BBC1, 1990). The sex lives of law graduates are explored using innovative camera techniques in *This Life* (BBC2, 1996). There are two gripping police series: *Cracker* (ITV, 1993), about a police psychologist played by Robbie Coltrane; and *Prime Suspect* (ITV, 1991), about a female detective played by Helen Mirren. By contrast, Nick Park's animated thirty-minute films, featuring Wallace and Gromit, bring smiles to the faces of adults as well as children. The most popular game show is *Who Wants To Be a Millionaire?* (ITV, 1998) and a notable comedy quiz show is *Have I Got News for You* (BBC2, 1990).

On 30 March 1997, Channel 5, the fifth terrestrial television channel, is launched. Soon it becomes a byword for substandard tabloid television.

A decade of Channel 4 (the most provocative channel):

- 1992: on *The Word*, Shabba Ranks, a Jamaican rapper, argues that gays should be crucified.
- 1993: *Brookside*, a soap opera, shows a lesbian kiss before the watershed time of 9 p.m.
- 1994: *Brass Eye*, a satirical spoof documentary by Chris Morris, fools celebrities into supporting absurd causes. In one episode, public figures warn of the dangers of Cake, a fictitious drug.

- 1994: On 5 April, during the last interview of terminally ill playwright Dennis Potter three months before his death, he says he has nicknamed his cancer Rupert, after the global media tycoon Rupert Murdoch.
- 1999: *Queer as Folk* is a gobsmackingly explicit series about gays living in Manchester.

Film

The decade is dominated by Hollywood cinema, with an emphasis on violent shoot-'em-ups and special effects.

- *Titanic* (1997), directed by James Cameron using innovative digital technology, is the most successful film of the decade, grossing almost $2 billion worldwide.
- Disney's *The Lion King* (1994) is the highest-grossing animated film. A musical, based on the film and directed by Julie Taymor with music by Elton John, premieres in the USA in 1997. London version opens in 1999.
- Quentin Tarantino, who makes *Reservoir Dogs* (1992), *Pulp Fiction* (1994) and *Jackie Brown* (1997), is the most controversial American director because of his use of stylised violence.
- One of the most iconic actors is Arnold Schwarzenegger, the protagonist of the dystopic *Terminator 2: Judgment Day* (1991), directed by James Cameron, a sequel to his *Terminator* (1984).

Brits in Hollywood: Oscar-winning best films include *The Silence of the Lambs* (Anthony Hopkins as serial killer Hannibal Lecter, 1991); *The English Patient* (Anthony Minghella's version of Michael Ondaatje's book, 1996); *Shakespeare in Love* (co-written by Tom Stoppard, 1998) and *American Beauty* (Sam Mendes's suburban drama, 1999).

Memorable British films: British films love historical and literary themes, and contemporary social issues. Most notable Shakespeare adaptation: *Much Ado About Nothing* (Kenneth Branagh, 1993).

Adaptations of plays: *Shadowlands* (William Nicholson, 1993); *Tom & Viv* (Michael Hastings, 1994); *The Browning Version* (Terence Rattigan, 1994); *The Madness of King George* (Alan Bennett, 1995); *Beautiful Thing* (Jonathan Harvey, 1996), *Little Voice* (Jim Cartwright, 1998), *The Winslow Boy* (Rattigan, 1999) and *East is East* (Ayub Khan-Din, 1999).

Adaptations of novels: *Howards End* (1992); *The Remains of the Day* (1993); *Sense and Sensibility* (1995); *Trainspotting* (1996); *Fever Pitch* (1997); *The End of the Affair* (1999).

Brit rom-coms: the Richard Curtis-written *Four Weddings and a Funeral* (1994) and *Notting Hill* (1999).

Historical films: *Land and Freedom* (1995); *Mrs Brown* (1997); *Elizabeth* (1998), *Topsy-Turvy* (1999).

Contemporary films: Stephen Poliakoff's *Close My Eyes* (1991); Danny Boyle's *Shallow Grave* (1994) and *Trainspotting* (1996); Mike Leigh's *Naked* (1995) and *Secrets & Lies* (1996); Ken Loach's *Ladybird Ladybird* (1994) and *My Name is Joe* (1998). *Brassed Off* (1996) and *The Full Monty* (1997) explored northern life.

Gangster films: *The Krays* (Philip Ridley, 1990) and *Lock, Stock and Two Smoking Barrels* (Guy Ritchie, 1998).

Newspapers
The *Sun* entertains and appals:
- Most famous headline on the day of the 1992 General Election: 'If Kinnock Wins Today, Will the Last Person to Leave Britain Please Turn Out the Lights'. Two days later The *Sun* boasts that it helped elect the Conservatives: 'It's the Sun Wot Won It.'
- In 1994–6, The *Sun*'s circulation peaks. Highest sale is in the week ending 16 July 1994, when the average daily figure is 4,306,000. The highest ever one-day sale is on 18 November 1995 (4,889,118), helped by cut cover-price of 10p.

- The *Sun* switches support to New Labour in March 1997, six weeks before the landslide General Election victory of Tony Blair.
- Other headlines include 'Up Yours Delors' (1 November 1990), attacking the French EU commissioner Jacques Delors, who promotes the euro currency, and 'It's Paddy Pantsdown' (6 February 1992), mocking Paddy Ashdown, leader of the Liberal Democrats, for having an affair with his secretary.

Other news
- 1990: first issue of the *Independent on Sunday*.
- 1990: on 11 May, tycoon Robert Maxwell launches the *European* (closes in 1998).
- 1991: on 5 November, Maxwell dies in a yachting accident.
- 1992: *Punch*, the UK's oldest magazine (1841), closes.
- 1993: the Guardian Media Group acquires the *Observer*.
- 1995: on 17 November, the *Today* newspaper stops publication (the first national newspaper to fail since the *Daily Sketch* in 1971).
- 1999: the *Sunday Herald* newspaper is launched in Glasgow.
- The *Independent* runs into deep financial problems, which prove intractable to editors Andrew Marr and Rosie Boycott. They soon quit. The *Indie* staggers on.
- Local newspapers all around the country are in steady decline.

Magazines: as well as celebrity gossip, the most popular magazines of the 1990s are lads' mags, such as *Maxim*, *Loaded* and *FHM*. They help to create a culture of laddism – in 1993 journalist Sean O'Hagan coined the term 'New Lad' in *Arena* magazine, which involves middle-class men ironically posing as sexist, anti-intellectual beer-swilling brutes. Such magazines specialise in images of semi-naked women, plus articles on other traditional male interests such as sport and cars. This is all evidence for those who see masculinity in crisis as being one of the themes of this decade.

Fashion

Designers create 'softer' fashions that are more relaxed than the 1980s look. Casual fashion sports T-shirts, combat trousers and chinos, while street fashion is influenced by hip-hop culture and characterised by baggy jeans, hooded sweatshirts, football jerseys and puffy jackets. Clothing fads include pre-ripped jeans, Ninja Turtles items, headbands and Reebok trainers. Retro styles, influenced by the 1960s and 1970s, abound. High designer fashion becomes increasingly diverse: for example, a Paul Smith suit mixes flamboyant patchwork fabrics from Afghanistan with 1950s tailoring, while a Helen Storey ensemble mixes modern street and sportswear influences with ethnic-inspired embroidery. Doc Martens boots, 1980s symbol of the well-hard individual, make a comeback, often in stylish new colours. In advertising, 'heroin chic' – the use of thin, druggy-looking models – becomes a controversial issue. Body piercing and tattooing become increasingly popular.

Comedy

The spirit of alternative comedy, which boomed in the 1980s, lives on – it is hyped as 'the new rock'n'roll'. This entertainment includes irreverent jokes, dark humour, observational comedy and political satire – most of which now find their niche in the mainstream. Double acts dominate televised comedy: Reeves and Mortimer (Vic Reeves and Bob Mortimer), Punt and Dennis (Steve Punt and Hugh Dennis), Newman and Baddiel (Robert Newman and David Baddiel) and Skinner and Baddiel (Frank Skinner). Newcomers include Graham Norton, Bill Bailey, Jack Dee, Angus Deayton, Sacha Baron Cohen and Harry Hill. Caroline Aherne introduces us to her Mrs Merton character in 1994 and then writes, with Craig Cash, *The Royle Family*, in which she also appears. Armando Iannucci's *On the Hour* on radio and *The Day Today* on television introduce a new sense of the ludicrous. On the radio, Jeremy Hardy's satire is fuelled by his radical beliefs. *The Fast Show* (TV) is an influential quickfire television show, while *Goodness Gracious Me*, with Meera Syal and Sanjeev Bhaskar, explores the Asian experience of British life.

Celebrity culture

Although glamour has always been part of society, in the 1990s the public obsession with celebrities plumbs new depths. Following the creation of *Hello!* magazine in 1988, soon followed by imitators such as *OK!* (1993), celebrity journalism booms as the rich and famous invite journalists into their homes. Saccharine articles inevitably follow. Royalty, film stars, television stars, pop stars and football stars are the main focus of attention: examples include Princess Diana, David Beckham and his wife, Victoria (formerly Posh Spice). Yet some celebrities are simply famous for being famous. But if much media coverage presents a sunny view of celebrity culture, this is equalled in popularity by a tabloid fascination with their divorces. Nor is the traditional media left out: in 1995, Princess Diana appears on the BBC's *Panorama* and tells all about the break-up of her marriage. In celebrity culture, the figure of the paparazzo (usually acting in a pack of paparazzi) looms large as a hate figure, whose intrusive lens provides the material for mass ogling of the famous. The death of Princess Diana in a high-speed crash in Paris while her car was being chased by paparazzi sums up the symbiosis between media and celebrity tragedy.

4. Culture[5]

Cool Britannia

The term 'Cool Britannia' is a media-inspired label which celebrates the creativity of British culture in the mid-1990s, acting as both tourist magnet and cultural boosterism. In 1996, *Newsweek* magazine calls London the 'coolest city on the planet', and the idea of 'Cool Britannia' brings together pop music, art, film, theatre, fashion and even eating out, hyping up national pride, exemplified by the use of the Union Jack to decorate the guitars of musicians or the clothes of celebrities. Examples of this phenomenon include Britpop, the YBAs, Brit films and new plays by young playwrights. Tony Blair – who once played in a band – cashes in on 'Cool Britannia' by hosting pop stars and other creatives at Downing Street. Because this phenomenon is London-based, other parts of the UK come up with their own brands of cultural revival, with Cool Caledonia for Scotland and Cool Cymru for Wales.

Music

Pop is dominated by boy bands and girl bands, characterised by catchy songs, choreographed dancing and a carefully constructed

14

image. Manager Nigel Martin-Smith creates Take That, while Louis Walsh creates East 17. Producer Simon Cowell manages Westlife, also created by Walsh. Take That features Gary Barlow, Howard Donal, Mark Owen, Jason Orange and Robbie Williams. Formed in Manchester in 1990, they sell more than 25 million records in 1991–6, especially their album *Everything Changes* (1993). Robbie Williams leaves in 1995 to pursue a solo career.

The most phenomenal of the girl bands is the Spice Girls, formed in 1994 by Heart Management. Band members Victoria Beckham, Melanie Brown, Emma Brunton, Melanie Chisholm and Geri Halliwell take on marketable identities as Posh, Scary (Mel B), Baby, Sporty (Mel C) and Ginger. In June 1996, they release their debut single 'Wannabe', and their first album *Spice* sells 25 million copies worldwide. In 1997, comes *Spiceworld: The Movie*. Their massive success make them iconic figures of 1990s pop culture. Geri Halliwell's Union Flag dress becomes a symbol of 'Cool Britannia', and the concept of 'Girl Power' helps to define the decade. In 1998, Halliwell leaves the group.

- 1992: Suede's 'The Drowners' and Blur's 'Popscene' signal the start of Britpop.
- 1993: Blur's *Modern Life is Rubbish*.
- 1994: Oasis's *Definitely Maybe*; Blur's *Parklife*.
- 1995: Oasis's *What's the Story (Morning Glory?)*; Blur's *The Great Escape*; Pulp's *Different Class*.
- 1996: Spice Girls' 'Wannabe'.

Britpop

As a reaction to the inauthenticity of boy bands and girl bands, Britpop develops in the indie (independent) music scene and changes pop culture. Guitar groups such as Blur, Oasis and Pulp are influenced by 1960s pop such as the Beatles and Kinks. Britpop bands also create their music as a reaction against American grunge music, which is popular at the start of the 1990s. Other Britpop bands include Suede, Supergrass, Sleeper, Menswear and Elastica. Liam Gallagher of Oasis becomes a tabloid celebrity for his bad-boy antics. In 1995, a chart battle between Blur's 'Country House' and Oasis's 'Roll with It' is labelled 'The Battle of

Britpop' by music magazines such as *NME* (Blur won by selling 274,000 to Oasis's 216,000). Britpop declines after Oasis's *Be Here Now* (1997) album flops. Attention shifts to bands such as The Verve, Radiohead, Travis and Coldplay.

- Prodigy's 1997 single 'Smack My Bitch Up' causes controversy because of its lyrics.
- American teenager Britney Spears releases 'Baby One More Time' and 'Oops I Did It Again!', helping to revive teen pop.
- Dance band D:Ream's 1994 hit 'Things Can Only Get Better' becomes the New Labour 1997 election anthem. (Off-the-wall: the band's ex-members include media physicist Professor Brian Cox, who played keyboards while studying.)

Clubbing

Following the Acid House parties of the late 1980s, clubbing and dance culture boom. Super clubs such as Ministry of Sound, the Laser Dome, the Fridge and Hippodrome in London (plus cool spots such as Helter Skelter in Manchester and Cream in Liverpool) are led by star DJs playing a variety of dance music. Alongside this, Rave culture, with its joyously illegal warehouse parties and Ecstasy-fuelled all-nighters/long-weekenders, is attacked by the media for its illicit drug use and unlicensed venues, and this results in the Criminal Justice and Public Order Act of 1994, which empowers police to stop such events. Abroad, Ibiza is a favourite holiday venue where clubbers of all countries unite. Many 1990s plays contain references to this clubbing culture and drug use.

Books
Ten memorable bestsellers:
Andrew Morton, *Diana: Her True Story* (candid royal biography).
Helen Fielding, *Bridget Jones's Diary* (humorous year in the life of a thirtysomething).
Bill Bryson, *Notes from a Small Island* (humorous travel book by American author).
Nick Hornby, *Fever Pitch* (autobiography of a football fan).
Joanna Trollope, *The Rector's Wife* (witty account of Anna's rebellion).

Andy McNab, *Bravo Two Zero* (behind-the-lines SAS patrol in Gulf War).

Stephen Hawking, *A Brief History of Time* (theoretical physicist's view of cosmos).

Louis de Bernières, *Captain Corelli's Mandolin* (Second World War love story).

J. K. Rowling, *Harry Potter and the Philosopher's Stone* (fantasy set in Hogwarts School of Witchcraft and Wizardry).

Sue Townsend, *The Queen and I* (Royal Family on a council estate).

American imports

One of the most influential kinds of literature is a new generation of young American writers called the 'blank generation'. Their writing is characterised by its detached coolness and a tone that feels flat, affectless and atonal, with offhand narrative voices describing urban life, violence, sex, drugs and consumerism. In these novels, awful things happen, but they leave the writers apparently unfazed. A good example is Bret Easton Ellis's *American Psycho* (1991), in which a serial killer recounts the details of his murders with the same sense of distance that he lists the designer clothes worn by himself and his friends. Other examples of this genre include the work of Douglas Coupland, Dennis Cooper, Jay McInerney, Chuck Palahniuk and Tama Janowitz.

Government can never do the work of creating. But it can and must support those who do.

> – Chris Smith, *Creative Britain*
> (London: Faber, 1998), pp. 141–2

Art

Young British Artists: YBAs is the name given to a group of conceptual artists whose notoriety dominates the decade. They include Damien Hirst and Tracey Emin. Many of them are taught at Goldsmith's College, University of London, and their work is exhibited and bought by cultural entrepreneur Charles Saatchi, who promotes the phenomenon of Britart. In 1997, the Royal Academy hosts the *Sensation* exhibition (items from Saatchi's personal collection). It includes Hirst's *The Physical Impossibility of Death in the Mind* *of Someone Living* (shark in formaldehyde) and Emin's *Everyone I Have Ever Slept With* (tent embroidered with names). One work, Marcus Harvey's *Myra* – a picture of Moors murderer Myra Hindley made out of the handprints of children – creates immediate controversy. Another, Chris Ofili's *The Holy Virgin Mary*, causes offence when the exhibits visit New York because it includes porn images and a lump of elephant dung. Other YBAs include Jake and Dinos Chapman, Rachel Whiteread, Sarah Lucas, Sam Taylor-Wood and Steve McQueen.

The Angel of the North: located on a hill overlooking the A1 road in Gateshead, north-east England, Antony Gormley's *The Angel of the North* is an iconic piece of public art. Erected in 1998 and costing £1 million of National Lottery funding, the statue is about twenty metres tall and has a wingspan of fifty metres. Although its initial reception is not enthusiastic, the statue soon becomes an emblem of local pride – in 1998, local football fans pay tribute to Newcastle United footballer Alan Shearer by draping a huge football shirt on the Angel.

The Millennium Dome: the largest building of its type in the world, the Millennium Dome is a huge white marquee designed by architect Richard Rogers and located on the Greenwich Peninsula in London. It is originally the idea of John Major's Conservative government, which wants a distinctive building to celebrate the arrival of the third millennium AD on 1 January 2000. After his election in 1997, Tony Blair hypes up expectations for the project, which opens to the public as The Millennium Experience, a one-year exhibition that lasts for the whole of 2000. It is widely derided. After this, the Dome becomes a white elephant, an empty monument to the hype generated by New Labour, until bought and rebranded as the O2 Arena in 2005.

Sport
Football:
- 1990: on 4 July, Germany beats England in a penalty shoot-out in the World Cup semi-final, held in Italy. Footballer Paul Gascoigne (Gazza) cries and his tears seem to symbolise a more

feeling nation. After this tournament, which is marketed with the song 'Nessun Dorma' (from Puccini's opera *Turandot*) sung by tenor Luciano Pavarotti, football in the UK gets a boost in popular support. The sport now has safer stadiums, and bigger and more mixed crowds.

- 1992: the FA launches new Premier League. Gary Lineker is voted Player of the Year.
- 1993: Paul Ince is the first black man to captain England.
- 1996: in the UEFA Euro 96 competition, Germany beats England in the semi-final after footballer Gareth Southgate fails in the penalty shoot-out.
- 1999: hat trick – in the UEFA Champions League final, Manchester United beats Bayern Munich 2–1, having already won the FA Cup and topped the Premier League in the same 1998–99 season. Manchester United are kings of UK football. In 1995, star player Eric Cantona is fined £20,000 for a kung-fu attack on a spectator.

Other matches:
- Cricket: English cricket is in decline, with many defeats, symbolised by hapless batsman Graeme Hick. Signs of revival in late 1990s under Nasser Hussain's captaincy.
- Tennis: despite the popular following of British star Tim Henman, no male Brit has won the Wimbledon tournament since 1936. Henman is the first player to be disqualified from Wimbledon when in 1995 he strikes a ball in a fit of anger and it hits a ball girl on the head.
- Boxer Lennox Lewis wins the world heavyweight title after defeating Evander Holyfield in 1999.
- Sprinter Linford Christie is the most successful British runner, winning an Olympic gold in 1992 and being the first to break the ten-second barrier for 100 metres. In 1999, Christie is, despite his denials, found guilty of using a performance-enhancing drug and banned for two years.

Travel and leisure

Cheap flights take off. In 1992 the air industry is deregulated by the EU. The winners are low-cost airlines, such as Ryanair and easyJet, which make flying cheap and available to everyone. Air becomes by far the most popular way of travelling.

By 1998, Stansted Airport is handling seven million passengers a year. Europe is the most popular destination (80 per cent of visits abroad). Since 1994, Spain is the most popular country, followed by France. Package trips to the USA become cheaper than trips to British resorts. With falling prices, a second holiday becomes possible, and Thailand, Bali and Australia are now on the map.

Most working people have four weeks' holiday a year and go away for two weeks in July and August. Seaside package holidays abroad are most popular, but more Britons also take a second holiday abroad in the winter (skiing for a week) or spring (short breaks to Europe).

At home, people enjoy various indoor and outdoor activities. The biggest cultural shift is towards home-based leisure. About 99 per cent of households have at least one television, which is the most popular leisure activity with an average viewing time of twenty-five hours per week – half an individual's weekly free time.

By the end of 1993, three million subscribe to satellite television channels. Video watching booms. In 1992, some 70 per cent of households have a video recorder, but only 20 per cent have a home computer. Video games rise relentlessly. But so does reading: for example, sales of books rose by 5 per cent in 1993.

People spend a quarter of their time on socialising with friends, and a little less on sports and hobbies. DIY and gardening are national obsessions.

In the 1990s, beer loses out to wine as the most popular alcoholic drink, with chilled Chardonnay a beverage of choice.

Retail therapy grows in importance.

5. Science, Technology and Industry[6]

Science
- 1990: Englishman Tim Berners-Lee implements the first successful communication between a Hypertext Transfer Protocol (HTTP) client and server via the internet at CERN (European particle physics laboratory) in Switzerland, where he works, leading to the launch of the World Wide Web in 1991.
- 1990: the Human Genome Project, a massive international effort to map the chemicals that make up the sequence of 20–25,000 genes of human beings, begins. By the end of the decade, DNA evidence is being used in criminal prosecutions.
- 1993: the Pentium processor for personal computers invented.
- 1994: Global Positioning System (GPS) becomes fully active.
- 1996: Scottish scientists at Roslin Institute clone the first mammal, a sheep named Dolly. Bioethics soon becomes a big issue.

Test-tube babies: a significant moment in the development of *in vitro* fertilisation (IVF), enabling women to become pregnant by the implantation of fertilised eggs, is the invention of a process for injection of single sperms by André Van Steirteghem in Brussels in 1992. This enables men with minimal sperm production to help achieve pregnancies. Also, the development of IVF using donated eggs helps women with ovulation problems achieve pregnancy.

Pop science: the public is keen on science, and the appetite for science journalism and books aimed at the general reader grows. A good example is Stephen Hawking, a Nobel laureate whose book on cosmology, *A Brief History of Time* (1988), stays in the bestseller lists throughout the 1990s, although it is more often bought than read. Sometimes pop science is intensely political, as when Richard J. Herrnstein and Charles Murray publish *The Bell Curve* (1994), which purports to prove that differences in intelligence between races are genetic in origin.

Technology

The digital revolution

The digital revolution has a huge impact on everyday life. In 1991 the World Wide Web is made available via the internet and by the middle of the decade everyone knows about it. For many people, their first experience is through a slow dial-up connection to send and receive emails. In 1994, the first internet café opens, and, in the following year, eBay and Amazon are started. The ability to create individual websites fires the expansion of the internet in the late 1990s. By 2000, 40 per cent of British households own a personal computer and access the internet. In general, the use of personal computers increases and mobile phones become widely available for the first time. Internet and mobile phones immediately speed up personal communications and various forms of human interactivity: with mobile phones, parents are able to better monitor the movements of their children. The use of text-messaging quickly spreads. During the decade, the use of Microsoft software – especially Windows – and Pentium Intel computers makes these brands household words. Handheld video games such as Nintendo Game Boy and Sega's Sonic the Hedgehog are massively popular. Many businesses find digital transactions easier. However, along with such benefits come new problems: the ability of the state and corporations to accumulate large amounts of information in digital format raises questions about personal privacy. Increased availability of new digital technologies makes older technologies obsolete. So CDs replace audio tapes and gramophone records, and DVDs replace VHS tapes; increased use of mobiles goes with a steady decline in pay phones; digital cameras replace traditional models. Emails gradually replace letter writing and postal communication.

The dotcoms: dotcom companies, which do most of their business on the internet, boom in the late 1990s, mainly funded by venture capitalists but often with poor business plans and wildly inflated expectation of success. A stock-market crash in 2000 ends the dotcom bubble.

Toys: the Tamagotchi, a handheld digital pet made in Japan, is invented in 1996 and the Furby, an electronic furry robot, goes on sale in 1998.

Use of cheque books is down by a quarter and plastic card payments triple. By 1999, almost a million people work in IT-related jobs, a sharp increase.

Industry

Ravenscraig steelworks closes in 1992. Heavy industry, such as steel and coal production, declines. Michael Heseltine, Conservative President of the Board of Trade, closes thirty-one mines with the loss of 30,000 jobs. By 1994, British Coal has only seventeen mines, employing 8,500 miners.

British and French engineers celebrate in 1990 as they meet under the English Channel while building the first tunnel linking the two countries. In 1994, the Chunnel opens, linking London to Paris and Brussels by means of the high-speed Eurostar train.

Farm industry madness: an epidemic of Bovine Spongiform Encephalopathy (BSE), commonly called Mad Cow Disease, begins in the late 1980s and spreads throughout Britain, with thousands of cases each week by 1993. Although the Conservative government at first plays down the problem, with Agriculture Minister John Selwyn Gummer feeding a hamburger to his four-year-old daughter Cordelia in May 1990, the outbreak soon affects thousands of cattle, and about four million are slaughtered. In 1996 it is confirmed that BSE also spreads to humans in the form of Creutzfeldt-Jakob Disease (CJD).

Rail privatisation: in 1993, British Rail, a government-owned railway system, is privatised by the Conservative government. This involves a new complex system of ownership by more than 100 private companies of the railway lines, trains, stations and mainte-nance companies. Despite its initial opposition, New Labour does not reverse the process. A series of horrific rail crashes, beginning at Southall in 1997 and Ladbroke Grove in 1999, and continuing early in the 2000s, are blamed on the cost-cutting involved in the now privately owned railways.

6. Politics[7]

United Kingdom
- 1990: on 22 November, Conservative Prime Minister Margaret Thatcher is forced to resign, soon replaced by John Major, her Chancellor. A two-year economic recession begins, with unemployment more than three million.
- 1991: the Maastricht Treaty, an agreement of European Union countries, is signed. In the UK, this is widely seen as a move towards greater political integration in Europe, and vociferously criticised by many Conservative Party members as a step in the direction of a European 'super-state', and thus an affront to national sovereignty.
- 1992: on 9 April, Major wins the UK general election. Labour leader Neil Kinnock resigns, replaced by John Smith. On 16 September (Black Wednesday), Major's Conservative government is forced to withdraw from the European Exchange Rate Mechanism (ERM). This is a political humiliation because the ERM aimed at harmonising European currencies and the UK's exit is seen as the failure of Major's aspiration to be 'at the heart of Europe'.

Fifty years on from now, Britain will still be the country of long shadows on cricket grounds, warm beer, invincible green suburbs, dog lovers and pools fillers.

– John Major on Britishness

- 1993: Conservative government ratifies the Maastricht Treaty in Parliament, but splits emerge in the party over European policy. Major launches 'Back to basics' campaign, which fails as sexual and financial scandals involving Conservative politicians are revealed. On 15 December, the Downing Street Agreement (a joint declaration by the UK and Irish governments for the self-determination of Northern Ireland) begins the Peace Process aimed at ending some twenty-five years of the Troubles.
- 1994: on 12 May, Labour leader John Smith suddenly dies,

replaced by Tony Blair, the youngest leader of the party. 'Cash for questions' scandal involving corrupt Conservative politicians symbolises the 'sleaze' of the administration. In Northern Ireland, the IRA calls a ceasefire in August as part of the Peace Process, but resumes operations in February 1996 after poor response from the government.

- 1995: in July, Major resigns and challenges the critics in his own Conservative Party to 'put up or shut up': he succeeds in being re-elected as the leader. Nolan Committee on Standards in Public Life publishes its report, calling for full disclosure of MPs' interests.

- 1996: On 15 February, Sir Richard Scott's report into the 'Arms for Iraq' enquiry is published and blames two Conservative government ministers for colluding in the sale of arms to Saddam Hussein by a British company. The IRA bombs the Docklands in London on 9 February and Manchester city centre on 15 June, causing huge damage.

- 1997: on 1 May, general election, Tony Blair elected Prime Minister in New Labour landslide. The government gives more independence to the Bank of England. In July, the IRA calls another ceasefire. On 31 August, death of Princess Diana. A referendum on political devolution in Scotland gets a yes vote; likewise in Wales.

> She was the People's Princess.
> – Tony Blair on Princess Diana

- 1998: On 10 April, the Good Friday Agreement marks an important step forward in the Northern Ireland Peace Process, which includes plans for a devolved assembly. In Scotland and Wales, plans for partially devolved government go ahead. On 15 August, the Omagh car bombing, carried out by the Real IRA, a Republican splinter group, kills twenty-nine people in the worst atrocity of the Troubles.

Wider world

- 1990: on 11 February, Nelson Mandela, leader of the African National Congress, is freed after twenty-seven years imprisonment by the South African Apartheid regime. Lech Walesa, former leader of the Solidarnosc trade union, becomes first President of Poland.

- 1991: in January–February, the Gulf War, during which a UN Coalition force, led by the USA, expels Saddam Hussein's Iraqi forces from Kuwait. In June, Boris Yeltsin elected President of Russia. On 27 December, Soviet Union dissolved; Russian Federation formed. South Africa repeals Apartheid laws. First McDonald's restaurant opens in Beijing.

- 1992: Bosnian War in the former Yugoslavia, a genocidal civil conflict that lasts until 1995. In April, in Los Angeles, riots follow the acquittal of four police officers videotaped beating Rodney King, a black man.

- 1993: Bill Clinton elected President of the USA, with a second term from 1997 to 2001. In Waco, the Branch Davidian cult is besieged by the police in a fifty-day stand-off that ends with the deaths of seventy-five people. World Trade Center bombed.

- 1994: genocide in Rwanda results in some 800,000 deaths. Nelson Mandela elected President of South Africa. O. J. Simpson arrested for murder of his wife Nicole and her boyfriend (acquitted in 1995).

- 1995: Oklahoma City bombing by Timothy McVeigh kills 168, perhaps in retaliation for the Waco siege. Members of the Aum Shinrikyo religious sect kill thirteen people in a deadly sarin gas attack in the Tokyo underground. Israeli Prime Minister Yitzhak Rabin assassinated at a peace rally in Tel Aviv, Israel.

- 1996: In September, the Taliban, a radical Islamist grouping, takes power in Afghanistan.

- 1997: Deng Xiaoping, leader of China, dies. UK returns Hong Kong to China.

- 1998: US President Clinton impeached but acquitted of

perjury after denying that he had had sexual relations with Monica Lewinsky, a White House intern.

I'm going to say this again: I did not have sexual relations with that woman, Miss Lewinsky.

– Bill Clinton

• 1999: On 1 January, the euro currency is introduced in Europe. Yeltsin appoints Vladimir Putin acting President of the Russian Federation. NATO forces attack Serbia in order to force its troops to withdraw from Kosovo.

In the emerging world, the relations between states and groups from different civilizations will not be close and will often be antagonistic. Yet some intercivilizational relations are more conflict prone than others. At the micro level, the most violent fault lines are between Islam and its Orthodox, Hindu, African, and Western Christian neighbors. At the macro level, the dominant division is between the 'West and the rest'.

– Samuel P. Huntington, *The Clash of Civilizations and the Remaking of the World Order*, New York: Simon & Schuster, 1997), p. 183

Liberal principles in economics – the 'free market' – have spread, and have succeeded in producing unprecedented levels of material prosperity.

– Francis Fukuyama, *The End of History and the Last Man* (London: Penguin, 1992), p. xiii

CHAPTER 1
THEATRE IN THE 1990s

Esme I have my life here in this theatre. My life is when the curtain goes up. My work is my life. I understand nothing else.
— David Hare, *Amy's View*, 1997

Background

Fall of the Berlin Wall

One of the key global events that defined the 1990s happened on 9 November 1989, when the Berlin Wall came down. On that date, the Communist East German government announced that all its citizens could visit West Germany, sparking off mass celebrations that signified the end of the Cold War (the worldwide conflict that had savagely divided a democratic and capitalist West from a totalitarian and Communist East since the end of the Second World War in 1945). Following the fall of the Berlin Wall, which had split Germany in two since 1961, the country was reunited on 3 October 1990, while, further east, the Soviet Union disintegrated and finally collapsed in 1991. These massive changes in the geo-political system led to what was widely seen as a New World Order. Some commentators, such as Francis Fukuyama, enthusiastically and prematurely announced the 'End of History' and the triumph of the capitalist system. Fukuyama's pronouncements find an echo in Mark Ravenhill's ironical 1997 play *Faust Is Dead*, in which Alain, the philosopher character, argues not only that history has ended, but also that 'Man is dead'.[1]

New World Order

Instead of a Cold War stand-off between two superpowers, the New World Order consisted of the USA as the one major superpower, while the Soviet Union fragmented into one large country, Russia, and several smaller independent states, such as Georgia and Kazakhstan. Likewise, the collapse of Communist regimes in Eastern Europe changed the political map of the continent. These changes provoked responses such as Howard Brenton and Tariq Ali's *Moscow Gold* (1990), a play about power struggles in the Soviet Union told in a living newspaper style, and Caryl Churchill's *Mad Forest* (1990), about the Romanian revolution which toppled the Communist regime in that country. China remained politically Communist even while its leaders allowed a market economy to flourish. If, elsewhere, the decade started off optimistically, with the freeing of Nelson Mandela and the ending of the Apartheid regime in South Africa, soon local conflicts reasserted themselves. Although some politicians spoke of a peace dividend, what actually happened was a series of small wars which had devastating local effects. The Middle East remained a flashpoint. The first Gulf War, fought by a US-led Coalition against Saddam Hussein, resulted in his expulsion from Kuwait and his containment in Iraq. During the 1990s, the Middle East Peace Process made some progress with the Oslo Accords between Israel and the Palestinians, signed in 1993. But, in Africa, the genocidal conflict in Rwanda in 1994 cost the lives of some 800,000 people. In Afghanistan, the Taliban, a radical Islamist grouping, took power in 1996. In the former Soviet Union, the brutal first Chechen war was fought by separatists in Chechnya who wanted independence from Moscow. In Europe, the Bosnian civil war (which influenced Sarah Kane's *Blasted*) lasted from 1992 to 1995, with horrific casualties and atrocities. As well as Bosnia, there were other problems in Europe. Widespread migration from the developing world and the former Eastern Europe, plus arguments over European political integration in the EU, created social tensions. Alive to these changes, David Edgar examined the new state of the world with *The Shape of the Table* (National, 1990) – which looked at the transition from Communism to capitalism in a fictional East European state – and *Pentecost* (RSC, 1994) – which examined cultural conflict in the new Europe – while David Greig's debut *Europe* (Traverse, 1994) focused on migration and European identity.

Major followed by Blair

In the UK, most of the decade was overshadowed by John Major's Conservative government, which became rapidly unpopular during the economic recession of 1990–1, a downturn costing thousands of people their jobs and their homes. Things got even worse when, after the Maastricht Treaty, the Conservative Party was split by furious arguments over Europe. The government continued Thatcher's policy of privatisation by selling off the railways in 1993, although it refrained from introducing university fees. Despite Major's efforts to promote a nation at ease with itself, his government became mired in sleaze and scandal, creating a climate of cynicism and apathy. On the Labour side, the reforms of the party begun by Neil Kinnock in the 1980s, and alluded to by David Hare in his semi-fictional *Absence of War* (National, 1993), failed to win him the 1992 election, but were continued by Tony Blair, who rebranded the party as 'New Labour'. Dropping the historic Clause Four of the party's constitution (which advocated nationalisation) in 1995, Blair moved the party on to the centre ground of British politics and narrowed the ideological gap between it and the Conservatives. Not everyone welcomed this move: one of the displayed scene titles in Caryl Churchill's *This is a Chair* (Royal Court, 1997) was 'The Labour Party's Slide to the Right'. In 1997, Blair was elected prime minister in a spectacular landslide victory. His youthful image was enhanced by stories of his guitar-playing past and by the fact that his son Leo was the first baby to be born to a serving post-war British prime minister. Among the elements of continuity between the Major and Blair administrations, the most important was the Peace Process in Northern Ireland, which gradually ended some thirty years of armed conflict. Constitutionally, the partial devolution of Scotland, Wales and Northern Ireland went forward, and the first steps to reform the hereditary House of Lords were taken. The first significant measure of the new government was the handing of policy over monetary control to the Bank of England, which signalled a light-touch attitude to regulating banking and credit. The first of Blair's wars was fought when he successfully advocated the NATO bombing of Serbia to force it to withdraw from neighbouring Kosovo.

Nineties culture

In the 1990s, despite the long political dominance of the Conservatives (who had been in power since 1979), there was a real sense of cultural change. Regardless of all the hype, the arrival of Britpop, Brit film and Cool Britannia contributed to a sense of cultural confidence, while the election of Blair brought a feeling of a new dawn, with the image of the nation rebranded as youthful, bright and optimistic. At the same time, British youth culture continued to be influenced by a darker sensibility, especially from North America. For example, the Canadian Douglas Coupland's 1991 cult novel *Generation X* had an enormous influence, becoming a book that 'distils the spirit of a moment and comes to represent a particular time'.[2] Such blank generation literature offered a more disenchanted view of the world to set against the pervading currents of optimism. This was also a time when the huge forces of globalisation, which expanded mental horizons as well as economic markets, made a powerful impact on Britain, while artistic responses to these new realities took many forms: a retreat into private concerns, a dismissive cynicism or a renewed criticism of consumer capitalism. All of these were present in British theatre of the time.

Heritage, culture and the Arts Council

In 1990, the system of arts funding in Britain was the traditional post-war cultural settlement of using the Arts Council of Great Britain, an arm's length public body, to distribute government subsidy to individual institutions in partnership with local authorities and, increasingly, with business sponsors. The effect of cuts in state subsidy during the Thatcher-led 1980s was twofold: first, it made the whole theatre system increasingly driven by commercial objectives and, second, it encouraged an embattled psyche, what critic Michael Billington called 'a siege-mentality, excessive prudence and the sanctification of the box-office'.[3] As well as state subsidy, local authorities also funded theatres, and this sometimes led to problems: when the Merseyside Metropolitan Council was abolished by the Thatcher

government, its successor was unwilling to subsidise Liverpool's theatres, so the Liverpool Playhouse almost went bankrupt in 1990 was
dark in 1998–2000, while the Liverpool Everyman closed in 1993.

During the 1990s, two important innovations were brought in by
the Major government: the Department of National Heritage and the
National Lottery. The Department of National Heritage was Britain's
first ministry for culture, responsible for the performing arts, film,
museums, galleries, heritage, sport and tourism, while the Lottery
rapidly became a national institution, whose weekly draws were
broadcast on primetime television and which distributed its profits to
the arts, charities and good causes. These two new institutions
symbolise the spirit of the Conservative 1990s: on the one hand, the
new government department offered a cosy, patriotic idea of heritage
and historical tradition; on the other, the Lottery suggested a casino
economy which mocked enterprise culture, and was regressive because
the poor bought the most tickets while the middle classes benefited
most from Lottery awards.

Conservative government policy was inconsistent. Timothy
Renton, Minister for the Arts in 1991, publicly contemplated abol-
ishing the Arts Council but, in the run-up to the 1992 General
Election, actually increased its funding to £194 million, so theatre
subsidy rose by 14 per cent. The Arts Council was thus able to bail
out the RSC, which had accumulated deficits and had been forced to
shut its Barbican base in London for four months in November 1990.
Then, in mid-decade, Arts Council funding was cut again.
Meanwhile, the organisation was restructured. By April 1994 ten
Regional Arts Boards were created and clients were distributed
between a central office (National Theatre, RSC and Royal Court)
and the RABs (regional theatres). At the same time, 'many of the
specialist units that the Arts Council had developed in the eighties to
promote general policies such as cultural diversity, the role of women
in the arts and attention to disability, were wound up'.[4] In 1993, the
last year of the old Arts Council of Great Britain, this body tried
various cost-cutting measures – such as reducing funding to ten theatres outside London – which all failed, and meant that the Arts
Council lost the confidence of both government and its own clients.

In 1994, the Arts Councils of Scotland and Wales were devolved, to be funded directly by the Scottish and Welsh Offices, and the London headquarters became Arts Council England. This restructuring was less important than pervasive fear of cuts to the arts' budget.

Following the Thatcher years, business sponsorship remained a vital ingredient of arts funding. By the early 1990s, government was aiding business sponsorship by topping up private deals: 'by 1994 the government had contributed twenty-one million pounds, in response to forty-three million in sponsorship'.[5] But business sponsorship fell during periods of economic recession. Still, the trend of the 1990s was for corporate sponsors (often from the financial sector) to become a vital part of every major theatre's core funding. In 1994, when the RSC concluded six years of sponsorship by Royal Insurance, it made a fresh deal with Allied Lyons worth £3 million over three years. This was, says Robert Hewison, 'the largest arts sponsorship deal in Britain'.[6] On a smaller scale, Barclays bank sponsored the Royal Court's annual festival of experimental new work. But such deals provoked controversies that even affected educational charities: when in 1998 a £3 million grant by the Jerwood Foundation to the Royal Court was made conditional on the theatre adding the name Jerwood to both its auditoriums, there was an outcry. Despite such bitter disputes, the main trends were those of increasing sponsorship and commercialisation.

In 1993, the new Department of National Heritage, in charge of the Arts Council, seemed to herald an optimistic future. After all, it had an arts lover, David Mellor, as its Secretary of State. Similarly, the National Lottery, launched at the end of 1994, promised 'to initiate the biggest expansion in cultural activity since the sixties'.[7] What could go wrong? Well, quite a lot. It was typical of the sleazy image of the Major government that Mellor soon resigned because of a sex scandal involving an actress, Antonia de Sanchez. And the Lottery was such an enormous, and unexpected, success that the Arts Council found itself distributing £340 million of Lottery arts funding (for capital projects such as building refurbishment) compared to £191 million of regular arts funding (for running costs).[8] The huge sums of money made available by the Lottery allowed new theatre building projects, such as the refurbishment of the Royal Court Theatre (completed in 2000). But decreases in core funding created 'the paradox of cultural institutions dying of revenue thirst while drowning in lakes of capital funding'.[9] Major's last Heritage Secretary Virginia Bottomley recognised that the arts had been underfunded, with theatre outside London alone carrying deficits of £8 million, and she set up a stabilisation fund in 1997 to bail out the worst-hit theatres.

The advent of New Labour in 1997 reversed some cuts, but added lots of spin. The Blair government changed the name of the Department of National Heritage to the Department for Culture, Media and Sport, and its first Secretary of State Chris Smith played a boosterish role in hyping the Blair government's cultural credentials: his book of speeches was called *Creative Britain*. Although this was part of what Jen Harvie calls 'a crucial paradigm shift', moving from talking about culture as art to marketing it as 'creative industries', the new government also did some good. For example, it commissioned the Boyden Report to look at the problems of theatre outside London.[10] Thus the benefits of New Labour policies would be reaped in the new millennium.

By the end of the decade, following twenty years of glorifying the market, two trends were of the utmost importance: first, the mixed economy of funding – part state subsidy, part business sponsorship and part box office – was in crisis, especially in respect to theatres outside London. Second, the entire theatre funding system had been thoroughly commercialised, so that even subsidised companies were under pressure to be successful businesses. The outward signs of this were everywhere: theatres rebranded themselves, acquired logos, learnt to use niche marketing, made sponsorship deals, redesigned their foyers and expanded their bar activities. Audiences became customers, and shows became product. The box office was king.[11] Added to this was a new creed: the arts should be assessed on their social impact: the hunt was on for new audiences and greater access. Within theatres, commercial pressure undermined the traditional relationship between directors and theatrical institutions, creating what Billington describes as a freelance culture in which directors found themselves in an open market: 'Where in the past it had been companies and buildings that possessed a defining aesthetic, now that was something imported by individual directors who came bearing their own particular brand and style.'[12] But how did these changes affect the shows that theatres put on?

Flagship theatres: West End, National and RSC

The mainstream theatre landscape was divided between a commercial West End and a subsidised sector which was headed by the National Theatre and the RSC. In the mid-1990s, theatre suddenly, if briefly, became part of Cool Britannia, when publications such as *Newsweek*, *Le Monde* and the London *Evening Standard* hyped London as both the theatre capital of the world and Europe's coolest city. As one epitome of traditional Englishness, *Country Life* magazine, put it: 'London is the greatest theatre city in the world – the West End has twice as many theatres as Broadway.'[13] Certainly, it is true that theatre was amazingly popular: critic Benedict Nightingale estimates that 'roughly twenty-five million visits were annually made to English theatres in the mid-1990s, four million of them by foreign visitors'.[14] Statistics suggested that about 30 per cent of tourists who came to London went to the theatre.

The commercial sector

West End theatres were owned and run by commercial giants such as Stoll Moss, Apollo Entertainments and Associated Capital Theatres, and individuals such as Stephen Waley-Cohen. In 1999, Andrew Lloyd Webber's Really Useful Group bought Stoll Moss, adding ten theatres to the three that the impresario and composer already possessed. This was a big move in a big business: in 1996, gross box office for West End musicals was more than £330 million per annum, with eleven million people paying an average ticket price of £30. Nearly 16,000 musical performances a year were given and tourists spent 12 per cent of their entertainment budget on watching actors singing and dancing.[15]

As far as West End musicals go, the 1990s consolidated the

triumphs of the 1980s. Andrew Lloyd Webber, the prince of entrepreneurs, made theatre history in 1991 with six shows running at the same time in London's 'Theatreland'. A year later, his support of the Conservative government was rewarded with a knighthood. In July 1993 his *Sunset Boulevard* opened with £4 million in advance bookings, and in January 1996 *Cats* (1981) – with its instantly recognisable yellow-eyed logo – became the longest-running musical in history. In 1994, he repeated his achievement of 1982 and 1988 by having three musicals running in London and three in New York at the same time.[16] In 1996, Madonna starred in the film version of his *Evita*. In the 1997 New Year's honours list, as a farewell gift from the departing Tories, he was made a life peer, a fitting climax to a decade in which he made regular appearances in the list of the top ten richest Britons. Likewise, Cameron Mackintosh, the other major musical producer, enjoyed continued success with Claude-Michel Schönberg and Alain Boubil's *Les Misérables* (1985), which had been developed by the RSC but was a commercial goldmine for Mackintosh. By 2000, *Les Miserables* had been running continuously for fifteen years and Lloyd Webber's *Phantom of the Opera* for fourteen years, both making billions at the box office worldwide. Thus the aesthetics of the spectacular, a form 'that seeks to impress an audience with financial rather than creative prowess', was more profitable than even the most successful films.[17] If the more sophisticated work of Stephen Sondheim was eclipsed by these mega-musicals, other work – such as Schönberg and Boubil's *Martin Guerre* (1996), Lloyd Webber's revamped *By Jeeves* (1996) or Cy Coleman's ironical *City of Angels* (1993) – was markedly less successful. And musical turkeys included Disney's *Beauty and the Beast*, which lost a rumoured $12 million, as well as Lloyd Webber's *Whistle Down the Wind* and *The Beautiful Game*. Jukebox musicals, led by *Buddy: The Buddy Holly Story* (1989), in which a back catalogue of pop music hits were strung together in a feeble plot, presaged an unadventurous future.

While in the past serious plays were regularly put on by the commercial sector, over the 1990s the number shrunk considerably. Producers such as Bill Kenwright and Duncan Weldon would bring plays in from Bath or Clywd, and you might see Jenny Seagrove, say, in a revival of William Gibson's *The Miracle Worker* (1994). Occasional new plays by Ronald Harwood or Simon Gray, with Harold Pinter directing, plus transfers of popular work by Alan Ayckbourn and John Godber, joined old-fashioned genres such as courtroom dramas, thrillers or Ray Cooney farces. But gradually the energy ebbed out of serious commercial West End drama. Instead, new plays were developed in the subsidised sector and then brought into the West End. This led journalists to write perennial features about the decline of the West End, a local variant of the myth of Britain's post-war decline. For although fewer and fewer commercial managements put on new plays, the West End was thriving. For example, three long-running entertainments – Agatha Christie's *The Mousetrap* (1952), Stephen Mallatratt's adaptation of *The Woman in Black* (1983) and Willy Russell's play with music *Blood Brothers* (1988) – offered shots of nostalgia, sensation and sentimentality throughout the 1990s. Comedy shows by Julian Clary or Eddie Izzard brought in the punters. And the decade saw one massive success which suggested that commercial theatre could be part of Cool Britannia: *Art* (1996), a play for three male actors by French playwright Yasmina Reza, translated by Christopher Hampton, and produced by David Pugh and Dafydd Rogers. The original cast was Albert Finney, Tom Courtney and Ken Stott, but the production held the attention of audiences by constantly recasting, and actors such as Richard Griffiths, Henry Goodman, David Haig and Nigel Havers, as well as an all-American cast led by Stacey Keach, ensured that the production ran for seven years. But if it is true that the West End was, in critic Michael Billington's words, 'the ultimate exemplar of market forces', it was also able to stage work with a critical attitude.[18] For example, more than one million people saw Stephen Daldry's revival of J. B. Priestley's *An Inspector Calls*, which started life at the National (1992) before running for almost six years in the West End. With its neo-Expressionist aesthetic and clear advocacy of Labour Party renewal, this play implicitly interrogated Thatcher's comment that 'there is no such thing as society'.[19]

Nor was all commercial theatre the same. When veteran director Peter Hall – who spent much of the decade presenting solid if unexciting revivals of the classics – took over as artistic director of the commercial Old Vic in 1996, he gave free rein to Dominic Dromgoole – formerly head of the tiny Bush fringe theatre – to stage new plays on this large stage. The main beneficiaries were playwrights Samuel Adamson, Sebastian Barry and April De Angelis. Hall also staged classics with star actors such as Ben Kingsley and Felicity Kendal. In central London, the 440-seat New Ambassadors Theatre, run by producer Sonia Friedman from 1996, staged the work of new playwrights Mark Ravenhill, Ayub Khan-Din and Gary Owen, as well as Lee Hall's popular *Spoonface Steinberg*. The New Ambassadors also hosted populist theatre such as Marie Jones's *Stones in His Pockets*, a two-hander that questioned Hollywood images of Ireland, and Eve Ensler's *The Vagina Monologues*, an orgy of feminism lite which recruited celebrities to lead mainly female audiences in reclaiming the word 'cunt'. Other notable West End entertainments included Arthur Smith and Chris England's *An Evening with Gary Lineker* at the start of the decade and Alan Bennett's *The Lady in the Van*, starring Maggie Smith, at its end. In mid-decade, even cutting-edge drama – *Trainspotting*, *Closer* and *Shopping and Fucking* – had respectable runs in Theatreland. Meanwhile, south of the river, another commercial venture, American actor Sam Wanamaker's wood-and-plaster reconstruction of Shakespeare's Globe, which opened in 1997 with actor Mark Rylance as its maverick first artistic director, was a monument to heritage which was to prove immensely popular with audiences.

The subsidised sector: National Theatre

In contrast to the commercial West End, the twin peaks of the state-subsidised sector were the National Theatre and the Royal Shakespeare Company.[20] The National, led by Richard Eyre in 1988–97, enjoyed a decade of what Dominic Shellard calls 'stability and growth'.[21] Eyre created a National that was both overtly populist and mildly oppositional, and his 'good commercial sense' was seen in repeated West End transfers and a renewed emphasis on national touring.[22] He programmed a judicious mixture of popular musical revivals – such as *Carousel* (1992) and *Guys and Dolls* (1996), with black actors Clive Rowe and Clarke Peters – along with more critical work, such as Jim Cartwright's *The Rise and Fall of Little Voice* (1992), with Alison Steadman and Jane Horrocks. Other memorable productions included Tony Harrison's *The Trackers of Oxyrhyncus* (1990), which debated high and low culture while featuring a fragment of a play by Sophocles, complete with satyrs sporting proudly protruding phalluses; and Alan Bennett's frequently revived adaptation of *The Wind in the Willows* (1990), with its riverbank animals and nostalgic atmosphere. Shakespeare was well served by Eyre's grand production of *Richard III* (1990), with Ian McKellen as a 1930s-style fascistic despot, Deborah Warner's intimate and lucid production of *Richard II* (1995), with Fiona Shaw playing the king in a discomforting performance, and a moving *King Lear* (1997), for which Ian Holm overcame years of stage fright to turn in a thrilling performance.

Eyre's National developed what has been described as the 'new mainstream' of new writing.[23] David Hare became the house playwright, penning *Racing Demon* (1990), *Murmuring Judges* (1991) and *The Absence of War* (1993), which anatomised the Church, the Law and the Labour Party, three national institutions in crisis. As well as writing these state-of-the-nation dramas, which were revived as a comprehensive trilogy on the huge Olivier stage, Hare wrote a book about his research for them in which he commented, 'A playwright above all other writers responds unknowingly to the mood of the times.'[24] Unknowing or not, the trilogy was, in Eyre and Wright's words, 'a crowning moment in the life of the National Theatre in 1994. The plays all ask the questions: How does a good person change people's lives for the better? Can an institution established for the common good avoid being devoured by its own internal struggles and contradictions?'[25] Hare followed up with *Skylight* (1995) and *Amy's View* (1997), two excellent plays which attacked the values of Thatcherism. In the former, the personal conflict between restaurant owner Tom (Michael Gambon) and younger teacher Kyra (Lia Williams), a couple who were once lovers, mirrors the tensions between Thatcherite market ideology (Tom, in Hare's words, represents 'capitalist endeavour at its most fleeting and heroic') and a more caring attitude.[26] At one point, Kyra cooks a spaghetti supper in real time, a scene archly parodied by Martin Crimp in his updated version of Molière's *The Misanthrope* (Young Vic, 1997):

Man   Remember all the good times that we had.

Woman   The times that you call good now all seem bad.

Man   Let's dine out at my restaurant. The limousine is ready.

Woman   I'd rather stay at home and cook my own spaghetti.

[. . .] *They kiss beneath the leaking skylight.*[27]

In *Amy's View*, Judi Dench played an actress, Esme, who is eventually bankrupted by the fallout from the 1990s Lloyd's insurance scandal. She is the mother of Amy (Samantha Bond), who marries Dominic, a television producer and symbol of the dumbing down of contemporary media. In Act Two, Esme and Dominic clash when the young man suggests that theatre is dead. Esme fights back, sarcastically characterising Dominic in this corrosive speech: 'The country's most famous, most influential programme which lays down the law on the arts. And it's run by a man who seems to have only one small disadvantage. What is it? Remind me. Oh yes, I remember. It turns out he doesn't like art!'[28] The rasp that Dench gave to this rhetoric lingered long in the memory. Yet, despite Hare's successes, the decade was characterised by a decline in political theatre: the most typical examples of new writing by new playwrights all focused on the personal rather than the political.

Eyre also had a love for history plays, tapping into a national love of the past. The success of veterans such as Alan Bennett, with *The Madness of George III* (1991), and Tom Stoppard with *Arcadia* (1993), proved that audiences enjoyed intelligent nostalgia. Bennett's play featured an outstanding central performance by Nigel Hawthorne, and its theme of royal distress, solidly and sympathetically based on historical research, seemed to resonate with a public fascinated both by history and by the troubles of the contemporary Royal Family. Even more brilliant was Stoppard's play, an immensely witty and stimulating story about present-day scholars Bernard and Hannah, who investigate what happened when Byron visited a country house, inhabited by Lady Croom, her daughter Thomasina and the tutor Septimus Hodge in 1809–12. With its sharp contrasts between the unfounded speculations of today's characters and the real actions of the nineteenth-century ones, plus its themes of literature, biography, duelling, landscape gardening and chaos theory, it created a mood of wonder at the playwright's virtuoso mix of imagination and hilarity from its first exchange, featuring the teenage Thomasina and the older Septimus:

Thomasina   Septimus, what is carnal embrace?

Septimus   Carnal embrace is the practice of throwing one's arms around a side of beef.[29]

With its superb cast – Bill Nighy, Felicity Kendall, Rufus Sewell, Harriet Walter and Emma Fielding – and confident director, Trevor Nunn, the play was a perfect marriage of ideas and emotions. Its use of chaos theory as a scientific metaphor was thrilling and its design, by Mark Thompson, conjured up an English country house while echoing the themes of order within uncertainty. The final stage image involved couples from both eras – contemporary teenage savant Gus and Hannah; historical Septimus and Thomasina – dancing on stage at the same time. As John Fleming says, 'music from both periods is heard, the moonlight and candlelight are joined by a lush, purplish glow that bathes the dancing couples. It is a beautifully, moving finale as these "bodies in motion" celebrate both the human intellect and the human heart.'[30] Other new plays during Eyre's regime included work by Caryl Churchill, Christopher Hampton, David Storey, Peter Gill and Patrick Marber. Yet the last one he chose to direct was another Stoppard play, *The Invention of Love* (1997), which starred John Wood as A. E. Houseman in an intriguing memory play set in several locations in early twentieth-century Britain and 1870s Oxford (with cameos of Ruskin, Pater and Wilde), and in which Houseman's older self meets his younger self. As one critic wrote: 'Eyre couldn't have hoped to leave the National in finer style.'[31]

During his reign, the National also hosted the best Irish and American plays. The visit of the Abbey Theatre production of Brian Friel's *Dancing at Lughnasa* showed the influence of Irish playwriting and Tony Kushner's two-part epic *Angels in America* or Arthur Miller's

Broken Glass illustrated the inspiring ambition of the American imagination. *Dancing at Lughnasa* is a tale set in the home of five Mundy sisters in Ballybeg in 1936, where their precarious way of life is destroyed by a modern economy. Its most uplifting moment is, in Nesta Jones's words, 'the magnificent dance sequence early in the first act, in which the sisters abandon themselves to "Marconi's voodoo"', a memorably exciting staging of a celebration of a harvest festival, Lugh the Celtic fertility god.[32] But the story's ending, when two of the sisters come to London and become destitute, gave it a sharp contemporary resonance. Later in the decade, Martin McDongah's *The Cripple of Inishmore* suggested a more satirical, postmodern, view of Irish heritage. By contrast, although the hugely ambitious *Angels in America* (1992–3) was partly set in the 1950s, it ranged over a whole landscape of contemporary issues from gay sexuality to green politics, and felt completely engrossing. It was also an inspiration to British playwrights. If Eyre's policy, as Shellard argues, of 'pragmatism and populism' echoed New Labour's redefinition of the political middle ground, both were highly successful strategies as far as the public was concerned.[33]

When Trevor Nunn took over from Eyre in 1997, the year New Labour came to power, he continued his predecessor's mission to produce a thoroughly populist programme – heavy on revivals of musicals such as *Oklahoma!* and *My Fair Lady* – with occasional sterling classics, such as his forceful *The Merchant of Venice* (1999), with Henry Goodman as Shylock. But he did not neglect new work. Despite producing duds from playwrights such as Stephen Poliakoff and Hanif Kureishi, Nunn staged one of the best new plays of the decade: Michael Frayn's *Copenhagen* (1998). Taking the form of a memory play which questioned whether we can ever be certain about either quantum physics or our recollection of the past, the piece examined the meeting of two scientists, Niels Bohr and Werner Heisenberg, in Denmark at the height of the Nazi occupation of Europe. Although the men certainly met, and may have discussed Nazi attempts to produce an atom bomb, Frayn advances various different explanations of their encounter. As Margrethe, Bohr's wife, says, 'When you tell the story, yes, it all falls into place, it all has a beginning and a middle and an end', but in her mind reality is entirely different: 'It's confusion and rage and jealousy and tears.'[34] Both science and memory are coloured by human emotion. *Copenhagen* was also part of a larger trend of plays about science, which suggested a keen public interest in the subject: two examples are Timberlake Wertenbaker's *After Darwin* and Shelagh Stephenson's *An Experiment with an Airpump*, both staged at the Hampstead Theatre. Although Nunn sometimes fell foul of controversy, as when he introduced invisible microphones for actors in the Olivier auditorium in 1999, his regime prepared the ground well for the even greater triumphs of his successor, Nicholas Hytner.

The subsidised sector: Royal Shakespeare Company

At the RSC, with its new patron Prince Charles, the decade started badly following the 'national scandal' of the closure of Barbican due to cuts in state subsidy.[35] But the story of the 1990s was the story of artistic director Adrian Noble. He took up his post in 1991, with the aspiration of making the theatre the best classical company in the English-speaking world, and began with star-studded productions of the classics: Kenneth Branagh played Hamlet (1992), Antony Sher was an athletic Tamberlaine (1992) and Robert Stephens's Lear (1993) was rich in pathos if painfully slow. After this, the latter's son, twenty-four-year-old Toby Stephens, played Coriolanus (1994), and was hyped as 'the youngest Coriolanus anyone can remember'.[36] The plays of both the older and the younger Stephens fed into the public debate, which had arisen in the wake of the Jamie Bulger murder, about violence in the media. After defending the representation of violence in the arts, critic Michael Coveney described one incident in *King Lear*: 'Simon Russell Beale as Edgar, disguised as Poor Tom, a madman, finally crosses the insolent servant Oswald and instead of merely killing him with his dagger, stoves in his face with a pike staff. Again and again and again. Until his body lies limp, and we flop weakly in our stalls.'[37] With similar in-yer-face directness, the poster for *Coriolanus* featured the younger Stephens's face covered with blood. As the RSC marketing manager wrote in the *Independent*, 'It is gratifying that sales of the poster to thrilled theatre-goers have soared.'[38]

43

In attempting to revitalise the RSC as a classical company that explored the repertoire, Noble also staged Sam Mendes's productions of *Troilus and Cressida* (1991), *The Tempest* (1993) and *Richard III* (1992), all of which had Simon Russell Beale in the cast. His barefoot Ariel was tough and sinister, although his active, humpback Richard had its London run cut short when he slipped a disc. But two of the decade's most striking Shakespeare revivals had nothing to do with the RSC: Canadian Robert Lepage's *A Midsummer Night's Dream* visited the National while American Peter Sellars's *The Merchant of Venice* was seen at the Barbican. Both were poorly spoken, but visually memorable – Lepage's muddy waterlands evoked dark fantasy while Sellars's video cameras and contemporary dress alluded to the Los Angeles riots. At the RSC, other classics were also tackled: for example, John Barton's *Peer Gynt*, with Alex Jennings in the title role, offered an original take on the play, seeing it as a dream.

Noble was also keen on using his theatre spaces more imaginatively. At the Swan Theatre, Chekhovian naturalism was well realised in Terry Hands's *The Seagull* and Noble's beautiful *Cherry Orchard*. But his unwillingness to maintain the RSC tradition of a permanent directorial team meant that some critics found his company lacking a coherent style or approach. Still, the appointment of Katie Mitchell as artistic director of the Other Place in 1997 opened an arena for experiment, and productions of Koltès's *Roberto Zucco* (in a translation by Martin Crimp) suggested a renewed interest in the best of modern European drama. Mitchell's *The Phoenician Women* and her *Ghosts* were characterised, like all her work at this time, by intense acting, visual austerity and psychological clarity. But, in general, British new writing was comparatively neglected, and Noble appeared to be obsessed with one American writer, Richard Nelson, five of whose now-forgotten plays were staged during the 1990s. Exceptions to this rule, such as Peter Shaffer's *The Gift of the Gorgon* (1992), were similarly unmemorable, although Peter Whelan's two Renaissance history plays *The School of Night* (1992) and *The Herbal Bed* (1996) successfully and engrossingly evoked the world of Elizabethan England. Most impressive, however, was David Edgar's *Pentecost* (1994), a superb example of an ambitious state-of-Europe play, boldly debating culture and politics in the wake of the fall of the Berlin Wall. Like *Arcadia*, *Pentecost* used a vivid theatrical image – in this case a newly discovered Giotto-esque fresco – to provoke a discussion about the history of Europe. The play mixed pessimism about a future during which Communist 'prolecult' has lost out to American Rambos and Schwarzeneggers with what one critic called 'the inspiring, hopeful message' that 'diaspora can create a rich cultural inter-weaving' and 'a non-tragic sense in which "we are the sum of the people who invaded us"'.[39] Its vision of a European culture where, in the words of the art historian, 'every frontier teeming, every crossroads thronged' felt both exciting and contemporary.[40] Despite this triumph, Noble's steward-ship of the RSC tended to neglect new work and seemed deaf to the political relevance of the classics he so assiduously promoted.

Artistically, Noble – like Nunn – was a conservative cultural popu-list, and his RSC was condemned by critic Michael Billington as retreating 'into a reactionary mode totally alien to the spirit of its founding fathers'.[41] As the company swelled in size, becoming an international entertainment corporation, Noble struggled to keep control over its productions and its budget, accumulating a £1.6 million deficit. He tore up the traditional idea of permanent company, favouring stand-alone productions, and developed a huge but hubristic plan, Project Fleet, which aimed to demolish the Royal Shakespeare Theatre in Stratford-upon-Avon in favour of a hugely expensive Shakespeare Village, while abandoning the Barbican, the company's London base. This over-ambitious idea provoked a crisis that led to his resignation in 2002, finally defeated by, in the words of Colin Chambers, 'the clash between the demands of monetarism and the desires of public service that was played out across society in the 1990s'.[42] The mixed fortunes of the National and the RSC exempli-fied the highs and lows of the decade's state-subsidised flagships.

Off-West End and companies

Surrounding the main flagships and the commercial West End was a vigorous Off-West End sector, which included a range of medium- and small-scale state-funded theatres. The best way of understanding the main Off-West End venues is to distinguish between the trendy boutique theatres and the less glamorous but equally significant community theatres. Boutique theatres, such as the Donmar Warehouse in the centre of town and the Almeida in Islington, north London, had a good decade. As Billington says, 'Depending heavily on private finance, they were perfect products of the post-Thatcherite era.'[43] Community theatres were led by the Theatre Royal Stratford East, once the home of Joan Littlewood, and the Tricycle Theatre in Kilburn, north London. Equally significant in the general ecology of British theatre were, for different reasons, touring companies such as Cheek by Jowl, Tara Arts and Tamasha.

Let's start with the boutiques. The trendy Almeida, led from 1990 by actors Jonathan Kent and Ian McDiarmid, specialised in well-cast and well-designed revivals of mainly European and American classics. At this fashionable but cramped venue, where in the foyer you might be jostled by a superior kind of person, there was a lot of world drama from Euripides to Lorca, and from Dryden to Brecht and Pirandello. As one critic wrote, what you'd expect at this address is 'A state-of-the-art Racine revival, perhaps, or something piquant and rare by Griboyedov. The world premiere of a lean-cuisine Pinter or a hot-off-the-grid avant-garde opera about a titled nymphomaniac would raise few eyebrows here.'[44] From the beginning, the Almeida attracted star actors: Glenda Jackson in Howard Barker's *Scenes from an Execution* and Claire Bloom in Ibsen's *When We Dead Awaken*. Exceptional performances included Diana Rigg in *Medea* (1992) and Kevin Spacey in Eugene O'Neill's *The Iceman Cometh* (1998). Dressed in a blazing red gown, Rigg's commanding presence combined the character's sharp intelligence with her ferocious, lacerating anger. Spacey's Hickey was both silver-tongued charmer, a born-again messiah of the bandwagon, and a man desperate for human connection. The theatre also played an important part in the 1990s rehabilitation of playwright Terence Rattigan – who had been eclipsed by the Kitchen Sink dramatists of the 1960s – by staging a 1993 revival of *The Deep Blue Sea*, with Penelope Wilton. As well as programming a repertoire that might be the envy of any national company, the Almeida also promoted new work, especially the last plays of Harold Pinter: *Party Time* (1991), *Moonlight* (1993) and *Celebration* (2000). The venue revived Pinter's *Betrayal* and *No Man's Land*, in which Pinter played Hirst opposite Paul Eddington's Spooner. As well as these, other productions of Pinter plays – *The Birthday Party* at the National and *The Hothouse* in the West End – indicated a late flowering for this playwright. Other Almeida premieres included David Hare's *The Judas Kiss*, his rather unsuccessful account of the last days of Oscar Wilde. Newer writing talents were represented by Phyllis Nagy (*Butterfly Kiss*) and Louis Mellis and David Scinto (*Gangster No 1*). The Almeida also pioneered the trend for a theatre company to expand out of its base and temporarily occupy other venues. So Ralph Fiennes was seen at the Hackney Empire giving his head-bowed and slump-shouldered *Hamlet* (1995), Rigg in repertory in the West End with two Racine tragedies – *Phèdre* and *Britannicus* – and Fiennes again in *Richard II* and *Coriolanus* at the Gainsborough Film Studios in Shoreditch in 2000.

If the Almeida was the prime boutique theatre of the decade, the Donmar ran it a close second. Opening in 1992, this small 250-seat theatre is located in a Covent Garden building that had once been a banana warehouse and then an RSC studio in 1977–82. The brainchild of director Sam Mendes, the new venue opened with the British premiere of Stephen Sondheim's *Assassins*, and – despite having to wait four years for Arts Council subsidy – Mendes ensured that it was a lively theatre which specialised in a mix of classic American work and revivals of neglected plays in the current repertory. Here you could see classy revivals of Brian Friel's *Translations* or David Mamet's *Glengarry Glen Ross*. Its musical hits included Sondheim's *Company* and Kander and Ebb's *Cabaret*, which starred a reptilian Alan Cumming. Acclaimed performances from glamorous actors secured the venue's reputation as a place which provided some of the decade's most memorable, and award-winning, theatrical experiences. Nicole Kidman starred in *The Blue Room*, Hare's adaptation of Schnitzler's *Reigen*, in a performance described by one critic as 'pure theatrical Viagra'.[45] Other starry revivals included Tennessee Williams's *Orpheus Descending* (Helen Mirren), the same playwright's *The Glass Menagerie*

(Zoë Wanamaker and Claire Skinner) and Alan Bennett's *Habeas Corpus* (Jim Broadbent and Imelda Staunton). Ace directors were also welcome: Katie Mitchell (Beckett's *Endgame*), David Leveaux (Stoppard's *The Real Thing*) and Michael Grandage (Peter Nichols's *Passion Play*). As Matthew Warchus, who directed Simon Donald's *The Life of Stuff* and Sam Shepard's *True West* at the venue, said, 'Although the Donmar is a small theatre, it has something epic about it: there is a kind of electricity in there; the fact is, there's no place to hide.'[46] Like the Almeida, the Donmar bowed to celebrity culture; unlike the Almeida, it avoided the more difficult corners of the international repertoire. While such Off-West End venues continued the tradition of sharply designed and well-acted revivals, other Off-West End theatre developed different traditions.

Under Nicolas Kent, the Tricycle Theatre was devoted to political theatre. Perceiving that the fall of the Berlin Wall, the Northern Ireland Peace Process and the end of Apartheid in South Africa had dampened some of the burning issues of yesteryear, Kent decided to investigate more contemporary scandals. The form he chose and pioneered was verbatim tribunal theatre – using a text made of edited speeches from public inquiries. By doing so he found an aesthetic alternative to the fictional political play, which was seen as old-fashioned and irrelevant. The first example of such tribunal theatre was *Half the Picture* (1994), a stage version of the Scott 'Arms to Iraq' Inquiry, written by veteran radical playwright John McGrath and journalist Richard Norton-Taylor, who had met Kent while playing tennis. In 1998, two other tribunal plays – *Nuremberg* and *Srebrenica* – examined the reality of genocide in the past and present. But the theatre's greatest triumph was *The Colour of Justice* (1999), a play composed of extracts from the Macpherson Inquiry into the Metropolitan Police's botched investigation into the murder of black teenager Stephen Lawrence. If the numerous instances of racism by police and white suspects made for grim watching, this kind of play was rather inert as a theatrical experience – consisting mainly of men in suits asking and answering questions. Yet *The Colour of Justice* did have two memorable moments: in one, a senior policeman dismissively screwed up a note given to him by Lawrence's mother and, in the other, at the very end of the play, the actor playing Macpherson, chair of the inquiry, said: 'Would you stand with me for a minute's silence.'[47] The whole audience rose in respect. Kent says, 'The piece has had a lasting impact on race relations. It's been reprinted and is used as a training tool and video at Hendon Police College. When it was televised, it was seen by millions.'[48] As well as promoting socially committed drama, the Tricycle also staged work which reflected the ethnic mix (Irish, Asian and black) of the local community. And Kent was not averse to presenting wonderfully entertaining work such as *Ain't Misbehavin'*, the celebratory 1995 Fats Waller musical, which he co-directed with Gillian Gregory.

A similar mix was on offer at the Theatre Royal Stratford East, where artistic director Philip Hedley programmed a lively mixture of plays. Like Joan Littlewood, with whom he'd once worked, Hedley used his venue to represent the experiences of the area's black and Asian community. Playwright Winsome Pinnock called the venue 'one of the few theatres in London that can lay claim to the description multicultural, both in terms of the plays produced and the audience that attends the performances'.[49] So vocal were audiences that critics were often tempted to review not only the show but also its spectators. Audience reactions frequently enhanced the meaning of the shows. For example, performances of Roy Williams's award-winning debut, *The No Boys Cricket Club* (1996), were often accompanied by protests from black matriarchs who objected to the fact that, at one point, the young Michael character hits his mother Abi. Hedley also wanted local people to use the theatre on a regular basis so he developed a contemporary version of variety entertainment, with sketch shows such as the Posse's *Armed and Dangerous* (1991–2), the Bibi Crew's black women's show (1992), the young Asian *D'Yer Eat with Your Fingers?* (1994) and *Funny Black Women on the Edge* (1995). On one occasion, when Angie Le Mar, in the last-mentioned show, came on after the interval, a woman in the stalls called out: 'You're the man!' Hedley also promoted *Moti Roti Puttli Chunni* (1993), the first British Bollywood musical. Other popular successes, and West End transfers, included Clarke Peters's jazz musical *Five Guys Named Moe* (1990) and Ken Hill's spoof Edwardian musical *The Invisible Man* (1991), with its enjoyable stage illusions. In 1999, Hedley began the Musical Theatre Initiatives scheme to encourage new writing in musical theatre.

Other Off-West End venues, such as the Young Vic and the Lyric Hammersmith, also staged a mixture of significant classics and new work. At the Young Vic, David Thacker promoted the work of Arthur Miller, especially his *The Last Yankee* (1993) and *Broken Glass* (1994), becoming the American playwright's foremost British interpreter. He was followed by Tim Supple, who had a poor first year and then directed an outstanding revival of John Byrne's *The Slab Boys Trilogy*, a seven-hour cycle of plays set in 1950s Paisley. Supple's vividly macabre and cutely surreal version of the *Grimm Tales*, written by Carol Ann Duffy, was the highly praised Christmas show in 1994. After that, Supple further redefined the venue's mission and raised its profile. At the Lyric, artistic director Neil Bartlett staged his own productions, such as *The Picture of Dorian Gray* (1994), and worked hard to show how complex a gay sensibility could be. His studio space hosted Ryan Craig's debut, *Happy Savages*, and Mark Ravenhill's *Handbag* in 1998. *Handbag* has two strands – a contemporary story about gay parenting and a historical story involving characters from Oscar Wilde's *The Importance of Being Earnest* – and said more about Wilde than many of the countless revivals of his work in the decade. Elsewhere, the Orange Tree Theatre, in Richmond, moved in 1991 from its room above a pub into a new theatre in the round, where the indefatigable Sam Walters programmed forgotten Edwardian classics, European plays from Vaclav Havel and Michel Vinaver, and new plays by local authors.

Some theatre companies, set up on a shoestring during the 1980s, matured during the 1990s into internationally significant players. Chief of these was Cheek by Jowl – led by director Declan Donnellan and designer Nick Ormerod – which explored English and European classics such as Alfred de Musset's *Don't Fool with Love* (1993), Webster's *The Duchess of Malfi* (1995) and Shakespeare's *Measure for Measure* (1994). The company was something of an unofficial acting academy, numbering Daniel Craig, Sally Dexter, Anastasia Hille, Paterson Joseph, Matthew Macfadyen, David Morrissey, Lloyd Owen,

Saskia Reeves and Michael Sheen among its more famous alumni. Added to this, Donnellan played an important, and occasionally controversial, role by casting black actors. In 1989, for example, his *Fuente Ovejuna* at the National was a milestone in the advance of colour-blind casting for European classics. Likewise, his revelatory all-male *As You Like It* (1991) starred Adrian Lester as Rosalind and Tom Hollander as Celia, with its gender-bending men playing women playing men playing women, and appealingly warm atmosphere. Other stylistic devices pioneered by Donnellan and Ormerod included overlapping scenes, spatially geometric oppositions, economy of gesture, austere costumes and colourful, streamlined designs. In the early years, the effect was described as a 'mannered exuberance', which 'burst afresh upon their audiences' (at the time of his *Angels in America* directed for the National in 1992), and Donnellan's distinctive style always embodied a theatre where the actors came first.[50] Cheek by Jowl concentrated on long rehearsal periods and constantly refreshed the acting during lengthy international tours.

Shared Experience, whose name emphasised the relationship between the actors and the audience, was a touring company which specialised in stage adaptations of classic novels. Led by Nancy Meckler, greatly aided by director Polly Teale and playwright Helen Edmundson, the group created vividly theatrical versions of *Anna Karenina* (1991), *The Mill on the Floss* (1993), *War and Peace* (1996) and *Jane Eyre* (1996). By concentrating on novels which the public might be familiar with, the company was able to sell tickets to shows which were remarkable for the overtly theatrical nature of their stagings. In most cases, the visual elements of the story were the most memorable, as for example, the image of Count Vronsky (in the famous racing scene of the book) riding his lover Anna Karenina onstage as if she were a horse: when Vronsky's horse falls and has to be destroyed, Anna is likewise destroyed by her affair. As with Cheek by Jowl, Shared Experience put simultaneous scenes to good effect. In *Anna Karenina*, for instance, 'We simultaneously watch Levin's ecstatic happiness as Kitty accepts his proposal, while on the other side of the stage, Anna is first bitterly rebuked by her husband and lies in feverish agony after childbirth. It is a scene that thrillingly captures the full emotional range of the book with its intersecting arcs of despair and hope.'[51] In *The Mill on the Floss*, an adaptation of George Eliot's novel, three actresses played the part of Maggie Tulliver, one the wild childhood Maggie and the others two different sides of her adult personality (spiritual and sensual), creating a thrillingly resonant view of women's experience in Victorian times. In *Jane Eyre*, the madwoman in the attic was the alter ego of the restrained governess, while the Russian epic *War and Peace*, presented at the National Theatre, was a rollicking, riotous re-creation in which a ball becomes a military charge and sexual temptation appears to a prude in the guise of a man with bandaged eyes. Edmundson's version also stressed the political aspect of Tolstoy's story by creating imaginary conversations between the hero, Pierre, and Napoleon, as the former matures from youthful debauchery into middle-aged radicalism – and ends up as one of the Decembrist conspirators against the Tsar. Finally, the company's production of Eugene O'Neill's *Desire Under the Elms*, directed by Teale, featured a scene in which two illicit lovers are drawn to each other, even though they are in different rooms in the house. As both undress, Eben in the downstairs kitchen pulls himself up on a beam and kisses the ceiling, while Abbie in the upstairs bedroom lies down, mouth to the floor. It was a stunning moment of magnetic desire.

Tara Arts – led by Jatinder Verma – specialised in Asian versions of European classics, as well as staging work from the subcontinent. It was briefly made welcome at the National, as the first all-Asian company to perform at this flagship, with an Asian take on Molière's *Tartuffe* (1990), set in Mughal India. Creating a rich linguistic tapestry which mixed Urdu and English, Verma also used Indian popular theatre conventions, such as Bhavi, which, like Commedia dell'arte, has a satirical edge. He also introduced theatrical conventions of his own – for instance, offering translations of Urdu passages – with an eye for the comic. At one point, he remembers,

Orgon's children exchange verses from the Indian epic romance of *Heer and Ranjha* (an equivalent of Shakespeare's *Romeo and Juliet*). As the verse-exchange in Urdu finished, one of the story-tellers strode forward to address the audience: 'Another translation!' she declared. By this stage of the performance, the convention having been well-established, a murmur of recognition would ripple through the audience. Pausing a moment, 'Why bother!', she'd say and run back to her position on stage, the house having erupted in laughter.[52]

Likewise, Tara Arts' version of Molière's *The Bourgeois Gentilhomme* (1994) – with a title that mixed French and English – transposed the story to seventeenth-century Pondicherry, a French colony in South India, and the farce dealt with an upwardly mobile colonised community which mimics their colonisers. Tara also produced versions of Shakespeare and, in 1992, the first English presentation of Waris Shah's Punjabi classic *Heer Ranjha*. In terms of new writing, they developed Parv Bancil's *Crazy Horse* (1997), a fierce father and son confrontation set in a run-down garage. Another company, Tamasha, also developed new work for Asian talent, creating popular musical shows and stage adaptations of novels. Set up in 1989 by Kristine Landon-Smith and Sudha Bhuchar, their work included the parodic but touching Bollywood homage *Fourteen Songs, Two Weddings and a Funeral* (1998), and stage adaptations of novels such as Ruth Carter's *Women of the Dust*. The company also documented history: *A Tainted Dawn* (1997), for example, was based on several short stories about the Partition of India. In terms of new writing, they commissioned Ayub Khan-Din's *East is East* (1996) and Sudha Bhuchar and Shaheen Khan's *Balti Kings* (1999).

Other companies included Talawa, an Afro-Caribbean group led by Yvonne Brewster, which worked hard to establish a black presence on the British stage. Their straight version of Wilde's *The Importance of Being Earnest* (1990) didn't alter a line, but the mere fact that the actors of this English classic were black was subversive of expectations – and boosted the comedy of the piece. Taking up temporary residence at the Cochrane Theatre, they staged shows such as Ntozake Shange's *The Love Space Demands* and Derek Walcott's *Beef, No Chicken*. By contrast, the aptly named Classics on a Shoestring was a company that provided a launching pad for director Katie Mitchell, while Stephen Unwin's English Touring Theatre (ETT) produced excellent versions of classics such as *Hamlet*, with Alan Cumming in 1993, or *The Seagull*, with Cheryl Campbell in 1997. ETT's new writing included Jonathan Harvey's *Hushabye Mountain*, with Andrew Lincoln. Finally, Actors Touring Company (ATC), under the leadership of Nick Philippou, produced strikingly contemporary versions of European classics such as *Miss Julie* or *Ion*, as well as some of the early plays of Ravenhill. On the other hand, a company such as Mike Alfreds's Method and Madness focused on ensemble acting. All in all, these touring companies provided the variety and the specialist skills so often missing in the mainstream building-based organisations.

New writing

New writing is a distinctive genre of contemporary work which is often, although by no means exclusively, written by newly arriving or young playwrights, and characterised by the distinctiveness of the author's individual voice, the contemporary flavour of their language and themes, and sometimes by the provocative nature of its content or its experimentation with theatrical form. As well as other major venues, there was a group of state-subsidised theatres in London which specialised in new writing: the Royal Court, Bush, Hampstead and Soho theatres. These were joined by two significant new writing theatres outside the metropolis – the Traverse in Edinburgh and Live Theatre in Newcastle upon Tyne – as well as some unsubsidised London fringe venues with a proven track record in staging new plays, often within a mixed repertoire. These included the Finborough, the King's Head and the Old Red Lion. Once again, some touring companies – especially Out of Joint and Paines Plough – made a vital contribution, despite their small size, to producing new writers.

Following cuts in state subsidy during the 1980s, the genre of new writing was widely perceived to be in trouble at the start of the decade. As playwright David Edgar remembers, there was 'a growing belief, among directors in particular, that new work had run out of steam'.[53] Other theatre people agreed, arguing that financial constraints led to 'small casts in simple sets, performing plays written for small spaces and expecting short runs'.[54] In May 1991, Michael Billington summed up: 'New writing for theatre is in a state of crisis.'[55] But just as the obituaries of new writing were appearing in the media, a revival was beginning in the smaller theatres and hidden corners of the British new writing system. In January 1991, Philip Ridley's debut *The Pitchfork Disney* was staged at the Bush, whose new artistic director Dominic Dromgoole noted that the play upturned expectations and, by introducing a new sensibility, 'was one of the first plays to signal the new direction for new writing'.[56] At the Traverse, artistic director Ian Brown was promoting playwrights such as Anthony Neilson, whose debut *Normal* shocked audiences at the 1991 Edinburgh Festival with its depiction of a brutal murder, and whose *Penetrator* (1993) successfully transferred from Edinburgh to London. On 21 November 1994, eighty-six playwrights felt confident enough to sign a letter to the *Guardian* challenging theatres nationwide to produce at least three new plays a year.

Gradually, the early work of Ridley and Neilson was joined by other new writing in London. Under the artistic directorship of Stephen Daldry, the Royal Court – London's prime new writing theatre – gradually became aware of these new voices from the periphery, and soon began vigorously promoting first-time writers. Although at first better known for his interest in gay shows, Daldry produced Joe Penhall's *Some Voices* and Judy Upton's *Ashes and Sand* in autumn 1994. Then, for January 1995, he programmed Kane's debut, *Blasted*, directed by James Macdonald, and the resulting media furore over the shocking content and unsettling form of the play put British new writing on the map. Despite the sheer hysteria of some of the show's reviews, which were answered by the stout defence of her work by Martin Crimp, Caryl Churchill, Edward Bond and Harold Pinter, a new and exciting sensibility had arrived. In the summer, Jez Butterworth's dazzling *Mojo* – hyped as the first debut play to be staged on the Royal Court's main stage since John Osborne's *Look Back in Anger* in 1956 – strongly suggested that new plays by young writers were both fashionable and a box-office draw. One year later, this was confirmed by the arrival of Ravenhill's *Shopping and Fucking*, which, says Dan Rebellato, 'insinuated itself into the popular consciousness more successfully than any play' since *Look Back in Anger*.[57] Soon journalists and cultural pundits were hailing the renaissance of new writing. This excitement tended to overshadow Daldry's other project, to revive modern classics, most memorably David Storey's *The Changing Room* in 1996. But although a couple of emerging young playwrights did enjoy West End transfers, most of their plays remained in the risk-free spaces of state-subsidised new writing theatres, often performed for short runs in small studios.

But the work was both disturbing and pertinent. Although Kane's *Blasted* played to a total of only about a thousand people, it was, in the words of Graham Saunders, 'one of the key plays of the 1990s'.[58] With its evocation of the violence of civil war, its stories of appalling atrocities, its fraught stage images – rape, blinding and cannibalism – and its raw language, it brought Bosnia unforgettably to Sloane Square. It was also an indictment of the media's failure to tell the stories no one wants to hear, in this case about the extreme horrors of war. A similar concern with storytelling was one of the themes of 1990s drama, as evidenced by Ridley's plays, and by Ravenhill's *Shopping and Fucking*, whose title inspired jokes as well as nervousness, and which showed a group of young people struggling to get by in a recognisably contemporary world where sex has been commercialised and consumption sexualised. It included rude stories about the royals, and an oft-quoted speech by one character, Robbie, which begins, 'I think we all need stories, we make up stories so that we can get by.'[59] By contrast, the stories in Neilson's *Penetrator* were paranoid, nightmarish or pornographic: they made for very uncomfortable viewing, and its knife fight was one of the few genuinely hair-raising experiences in the decade's theatre. Also at the Court, Judy Upton's *Ashes and Sand* was the first play to focus on a girl-gang while Nick Grosso's laddish *Peaches* and *Sweetheart* explored the bewilderment wrought by testosterone. Most of the plays were angry at social injustice: Penhall's thrilling *Some Voices* was fuelled by his disgust at the iniquities of the Conservative government's policy of Care in the Community, while Rebecca Prichard's *Essex Girls* portrayed teen pregnancy, and suggested reasons for its prevalence. David Eldridge's

Serving It Up at the Bush was an emotionally powerful tale of working-class kids.

This loose group of young writers formed something of an avant-garde, sharing a similar sensibility, which has been labelled 'in-yer-face theatre'.[60] The term itself appears in several reviews in the 1990s: for example, in April 1994, the *Independent*'s account of Philip Ridley's *Ghost from a Perfect Place* described the play's girl-gang as 'the in-yer-face castrating trio', and when, in 1995, *Trainspotting* transferred to the West End, *The Times* commented: 'The two previous productions of the play brought actors within inches of the audience, and such in-yer-face realism is inevitably reduced when it is staged, this time by Gibson, for a tour of proscenium arch theatres.'[61] In November 1995, Neilson told a journalist that 'I think that in-your-face theatre is coming back – and that is good.'[62] Indeed, during this decade, some of the clearest examples of this style of playwriting came from the keyboards of Ridley, Neilson, Kane and Ravenhill, with the latter two especially having been influenced by, among others, the work of Crimp, which seemed to be at once coolly detached, cruelly direct and also experimental in form. In the wider culture, the term 'in-yer-face' seemed to echo with the zeitgeist. Simon Napier-Bell's account of pop culture exclaimed, 'This was the nineties – the "lottery age" – the "in-yer-face" age.'[63] As early as 1991, 808 State named a dance track 'In Yer Face', and in 1996 the iconic song of the moment of Cool Britannia, the Spice Girls' 'Wannabe', included the line: 'We got Em in the place who likes it in-yer-face.'

In-yer-face theatre was both a new sensibility and a series of specific theatrical devices. In terms of sensibility, these playwrights were drawn to the depiction of psychological and emotional extremes, some of which – such as sexual abuse or viciousness – were truly distressing. They insistently broke taboos and used direct, powerful language, often with fast and furious dialogue. Their sensibility relished the idea of provocation. As a series of theatrical techniques, in-yer-face theatre involved a stage language that emphasised rawness, intensity and swearing, stage images that showed acute pain or comfortless vulnerability, characterisation that preferred complicit victims to innocent ones, and a ninety-minute structure that dispensed with the relief of an interval. In-yer-face theatre depended on certain material conditions, mainly the ready availability of studio spaces (typically seating between fifty and eighty people) which provided ideal conditions for the kind of experiential theatre where audience members felt as if they were actively sharing the emotions being depicted by the actors. Unlike other names, such as 'New Brutalism', which have been used to characterise these plays, in-yer-face theatre describes not just the content of a play but rather the relationship between the stage and the audience. In other words, it strongly suggests what is particular about the experience of watching extreme theatre – the feeling of your personal space being threatened, or violated. This kind of theatre was a radical break with much of the drama of the 1980s. At its best, its aim was to use shock to awaken the moral responses of the audience – its desire was no less than to help change society.

Despite its wide acceptance by theatre practitioners, critics and commentators, the term in-yer-face theatre remains controversial. Sceptics have pointed out that although playwrights such as Ridley, Neilson, Kane and Ravenhill shared some of the same contemporary sensibility in their work, they all wrote in distinctly different styles. While the Kane of *Blasted*, *Phaedra's Love* and *Cleansed* seems to share many of the preoccupations of her peers, her final two plays – *Crave* and *4.48 Psychosis* – align her more with older playwrights such as Crimp and Churchill, and with a more Continental modernist tradition, than with the more naturalistic styles adopted by playwrights such as Penhall and Upton. In a similar vein, the initial response to the undoubted sensationalism of some 1990s drama has now given way to a consideration of its moral seriousness, and its pictures of a fragmented society and alienated individuals.[64] On the other hand, Mike Bradwell, artistic director of the Bush Theatre in the second half of the decade, is surely not alone in pointing out that 'there are as many clichés in "In Yer Face" Theatre as there are in Boulevard Comedy'.[65] Other critics of the concept of in-yer-face theatre argue that foregrounding the much-hyped geezer-chic Royal Court plays, such as Butterworth's *Mojo*, with its motormouthing gangsters and casual viciousness, neglects quieter talents. Lauding the loud and violent boys eclipses many of the female playwrights of the era. The achievements of Max Stafford-Clark's final years at the Royal Court – he was the venue's longest-serving artistic director (1979–93) – tend also to be downplayed in this rush to applaud the new. Yet, under his leadership, the venue bravely battled against grant cuts and in the early 1990s staged important plays such as Marlane Meyer's *Etta Jenks*, Winsome Pinnock's *Talking in Tongues*, Ariel Dorfman's *Death and the Maiden* and Timberlake Wertenbaker's *Three Birds Alighting on a Field*. [66]

Likewise, too great an emphasis on in-yer-face plays artificially elevates a London-centric phenomenon. 'In terms of sensibility,' says Ben Payne of Birmingham Rep, 'there are several writers who don't really fit into London scene', such as Bryony Lavery, Paul Lucas and Sarah Woods.[67] Some commentators also argue that Scottish playwrights 'set themselves an agenda very different to the fashion-victim, "shopping and fucking" introspection of 1990s London'.[68] As the editors of one collection of studies point out, 'a far greater degree of variety and complexity existed within the various forms of playwriting in the 1990s' and these powerfully 'challenge certain tenants of in-yer-face theatre'.[69] Similarly, the *Encore Theatre Magazine* website comments that 'the wave of new writing which followed [*Blasted*] swept away an intriguing moment in British theatre when new writing was represented by Paul Godfrey, and Gregory Motton, and early Martin Crimp'.[70] A revisionist account of the decade has to remind people that Godfrey's imaginative vision, Motton's dense texual poetry and Crimp's severity with form were all once part of a playwriting avant-garde. It could also look at other new talents of the early 1990s, such as Nick Ward, Clare McIntyre and Karen Hope (not to mention older writers such as Timberlake Wertenbaker, Sarah Daniels and Winsome Pinnock), who were swept aside by the wave of in-yer-face plays. As indeed were quieter voices, such as those of Peter Gill, Robert Holman and Richard Cameron. Who today remembers Sheila Yeger?

One influential playwriting style that was distinctly different from the in-yer-face brashness of many UK metropolitan playwrights came from Ireland. At the start of the decade, the Bush Theatre staged Billy

Roche's *The Wexford Trilogy*, three life-affirming plays that explored the claustrophobic mindset of a small town with Chekhovian preciseness and absorbing characterisation. Equally lyrical and emotionally true was Conor McPherson's *The Weir*, which began life in the Royal Court Theatre Upstairs in 1997 and then transferred to the West End for almost three years, then Broadway, its box-office success being crucial to the theatre's fragile finances. Dromgoole describes its redemptive magic as 'the most awesomely assured bit of storytelling, controlling and manipulating the audience with a sure and kind touch'.[71] Many Irish plays were deeply felt, a sublime example being Sebastian Barry's magnificent *The Steward of Christendom* (1995), with a riveting central performance by Donal McCann as Dunne, the Roman Catholic police chief of Dublin who once served the colonial Brits, and now finds himself in a home, aching for the vanished world of the past. One critic summed up McCann's striking appearance: 'He looks like a medieval saint with sad simian features and a mouth that opens to an O, then freezes in twisted contemplation of the story it tells.'[72] Likewise Marina Carr, whose *The Mai* and *Portia Coughlan* visited London, gave voice to an Irish female experience, along with echoes of tragedy and myth, which with 'her attention to narrative, her rich use of language and dialect, and her choice of rural settings arguably situate her as the contemporary heir to a Syngean legacy'.[73] Other writers whose work pulsed with the distinctive linguistic rhythms of Ireland, as well as having a joy in wordplay, include Enda Walsh, whose unique talent was first evident in the exciting *Disco Pigs*, one of the most adrenaline-fuelled plays of an exciting decade, and Martin McDonagh, a London-born writer whose highly successful *Leenane Trilogy* was thrillingly plotted and hilariously satirical. In his work, as Patrick Lonergan argues, 'there are few accurate references to local geography', despite the real names of their settings – McDonagh cares more about character, plot and laughter than rooted authenticity.[74] In such plays, 'the mythical surface of the Irish island idyll is hollowed out by homophobia and almost atavistic violence'.[75] Other new Irish playwrights, such as Daragh Carville and Dermot Bolger, abandoned rural locations and embraced the same kind of urban settings as their English contemporaries. At their best, as for example in Mark O'Rowe's blistering *Howie the Rookie*, their plays mixed bravado storytelling with a strikingly vivid sense of fantasy.

While equally vibrant, Scottish new playwriting was less successful – for no good reason – in London. The main exception, *Trainspotting*, Harry Gibson's stage adaptation of Irvine Welsh's contemporary novel about Edinburgh junkies, was successfully staged all over the country in the early 1990s. The work of David Greig – *Europe*, *The Architect*, *Caledonia Dreaming* and *The Speculator* – was clearly innovative and superbly written, yet failed to journey southwards. Only occasionally, as with his *Cosmonaut's Last Message to the Woman He Once Loved in the Former Soviet Union* (1999), did metropolitan audiences get to see his plays. Likewise, an international hit such as David Harrower's lyrical *Knives in Hens* (1995) was preferred, south of the border, to his more contemporary work, such as *Kill the Old Torture Their Young* (1998). The plays of older writers, such as Chris Hannan (*The Evil Doers* and *Shining Souls*) and Simon Donald (*The Life of Stuff*) were performed in London, but Mike Cullen, whose *Anna Weiss*, a sex abuse drama starring Catherine McCormack, moved from the Traverse to the West End in 1999, was an exceptional case of a young Scottish writer finding success in the metropolis.

Although many critics and commentators applauded young play-wrights – often specifying the ages of new arrivals such as Eldridge or Prichard – older playwrights were similarly productive. As well as safe hands such as David Hare and David Edgar, a younger generation which had emerged in the 1980s – especially Crimp, Doug Lucie and Terry Johnson – all produced excellent work. In 1997, Crimp wrote *Attempts on Her Life*, arguably the most influential play of the decade. Jettisoning traditional ideas of character and plot in favour of staging a series of scenarios in which an unspecified number of onstage actors tell stories about a woman named Anne, the play was thrilling in its originality and aptness to the theme of the construction of individual identity. At one point, Anne is even imagined as a make of car. Other Crimpian images, of terrorism, pornography and war, infused this fierce tone-poem of a play, making it both contemporary and visionary at the same time. Another Crimp play, *The Treatment* (1993), anticipated the in-yer-face sensibility with its stage images of explicit sex and violence. Older veterans also broke new ground. Churchill collaborated with choreographer Ian Spink in *The Skriker* (1994), a typically imaginative play about death, which featured Kathryn Hunter in the title role, her shape-shifting presence 'evocative of the twisted, distorted body of the hysteric' in a story that challenged both conventional and feminist views about the role of women in society.[76] Equally provocative was Churchill's breathtaking *Blue Heart*, two plays which tackled the highly emotive subject of fractured families and lost children by using the linguistic devices of manic repetition and language collapse. As Philip Roberts notes, 'Like a computer virus, all normative language is replaced' by the words 'blue' and 'kettle' in the second play, yet a convincing 'picture of longing and distress' emerges.[77] Similarly powerful was Pinter's *Ashes to Ashes*, staged at the Royal Court in 1996, a visionary two-hander in which a couple talk about an abusive sex game while remembering an incident that suggested a genocidal regime in Britain. Work such as this seemed to be responding to the challenge thrown down by playwrights such as Kane.

Equally important was the renaissance of gay and lesbian drama, which gradually shook off the heritage of the militant coming-out dramas of the 1970s and of the AIDS plays of the 1980s, to present a more rounded view of life and sex. (An exception was Bill Russell's *Elegies for Angels, Punks and Raging Queens*, a 1992 review of AIDS victims based on America's Aids Memorial Quilt.) More typical were Kevin Elyot's *My Night with Reg* (Royal Court, 1994) and Jonathan Harvey's *Beautiful Thing* (Bush, 1994), which gave the genre of gay theatre a makeover, avoiding clichés and grounding their stories in character. The first, which starred comedian John Sessions, was about a group of friends whose relations are all gradually revealed as having been affected by Reg, who never appears, and who symbolises the thrills and threats of promiscuous sex. The second was a tender love story about two working-class teens, which also featured a hilariously eccentric neighbour, Leah, who is into drugs and the records of Mama Cass. Both plays were widely influential, the first being screened on BBC2 television, and the second made into a film in 1996. Yet, in mid-decade, gay theatre was still controversial when it moved into the mainstream. In September 1994, the *Evening Standard*'s former critic, Milton Shulman, bemoaned the fact that plays such as *Beautiful Thing* and *My Night with Reg* successfully transferred to the West End. Yet the 'Stop the Plague of Pink Plays' controversy didn't last, and within a couple of years such views were laughable. But gay theatre itself remained controversial. As Alan Sinfield says, commenting on the genre's dissident origins in the 1970s, 'Gay/lesbian drama doesn't have to be dissident [. . .] I don't think Kevin Elyot's *My Night with Reg* is dissident.'[78] On the other hand, Nicholas de Jongh argues that '*Beautiful Thing* was revolutionary. It did away with a theatrical tradition in which gay men were usually depicted as middle-class, arty, adult, well-dressed and neurotic.'[79]

Over the decade, the Royal Court, the Traverse and the Bush led in the discovery and development of gritty urban dramas. By contrast, two other new writing venues in London – the Hampstead and the Soho – dealt with different sensibilities. The Hampstead was headed by Jenny Topper, who disliked 'tiny slices of life or cocky lad's plays', preferring 'the well-made play that is crammed full of ideas and hides its subversive heart in a cloak of laughter'.[80] Although she supported dangerous new writers such as Ridley, she also staged a wide variety of plays, from the likes of Michael Frayn, Stephen Poliakoff and Jonathan Harvey. One big success was Frank McGuinness's *Someone Who'll Watch Over Me* (1992), a Beirut hostage drama involving an Irishman (Stephen Rea), an Englishman (Alec McCowen) and an American (Hugh Quarshie). By contrast, the Soho, led by Abigail Morris, concentrated on first-time playwrights, which meant that other venues benefited from the development work this venue put into emerging talents. Both these theatres held well-received new writing seasons; both promoted female playwrights, often in the teeth of the fashionable laddish tendency of the decade. Playwrights Timberlake Wertenbaker and Phyllis Nagy had plays staged by the Royal Court, namely Wertenbaker's *Break of Day* and Nagy's *The Strip*, but they could see which way the wind was blowing. Nagy criticised 'this ridiculous promotion of men and bad plays and misogyny' and Wertenbaker condemned the Royal Court, saying that 'suddenly they were hungry for a different kind of play: male violence, homoerotica'.[81] Here, the aesthetic policy of a theatre works, in the words of Elaine Aston and Janelle Reinelt, 'as a form of censorship', a way of excluding other sensibilities. [82] This can be seen by contrasting Royal Court productions of April De Angelis's *Hush* (1992), a poetic account of politics, with Prichard's *Yard Gal* (1998), a much more visceral account of a girl-gang. Other female playwrights had a good decade. As well as Churchill, Pam Gems had a National success with *Stanley* (1996), about the painter Stanley Spencer, and a West End success with *Marlene* (1999), about the film star and cabaret artist Marlene Dietrich. Both plays illustrate the popularity of the biographical play. Elsewhere, one of the most popular plays at the Hampstead was Shelagh Stephenson's *The Memory of Water* (1996), a wonderfully warm comedy directed by Terry Johnson, about three sisters and their memories of their mother, infused with the playwright's characteristic obsession with death. In the early 1990s you might have seen Moira Buffini perform the often-remounted *Jordan* – a play she co-wrote with Anna Reynolds about a woman who kills her own baby – before Buffini became a versatile playwright, penning *Gabriel* (1997) and *Silence* (1999). And the most popular plays produced by the Soho, often making temporary use of venues such as the Cockpit Theatre, included Diane Samuels's *Kindertransport* (1993) and Amanda Whittington's *Be My Baby* (1998), both of which gave sympathetic views of female experience in the past, the first treating the subject of Jewish child refugees from Nazi Germany and the second looking at pregnant teenagers confined in a mother-and-baby home in 1960s Britain. So despite all the complaints about macho plays, the 1990s offered more opportunities to female playwrights than ever before.

Occasionally, the National also discovered a new writer. The best example is Patrick Marber. His plays *Dealer's Choice* (1995) and *Closer* (1997) thrilled critics and audiences with their punchy, frank dialogue. The highly popular *Closer* especially seemed to capture the essential facts about contemporary relationships between the sexes. The sharpness of the writing – at one point the human heart is called a 'fist wrapped in blood' – and its perceptiveness led one critic to write 'of the many four-letter obscenities in Patrick Marber's thrilling London love story for the Nineties, "love" is undoubtedly the most brutal'.[83]

The play has an early example of an internet exchange realised on stage by means of a projection of an online chat, and there was also a scene set in a lap-dancing club which, together with such moments as the phone-sex scene in *Shopping and Fucking* and the porn actress scene in *Attempts on Her Life*, criticised pornography while perhaps being inadvertently part of its domestication. But, as well as promoting Marber, the National also contributed to the decade's new writing trends through its Studio, which offered facilities to writers to develop their work, and then passed their plays on to other theatres. Tanika Gupta's *Voices on the Wind* (1995), about her great-uncle Dinesh Gupta, a fighter against colonial rule in India, was developed by the Studio.

Elsewhere, black writers such as Roy Williams joined Gupta in taking the journey from exploring the worlds of their own heritage to dealing with contemporary urban problems. Williams's 1999 Royal Court play *Lift Off*, for example, examines the appeal of black street culture to both white and black urban youth, while using his trademark street-hard dialogue. As Amelia Howe Kritzer says, the young men 'admire and emulate a particular black stereotype. The young men's ideal, which accords with Thatcherism in some respects, combines toughness and self-sufficiency.'[84] Similarly contemporary was the plight of the women in Winsome Pinnock's *Mules* (1996), commissioned by Clean Break Theatre Company (which makes theatre by and for women prisoners), and whose theme is the exploitation of young black women as 'mules' in drug trafficking. Other black writers such as Zindika, Biyi Bandele and Trish Cooke also emerged. By contrast, one of the most successful Asian plays of the decade mixed comedy with its sorrows: Ayub Khan-Din's *East is East* (1997) is a semi-autobiographical look at a 1970 Salford family, which has a Pakistani father and a white mother who run the local fish and chip shop. Known as 'Genghis' Khan to his kids, George the tyrannical father has to deal with the aspirations of his six offspring. What's beautifully observed are the arguments not only between the parents, but between the children. Each asserts their own identity in a different way – each has to cross a no man's land between being Pakistani and being British. Each has to redefine their relationship with their parents.

A lot of the fuel powering 1990s new writing came from America. After Crimp read the work of David Mamet, his own dialogues became more energetic.[85] When Ravenhill saw Canadian Brad Fraser's *Unidentified Human Remains and the True Nature of Love*, he was inspired to write his own version of American blank fictions. Talking of American dramatists, the Royal Court successfully staged John Guare's glittering if brittle *Six Degrees of Separation*, starring Stockard Channing, in 1992, and one of its greatest successes came from South America: Chilean author Ariel Dorfman's *Death and the Maiden* (1991), a political play in which Juliet Stevenson gave an inspired performance as Paulina, the torture victim who meets, or thinks she meets, her torturer from fifteen years previously. In 1993, the Royal Court *American Season* included Mamet's *Oleanna*, a controversial play in which a university lecturer is confronted by a feminist student (David Suchet and Lia Williams directed by Pinter in this production). Seen by many as a misogynist attack on political correctness, the lecturer physically assaults the student at the climax. At one performance, men in the audience called out, 'Smack the bitch', and the show report for 3 July stated that 'there was loud applause for the fight but those clapping were told to stop by others [in the audience]'.[86] In the same season, Crimp's *The Treatment* was especially memorable for its stage picture of a blind New York taxi driver. Elsewhere, the vogue for the dirty realism of some American writers was so strong that Tracy Letts's *Killer Joe*, which opened just after Kane's *Blasted* in January 1995, got much better reviews. In general, American theatre was as inspiring as Irish theatre. David Edgar says, 'The two texts that really turned things around were Tony Kushner's *Angels in America* and David Mamet's *Oleanna* in 1993 – they reminded British theatre of the sort of play we used to do so well. A lot of people sensed that if American writers could write seriously and imaginatively about today's issues, then so could younger British writers.'[87]

Touring companies were also vital to the development of new writing. After leaving the Royal Court in 1993, Max Stafford-Clark set up Out of Joint with producer Sonia Friedman, and this small company was responsible for some of the most striking work of the decade, from *The Steward of Christendom* to *Shopping and Fucking*. They also produced Wertenbaker's *Break of Day*, Churchill's *Blue Heart* and Ravenhill's *Some Explicit Polaroids*. As Philip Roberts and Stafford-Clark say, other plays by April De Angelis, Simon Bennett, Judy Upton and David Hare reflect the company's 'lifelong preoccupation with new writing'.[88] Building on his experience with both the Royal Court and Joint Stock in the 1970s, Stafford-Clark developed the workshopping approach to theatre making by involving the actors with the playwright in generating ideas. Similarly, the touring company Paines Plough, led by Vicky Featherstone, helped Kane, Ravenhill, Greig, Parv Bancil and a host of other new talents. The feminist touring company Sphinx produced work such as Bryony Lavery's *Goliath* (1997), a tough piece inspired by Beatrix Campbell's book about the riots that exploded across Britain's housing estates in 1991. Other touring companies, which had an explicitly political remit and had been important in previous years, such as 7:84, died a slow death in the 1990s.

Over the decade, the main thematic trends in new writing, as summarised by David Pattie, were 'a preoccupation with masculinity', 'a welcome tendency to treat gay and lesbian relationships as entirely normal', 'an interest in the marginalised and excluded' and 'a wider exposure for writers from other parts of the British isles'.[89] If the dominant themes were the crisis of masculinity, violence and sexuality, and one of the commonest settings the poverty-stricken underclass estate, the idea of storytelling also interested playwrights. In the final analysis, the sheer variety and richness of British playwriting left a lasting impression on both critics and audiences. The following examples all successfully transferred: Hare's *Via Dolorosa*, a monologue performed by the playwright himself, was an autobiographical account of a visit to the Middle East, and addressed questions of faith; Johnson's *Hysteria* and *Dead Funny* were superbly structured farces – one about Freud and Dali, and the other about the British comic tradition – whose lightning wit and emotional depth delighted audiences; plays such as Lavery's *Frozen* (1998) and Charlotte Jones's *In Flame* (1999) presented different and occasionally difficult aspects of women's experience; populist entertainments such as Lee Hall's *Cooking with Elvis* (1998) and Ben Elton's *Popcorn* (1996) covered disability, movie violence and pop culture. If new writing began the decade in a parlous condition, it ended it on a high. Given its richness, and its success in many countries abroad, it is surely not absurd to claim that it gave British theatre an international boost.

Experimental, fringe and live art

In the 1990s, many experimental companies moved decisively into the mainstream. The best example is Théâtre de Complicité, a so-called physical theatre company which since 1983 had explored the visual and movement aspects of theatre in highly innovative productions. It was welcomed by the National, where it staged *Street of Crocodiles* (1992), based on the work of Polish-Jewish writer Bruno Schultz, and *Out of a House Walked a Man* (1994), based on the writings of Russian absurdist Daniil Kharms, as well as enjoyable versions of Dürrenmatt's *The Visit* (1991) and Brecht's *The Caucasian Chalk Circle* (1997). *The Visit* was memorable both for the manic miming of the railway station scenes and for Kathryn Hunter, whose Clara had a viciously rasping voice, hoarse from decades of cigarette smoking. Led by director Simon McBurney, who worked with regulars such as Hunter, Marcello Magni and Lilo Baur, the company's other notable successes included *The Three Lives of Lucie Cabrol* (1994), an unsentimental view of French peasant life based on John Berger's *Pig Earth*, and *Mnemonic* (1999), the company's most resonant, meaningful and inspiring production: at its start, audience members had to put on an eye mask and hold a leaf, with McBurney – who also playfully took a call on his mobile phone – asking them to think of its veins as their family tree. Then the epic play unfolded through two strands: twenty-something Alice's journey across Europe in search of her father's identity, and the discovery in the Alps of an ice-man, a body from prehistoric times, which spoke of humankind's collective heritage and identity. When a Neolithic mass grave was mentioned the parallels with Bosnia were strongly suggested.

Here and in its other work, the company's style was distinguished by imaginative use of simple props and the bodies of the performers. Typically, the performers' fingers would become bushes or books become birds. McBurney describes how, in *Street of Crocodiles*, through a process of improvisation, 'the actors physically learned to shift together, like a flock of starlings. They learned to dip and wheel and found a fantastic pleasure in it.'[90] Other magic moments included the haunting slow-motion procession from Bohemia to Sicilia as the cast of *The Winter's Tale* (1992) changed from being travellers into mourners, in funeral garb; the breathtaking opening of *Street of Crocodiles* when an echoing library came to life, as one character 'walked' down a wall, another emerged from a packing case and others rolled across the stage; in *The Three Lives of Lucie Cabrol*, the company became trees, or offered their fingers to Lucie for her to pick berries from them; in *Mnemonic* a wooden chair tenderly becomes a corpse. But as well as using these poor theatre techniques, the company was also well marketed. Rebranding itself as Complicite (dropping the foreign elements of its name) it toured internationally to great acclaim during the decade.

Straddling the divide between live art and written theatre were companies such as the Sheffield-based Forced Entertainment, which adopted a style of quiet conversational delivery, suggesting through its fragmentary scripts that its grip on reality was tentative. Led by Tim Etchells and a handful of regular performers, the company also delighted in childish props, animal masks, pop-culture references, and often parodied other forms of entertainment such as cabaret or children's TV. Their best shows – *Speak Bitterness* (1994) – involved using everyday expressions and language to create an emotional crescendo. In *Speak Bitterness* a line of seven performers at a long steel table on a bare stage delivered a script made up of real and imaginary confessional statements, from murder and mayhem to white lies and cowardice, delivered deadpan to the audience. Other shows offered more visual variety: in *Emmanuel Enchanted* (1992), performers came on and off the stage wearing placards with names such as 'The Hypnotised Girl'; in *Club of No Regrets* (1993), a character called Helen X bossed around a pair of performers inside a tiny box set, helped by two incompetent assistants; in the comical *Showtime* (1996), one performer was dressed in a suicide bomber vest and another as a dog; in *Pleasure* (1997) a sexually aroused pantomime horse was teamed up with a weary, melancholic nightclub MC.

Some of the most exciting experiences of the decade came from the mixture of dance and theatre. The most impressive and influential company was DV8 Physical Theatre, with its director-choreographer Lloyd Newson and performer Nigel Charnock, who developed a style of narrative-led dance that used contemporary music and movement in a particularly forceful way. DV8's masterpiece, *Enter Achilles* (1995), featured a group of men drinking and fighting in a pub, and was – like so many written plays in this decade – a meditation on masculinity. As Newson wrote in the show's programme, '"Unmanly" behaviour is often considered threatening, particularly by those who uphold rigid precepts of how men should behave. Why should non-conformity produce so much abhorrence and fear? [. . .] we will look at how the pint, shared between men, can become a metaphor for bodily fluids / our life source, and how the qualities of the glass (the pint) can represent our rigidity, fragility and transparency.'[91] Other shows had similarly provocative subject matter: *Strange Fish* (1992) was about religion and belief; *MSM* (1993) – whose title derived from the sociological term Men who have Sex with Men – used interviews with gay men who had experience of cottaging. Likewise, *The Happiest Day of My Life* (1999) was about the desire for sexual excitement and romance, featuring a first half in which the idea of 1990s hedonism was to the fore, and a second half set on a small island in a swimming pool, a visual metaphor for one married couple's emotional estrangement: will this couple sink or swim? Striking visual effects included a larger-than-life film of a gyrating woman projected on to the spray from a shower and a lone man dancing with an upended sofa. Other similarly dynamic dance companies included V-TOL (Vertical Take-off and Landing), formed in April 1991 by artistic director Mark Murphy, and Matthew Bourne's Adventures in Motion Pictures, whose 1995 all-male *Swan Lake* was an enormous success. These developments were partly indebted to the work of German choreographer and dancer Pina Bausch.

All of these companies continued to inspire each other. For example, Volcano, a physical theatre company resident in Swansea and specialising in provocative work, inspired Frantic Assembly. Set up in 1994 by Scott Graham, Steven Hoggett and Vicki Middleton, Frantic Assembly mixed dance moves and thumping music with a playwright's text. Their first manic phase involved *The Generation Trilogy* – three hip, rave-infused plays called *Klub*, *Flesh* and *Zero* (1995–7) – the first two with texts by Spencer Hazel and performed with hazardous physical energy. The subject matter was thrillingly cotemporary: drugs and club culture (following the death of Leah Betts), selling your body (from performance to prostitution) and millennium angst. Regularly characterised as the future of British theatre, Frantic Assembly ended the decade with a 1998 hit *Sell Out*, text by Michael Wynne, and *Hymns* (1999), written by Chris O'Connell. The process of creating *Sell Out* involved a questionnaire put together by Wynne, which asked about relations and emotions. The resulting show was, in the words of Graham and Hoggett, 'full of back-stabbing and sexual shenanigans' which 'debunked the "friends are the new family" notion so popular at the time'.[92] By contrast, *Hymns* was about a funeral, death and male competitiveness.

Old campaigners from the 1960s, such as the People Show and Welfare State International, soldiered on during the 1990s, but their energy was on the wane. The Bethnal Green-based People Show continued with their edgy brand of surrealism: in *The Solo Experience* (1992), actor Mark Long expounded Einstein's Theory of Relativity; in *Fetch the Gramophone Out* (1997), old age was explored using waltzing armchairs; and shows such as *A Song without a Sound* (1999) featured Josette Bushell-Mingo, a People Show regular. Whenever the company couldn't think of a title, it just gave their shows a number. Meanwhile, the Cumbria-based Welfare State International, led by John Fox, specialised in large-scale participatory public spectacles, using processions, puppets, folk song and fireworks. In 1990, they delivered the biggest lantern festival in Europe for Glasgow City of Culture, as well as creating the *Feast of Furness*, the climax of a bold seven-year project at Barrow in Furness, with eleven shows devised in collaboration with local community groups. The grand finale, *The*

Golden Submarine, an outdoor spectacle which played to a local audience of about 5,000, was characterised, says Baz Kershaw, by huge 'extraordinary' visual effects, although this 'spectacular imagery' was offset by a story 'which had all the simple predictability of agit prop at its crudest'.[93] Being inclusive and celebratory, this kind of local carnival was also heavily dependent on local government funding.

In the context of experiment, there were two playwrights whose work was sufficiently distinctive to merit special attention. Howard Barker, with the Wrestling School – a state-subsidised company devoted exclusively to his work – continued his mission to trouble the audience's notion of naturalism, developing a drama that dissolves literal representation and connects more with the passions of the unconscious than with conscious reason. Instead of reconciling audiences in togetherness, he aimed to fragment responses. Most successful was *The Europeans* (1991), a dark drama set in the aftermath of the 1683 Siege of Vienna and featuring Katrin, a woman whose agonising ordeal exposes a world of unreason in a poetic text that felt like a chance meeting between Voltaire's Candide and Lautréamont's Maldoror. As a mutilated victim of the Turks, she refuses either to turn the other cheek or to suffer in silence. With its strong stage images and visionary intimations of a cultural struggle between Christianity and Islam, this is one of the most underrated plays of the decade. Barker's prolific output included *Uncle (Vanya)* (1993) and *Hated Nightfall* (1994), which revisited Chekhov's play and the death of the Romanovs in 1918, respectively. Towards the end of the decade, *Und*, Barker's one-woman show about the symbiotic relationship between the torturer and victim in the Holocaust, pushed the boundaries of his theatre. Likewise, *Ursula* was a richly poetic play about the violent tensions between sexual love and spiritual sacrifice. Although many of his plays had a historical subject, Barker was clear that 'the only things worth describing now are things that did not happen' and his plays created a highly emotional and allusively imaginative world.[94] They were not historical documentaries. Similarly, Edward Bond continued with his project to write difficult, non-naturalistic work, and to devise a distinctive dramaturgy with which to present it, one aimed at forcing audiences to make a moral choice. In the 1990s, he directed, for the RSC, his Shakespeare-inspired, if long-winded, *In the Company of Men* (1992) – which looked at the connections between capitalism and violence by examining the relationship of an arms manufacturer and his son – to largely uncomprehending reviews, and this contributed to his marginalisation from the mainstream. In response, he moved increasingly into theatre-in-education, especially with Big Brum in Birmingham, while at the same time enjoying productions of his work on the Continent, especially in France. For Big Brum, he wrote plays such as *At the Inland Sea* (1995) and *Eleven Vests* (1997), which examine humanity in times of authority and genocide. His most important 1990s play was *Coffee* (1996), which imagines a nightmarish war, in which civilians are executed and the individual's left-field moral stand is seen as vital to survival. It was produced by a mixed company of amateur and professional actors in Wales. In the words of David Rabey, 'Rather than present an allegory or thesis in fundamentally consistent terms which imply a correct explanation, *Coffee* provides an expressionistic dreamworld odyssey of dislocating experience and discovery, like *Early Morning*.'[95] Other once-experimental practitioners such as Steven Berkoff lost much of their energy in the 1990s. Berkoff's 1990 version of Kafka's *The Trial* at the National, for example, featured a quietly intense performance by Antony Sher along with an immensely self-indulgent one by Berkoff himself. The most characteristic Berkoff play of these years was 'Dog', one of his three-part *One Man* show (Garrick, 1993), in which he played a rabid Rottweiler and its skinhead owner, a binge-drinking Millwall supporter.

London fringe

As well as companies and playwrights some venues were important. The most notably experimental fringe theatre was BAC (Battersea Arts Centre) in south London, headed by Tom Morris from 1995, who provided countless opportunities for theatre companies to develop their work at this venue. Beneficiaries included Complicite (*Mnemonic*, later staged at the Riverside Studios), Frantic Assembly, Told by an Idiot, Improbable Theatre and Ridiculusmus. New directors such as James Menzies-Kitchin plied their craft. At BAC, a handful of resident producers monitored the projects of dozens of groups and individuals, covering everything from opera to puppetry. BAC pioneered adventurous seasonal programming, the idea of 'scratch nights' (when work in progress could be shown), and hosted an annual festival of visual and devised theatre which brought in performers from all over the world, and even gave mime a good name. As one journalist summed up, 'Under Morris's artistic directorship, BAC has been transformed from a marginal fringe venue into a buzzing powerhouse of experiment and development that is setting the agenda for the next generation of theatre-makers.'[96] But while BAC often produced new work, equally important in London in the early 1990s was the ICA, which hosted companies from all over the UK, such as Forced Entertainment. Another fringe venue, the Drill Hall, specialised in gay theatre and one of its big successes was Claire Dowie's *Easy Access (for the Boys)* in 1998, a riveting but excruciatingly painful show about child abuse, in which Dowie controversially used a video of her own daughter playing in the park, with a voiceover describing a sexual fantasy. While plays such as *My Night with Reg* and *Beautiful Thing* showed that gay theatre could succeed in the commercial mainstream, other gay performers – such as Neil Bartlett's Gloria company, Bette Bourne and Bloolips – played to a narrower audience. Gloria (*Night after Night*, 1993) was especially significant in its attempts to reclaim the genre of the musical and the notion of theatrical pleasure from the exigencies of sentimental commercialism.

Some fringe theatres in London, often located above a pub and completely unfunded, played a crucial role in the mid-1990s in staging the first plays of writers who later came to wider prominence. In May 1993, the Old Red Lion theatre hosted the London New Play Festival, run by Phil Setren, which included early plays by Mark Ravenhill and Joe Penhall. Eighteen months later, Ravenhill's *Fist* at the Finborough pub theatre attracted the attention of Out of Joint's Max Stafford-Clark, and led eventually to his production of *Shopping and Fucking*. As Dominic Dromgoole remembers: 'In the mid-1990s, there was a more vibrant garage-band feel when anyone could get their play on at the Old Red Lion or the Finborough. And people would enjoy that. [. . .] You were as likely to have a good evening on the fringe as at the National.'[97] This ferment of youthful energy at the margins fed into the main new writing theatres and, occasionally, reached the West End. For example, American playwright D. M. W. Greer's *Burning Blue*, about anti-gay prejudice in the US Navy, travelled from the King's Head pub theatre to the Theatre Royal Haymarket in 1995. Likewise, a tiny theatre such as the Gate in Notting Hill was completely unsubsidised but managed to stage artistic director Stephen Daldry's revelatory season of Spanish Golden Age plays in 1991; at various times, you could see a rare Botho Strauss or Thomas Bernhard here or even work by Kane; other heads of this hot venue were director and writer David Farr and director Laurence Boswell.

Experimental and international

Most fringe theatre took place in traditional theatre spaces. However, a theatre could also be an attic, basement, converted cinema, abandoned warehouse, hillside or an open street. Director Deborah Warner's *St Pancras Project* (1995) used the ruined neo-gothic Midland Grand Hotel next to King's Cross railway station as a site-specific venue for a fantastical walk in which audiences of one person at a time followed a route which felt as if it was haunted by ghosts from a past era, with glimpses of maids, bell-boys, tea services, leather shoes and petticoats. One room was planted with grass; in the distance a girl sobbed. Several other companies such as Artangel, Artsadmin and Station House Opera explored the possibilities of site-specific work, which crossed over into art installations such as the Artangel project of Rachel Whiteread's controversial concrete *House* (1993) in east London, a Turner Prize winner. Even when a play was confined to a traditional theatre, there was room for experiment. Warner's version of Beckett's *Footfalls* in 1994 spread itself across the balconies and gangways of the Garrick Theatre in the West End, and was promptly stopped by the Beckett estate for failing to obey the author's strict stage directions. In 1994, Daldry remodelled the whole of the Royal Court's auditorium to stage his revival of Arnold Wesker's *The Kitchen* and in 1997 the National's Olivier auditorium was given the same treatment for Complicite's version of *The Caucasian Chalk Circle*.

The *St Pancras Project* was produced by the London International Festival of Theatre (LIFT), an event which occurred every two years and was a strong reminder of the ability of London to attract, and be inspired by, international talent. Over the decade LIFT brought many delights from afar, such as George C. Wolfe's *The Colored Museum*, a hilarious show in which black Americans satirised themselves, as well as several visits from Bobby Baker, performance artist extraordinaire who took the mickey out of shopping, cooking, female roles and performance art itself. The Market Theatre from South Africa and the Maly Theatre from Russia, the Craiova Theatre from Romania and Societas Raffaello Sanzio from Italy, all testified to a new internationalism and opened the eyes of local audiences to different theatrical possibilities. Most spectacular of all was *Periodo Villa Villa*, by Argentinian group De La Guarda, a wild and joyous airborne show which sprinkled the audience with water and amazed it with the performers' sense of sheer euphoria. LIFT also produced straight plays, most notably Dorfman's *Death and the Maiden*. Other festivals included the National Review of Live Art (held in Glasgow and at the ICA), It's Queer Up North (Manchester) and Mayfest (Glasgow).

Live art

Elsewhere, much experimental theatre was hived off into the ghetto of live art. As Baz Kershaw comments, following the partial demise of the state-of-the-nation play, 'Live art – or time-based art, or performance art – became the new "political theatre" of the rising generation.'[98] New groups such as Blast Theory (1991), Stan's Café (1991) and Third Angel (1995) devised various ways of creating fresh forms of theatre entertainment. Blast Theory's early work used club culture for multimedia performance; their *Invisible Bullets* (1994) was a crime scene reconstruction in Hoxton, and in *Kidnap* (1998) two willing members of the public were sequestered while the event was streamed online. Stan's Café's *Voodoo City* (1995) involved a long incantation, wild dancing and slapstick magic; their *Simple Maths* (1997) was an hour-long show in which five performers changed the order in which they sat on six chairs. Third Angel collaborated with Forced Entertainment in *On Pleasure*, a short film about the latter's devising process. In *Senseless* (1998) three corridor spaces held three blindfold performers for three ten-hour days, each with a different task: measuring time, taking photographs, drawing every room they'd ever lived in. Other performers were even more extreme. In 1996, at the ICA, body artist Franko B – in the several parts of *I'm Not Your Babe* – cut himself and bled, using his body as a site of mutilation and pain, which was a powerful statement about human fragility, an image of self-sacrifice and an echo of the concerns of many playwrights with physical mutilation.[99] In Scotland, Suspect Culture – led by director Graham Eatough and playwright Greig – produced two experimental masterpieces, *Timeless* (1997) and *Mainstream* (1999). Other UK companies, such as Red Shift or the David Glass Ensemble, strove to inject some physicality into stale stagings. Although these kinds of experiments did push out boundaries and troubled taboos, the commercial sector also benefited by assimilating softer versions of many of these techniques. In the words of John Bull, 'the relationship between the mainstream and the *avant-garde* is more parasitic than symbiotic'.[100] In the 1990s, commerce proved stronger than experiment.

Outside London: England, Scotland, Wales and Northern Ireland

England

Theatres outside London had a bad decade: they were the main victims of the cuts in Arts Council funding and, by 1998, about thirty regional reps had deficits totalling more than £10 million. The situation was so bad that John Bull could accurately comment that 'regional theatre has fallen into a state of financial panic in which even the proven products of the established mainstream appear a dangerous risk'.[101] The strains of creaking budgets in the regional reps, that network of established repertory theatres most of which had a proud tradition of productions of all kinds, could be felt all around the country, from Bristol and Bath to Birmingham, Manchester and Leeds, and in places as diverse as Stoke or Salisbury, with news that first one and then another of the smaller theatres outside London was in serious trouble. For example, the Cheltenham Everyman stopped producing its own shows in 1993, the Redgrave in Farnham closed in 1995, the Thorndike in Leatherhead followed suit in 1997, and the Wolsey in Ipswich went dark in 1999. By 1997, when New Labour came to power, the years of Conservative underfunding of theatres outside London meant that, in Olivia Turnbull's words, 'approximately three-quarters of Britain's provincial producing houses had had to severely pare down activities and had proclaimed imminent close in the face of enormous accumulated and operational deficits'.[102] In 1999, Peter Boyden – on behalf of Arts Council England – undertook to investigate the *Roles and Functions of the English Regional Producing Theatres*, and his findings were that of forty-five producing theatres, thirty were operating with a deficit, and this was reported as a crisis in which 'most of the country's best regional theatres are technically insolvent after 20 years of chronic underfunding', followed by the obvious conclusion that 'a failure to take risks for fear of further losses was cramping creativity'.[103]

Lack of funding did indeed lead to a contraction of the repertoire, which was characterised by David Edgar as a nation witnessing 'major outbreaks of *Seagulls*, *Blithe Spirits*, *Doll's Houses* and various Ostrovskis; as the 1990s draw to an end, it appears that it is once again *Three Sisterses* and *Hamlets* that are breeding beyond epidemiological control'.[104] In most of the reps, revivals of classics were seen as less risky to stage in box-office terms than new work because at least the public was familiar with the play titles. Such brand recognition also extended to star actors, who preferred to act in classics than in new plays. This also meant that many young directors gravitated towards the classics because that was where the work was. In general, costs meant that managements preferred plays with small casts to plays with large ones. New plays with large casts by unknown writers were simply rejected. The most frequently revived living authors were Ayckbourn, Godber and Willy Russell, whose plays could be characterised as new writing lite. In many places, even being a museum of safe plays was not enough for some theatres – there was a strong trend towards musicals, comedy shows and other populist entertainments.

As Kate Dorney and Ros Merkin comment, 'crises run like a sore' for the past quarter century in theatre outside London.[105] In the early 1990s especially, Conservative government policy exacerbated the problem. By 1993–4, the whole network of regional reps appeared to be under attack: the government cut £5 million grant-in-aid to the Arts Council, there were news reports of a hit list of ten theatres, and the resignation of veteran farceur Brian Rix from the Drama Panel of the Arts Council contributed to a sense of acute turmoil. The 1990s saw an erosion of artistic leadership as the new managerial culture supplanted artists with executives, and marketing departments grew. Despite this dismal picture, there were resourceful theatres and some glimmers of hope. The Theatre Royal in Plymouth, led by Simon Stokes, managed to stay out of debt, and so did the Palace Theatre in Watford, under Lawrence Till. Although it ended the decade in the red, the West Yorkshire Playhouse, newly created in 1990 and headed by Jude Kelly, was a regional powerhouse. A typical example of its imaginative resourcefulness was getting Complicite's Kathryn Hunter to play the title role in *King Lear*. Kelly also promoted new writing, such as Crimp's *Getting Attention* (1991), a child-abuse drama, and Trevor Griffiths's *The Gulf Between Us* (1992), a political play about the first Gulf War. Its co-production of Ben Elton's *Popcorn* (about Hollywood movie violence) with the Nottingham Playhouse in 1996 transferred to the West End. In 1997, the West Yorkshire Playhouse also produced Dona Daley's *Weathering the Storm*, a love story set in the context of post-war migration from the West Indies.

Other high-profile theatres experienced a chequered decade. The Birmingham Rep, for example, in 1992 staged a disastrous production of *Biko*, a chamber opera about the black South African political activist Steve Biko. But the arrival of Bill Alexander as artistic director in the same year raised the theatre's profile nationally. As Claire Cochrane sums up: 'National critical approval, awards, regular London appearances: all were indicative of a company which was establishing itself as an artistic force.'[106] Despite ongoing deficit problems, Alexander promoted multi-racial casting for classics and directed memorable shows such as Jonson's *The Alchemist*; under his eye, Terry Hands's *The Importance of Being Earnest* came to the Old Vic, and

Lucy Bailey created a version of Tennessee Williams's *Baby Doll* (1999), which transferred to the National. The theatre hosted ace Romanian director Silviu Purcărete. New work was developed by Anthony Clark, who in 1992 staged Rod Dungate's *Playing by the Rules*, about male prostitution, and Sarah Woods's *Nervous Women*, a post-feminist ghost story (both writers had been students on Edgar's influential MA in Playwriting course at Birmingham University). Other new playwrights included Kate Dean, Bryony Lavery, Paul Lucas, Nick Stafford and novelist David Lodge. Ben Payne's appointment as literary manager in 1995 led to the creation of the Door, a studio dedicated to new work. Memorable work included *East is East*, a co-production, which, says the historian of the rep, 'came across in Birmingham as simultaneously comic, shocking, surreal and warmly sympathetic'.[107] Likewise, Andy de la Tour's *The Landslide* (1997), co-produced with West Yorkshire Playhouse, correctly anticipated Labour's election victory, while Bryony Lavery's *Frozen*, a paedophile murder drama with *EastEnders* star Anita Dobson, was a hit.

New writing was evident at many venues, and especially at Live Theatre, Newcastle, a specialist new writing theatre, where artistic director Max Roberts worked with local writers such as Peter Flannery, Michael Wilcox, Peter Straughan and Julia Darling. Other talent included Alan Plater and Lee Hall, whose successes *Cooking with Elvis* and *Spoonface Steinberg* (starring Hunter) began life on Tyneside and Sheffield before transferring to London. In Coventry, Chris O'Connell worked at the Belgrade Theatre, for example staging *Big Burger Chronicles* in 1996, and his Theatre Absolute produced *Car* (1999), about four joy riders, the first in his *Street Trilogy* of plays about youth, poverty and violence. In Scarborough, in 1996, after six years of fundraising, Ayckbourn opened a two-stage home in the Stephen Joseph Theatre, a former cinema. Occasionally a local writer would move towards the metropolis: for example, Richard Cameron (born in Doncaster and for many years a teacher in Scunthorpe) had his plays produced by the Bush.

All over the country, the main centres had mixed experiences. Manchester Royal Exchange, led by Braham Murray and Gregory Hersov, did good work but was badly damaged by an IRA bomb in

1996, reopening some two years later. The first production in the restored and refurbished theatre was a restaging of Stanley Houghton's classic *Hindle Wakes*, which had been running when the bomb went off. Andy Hay's Bristol Old Vic, based at the Theatre Royal, which opened in 1766 and is the oldest theatre in the UK, managed to produce large-scale shows such as a revival of *The Marat/Sade*, *A Midsummer Night's Dream* and an admirable version of Williams's *A Streetcar Named Desire*, with Tara Fitzgerald. New work included plays by Jim Cartwright, Catherine Johnson and Kwame Kwei-Armah. At the Newcastle Playhouse, the internationally minded director Alan Lyddiard produced Orwell's *Animal Farm* (1993), which stayed in the repertoire for twelve years, touring extensively abroad. In 2001 he created a version of the same author's *Nineteen Eighty-Four*. Anthony Burgess's own stage adaptation of his novella *A Clockwork Orange* (1995) was another keynote production. Elsewhere, venues such as the Sheffield Crucible and the Leicester Haymarket soldiered on. Lesser theatres, such as the Derby Playhouse, sometimes struggled to find populist plays: it often fell back on John Godber's populist work, a big success being his *On the Piste* in 1991.[108] Sometimes, a theatre could have a crucial if barely visible role: Daldry's outstanding National revival of *An Inspector Calls* was first mounted in a smaller version at the York Theatre Royal, where a lack of money paradoxically freed his imagination.[109]

Some English companies were formed as an explicit challenge to the theatre of the metropolis. Based in Halifax, Barrie Rutter's Northern Broadsides was set up in 1992 with a mission to perform Shakespeare and the classics with what Shellard calls 'a Yorkshire sensibility and celebrating the region's distinctive speech patterns'.[110] Performing with a fast pace, minimal props and often in unconventional spaces (cattle markets, riding stables, churches, mills), the company created memorably fresh productions of *Richard III* (1992), with Rutter in the title role, *A Midsummer Night's Dream* (1994), and Yorkshire writer Blake Morrison's version of Kleist's *The Cracked Pot* (1995). Elsewhere, touring companies such as Kneehigh, Trestle, Millstream and Compass did good and often innovative work, while community plays all over the country offered exceptional opportunities for large-scale participation by local people, and could be anything from a nostalgic celebration of a place's historical past to an innovative, site-specific experiment.

Scotland

In the 1990s, Scottish theatre expanded its vision. Due to changes in the political structure after New Labour introduced partial devolution, theatre shifted from being, in Adrienne Scullion's words, 'much preoccupied with issues of colonialism, marginalism and parochialism' to being a 'site of national political and social debate, as well as of aesthetic and dramaturgical innovation and experiment'.[111] At the forefront of this was the Traverse Theatre, which promoted not only Neilson, but also David Greig and David Harrower, whose *Knives in Hens* was one of the best new plays of the decade. Set in a rural society that was deliberately ambiguous in its historical reality, this resonant and evocative piece explored language, literacy and desire while at the same time telling a clear story with a freshly minted language. By contrast, his *Kill the Old Torture Their Young* (1998), with its figure of the Rock Star whose life spent flying across the globe means that he is almost untouched by the various problematic local identities of the other characters, was less successful. It was, however, Greig who emerged as the country's most influential playwright. At the start of his career, he immediately dropped the clichés of Scottish playwriting and, with *Europe* (1994), presented a powerful image of a railway station in central Europe at the crossroads of change, in a finely wrought play which ends with its female characters embarking on a migratory lifestyle as the burning station consumes their fathers. Greig's work is highly individual because, in the words of Dan Rebellato, of 'the conscious and artful way in which he is trying to come to terms with the immense changes being wrought across the world by globalisation: a perspective shaped and enhanced by his experience of a multiple and ambiguous Scotland'.[112] Greig's characteristic themes – the struggle to communicate along with intersecting lives – were beautifully realised in both *The Architect* (1996) and *The Cosmonaut's Last Message to the Woman He Once Loved in the Former Soviet Union*, whose exploding space rocket resonates through the lives of a variety of characters. Greig was also a powerful advocate for Scottish playwriting, arguing as early as 1995 that there was a 'flowering of Scottish plays' while at the same time urging the theatre community to trust and support new playwrights.[113]

In terms of identity politics, Scottish playwrights threw aside clichés of traditional Scottish identity and created, in David Pattie's words, 'a sense of identity in general that is fluid and transforming itself – while at the same time showing themselves to fully aware of how divisive and fragmented the experience of identity in the modern world might be'.[114] So older writers such as Chris Hannan and Simon Donald produced work which was contemporary in its language, sensibility and visual images: in Hannan's extraordinary and anarchic *Shining Souls* (1996) themes include the search for spiritual meaning and the politics of place. In his *The Evil Doers* (1990), set in Glasgow, the characters exist in a limbo land in which the working-class Sammy renames himself Danny Glasgow, and offers to guide tourists through a city that is fast becoming unfamiliar to him. Similarly, Stephen Greenhorn's 'road movie' *Passing Places* visualises Scotland as a new country full of newcomers from other parts of the UK and Europe. In Donald's *The Life of Stuff* (1992), there a grimly humorous episode when a stoned young woman nibbles a severed toe she has mistaken for a sausage: the picture the play paints is a bleak urban nightmare of violence as well as laughter. More traditional in content, although presented in an excitingly theatrical way, Sue Glover's *Bondagers* (1991) – about women who worked the land in the 1860s – was the latest in a long line of plays that reclaim the lives of women lost to history. Similarly, former pitman Mike Cullen's *The Cut* (1993) explored the world of the miners, a traditional subject, by using a punchy, revenge-thriller format. On the populist side, Liz Lochhead's crisply written *Perfect Days* (1998) brightly explored the desire of Barbs – a thirty-eight-year-old hairdresser played by Siobhan Redmond in a shockingly carrot-coloured wig – to have a baby in a show that was part sitcom, part contemporary issue play. Other women playwrights such as Rona Muro, Nicola McCartney and Zinnie Harris also made their debuts, plus gay writers such as John Binnie. Indeed, the 1990s saw a huge variety of work in Scotland. For example, the Glasgow Citizens – run by Giles Havergal, Philip Prowse and Robert David MacDonald – created an appealing version of Graham Greene's *Travels with My Aunt*, which made it to London's West End in 1993. Another Glasgow venue, The Tron Theatre, also produced both new writing and revivals of the classics. Director Annie Wood led a renaissance in theatre for children, TAG worked in schools and 7:84 took drama to local communities.

Although most Scottish playwriting developed independently and had its own agendas, it also had a profound effect on English playwrights, and on the in-yer-face sensibility. If Irvine Welsh's 1999 play *You'll Have Had Your Hole* seemed to glory in its own sadism, the adaptations of his novels *Trainspotting*, *Maribou Stork Nightmares* and *Filth* brought in new young audiences. Especially important were the various productions of *Trainspotting*, which with its dirty, nihilistic image of hopeless urban squalor resounded in the minds of metropolitan playwrights. Other influences were more subtle, if equally deep. Ian Brown at the Traverse staged influential playwrights such as the Canadian Brad Fraser, whose *Unidentified Human Remains and the Nature of Love* (1992) had scenes of explicit sex that London theatres had been too frightened to touch. Similarly, the Traverse promoted the work of Neilson, very much a pioneer of experiential theatre, and, of course, Kane's style of playwriting was heavily coloured by her experience of Jeremy Weller's Grassmarket Project, in Edinburgh, which used non-actors and improvisation to create compelling, fraught and hard-hitting dramas. These were not just casual influences; they were crucial to the development of each of these writers. Seen in this perspective, London's in-yer-face theatre was kick-started by an injection of Scottish theatricality.

Wales and Northern Ireland

Neither Wales nor Northern Ireland could compete with Scottish theatre. In Wales, Clwyd Theatre in Mold increased its reputation as a producer of fine revivals, some of which even came to London. Brit Goff, led by Mike Pearson, investigated local Welsh myths and traditions in a site-specific performances – *Haearn* (1992) and *Lla'th (Gwynfyd)* (1998) – which were innovative in their use of disabled or amateur actors along with a core of professionals. The major play-wright of the 1990s was Ed Thomas, whose *Gas Station Angel* was a co-production with the Royal Court. As Roger Owen says, 'Thomas used theatre as a means of creating exciting new myths for Wales, by releasing any previously held view of Welsh identity from its historical shackles, and by injecting an anarchically playful, consciously self-inventive element into his dramatic dialogue and its perform-ance.'[115] Thomas's work, including *East from the Gantry* (1992) and *Song from a Forgotten City* (1995), might be derided as verbose by English critics, but the picture it painted of Wales was contemporary and true. In a similar vein, the influential Swansea-based and politi-cally radical Volcano Theatre Company toured extensively outside Wales, and tried to connect with its local community. In the 1990s, provision for the arts was devolved in Wales, as it was in Northern Ireland, where the much larger political changes following the Peace Process meant that the traditional 'Troubles play' soon went out of fashion, and playwrights began to address the new realities of the place. Foremost among them was Protestant Gary Mitchell, whose work – especially *In a Little World of Our Own* (1997), *As the Beast Sleeps* (1998) and *Trust* (1999) – investigated the psychology of Loyalism in a context of rapid social and political change. Other local writers include Marie Jones, whose highly successful one-man show *A Night in November* (1994) examined Protestant identity, Anne Devlin, Owen McCafferty and Daragh Carville. New companies such as Tinderbox became more important as older companies, such as Field Day, lost momentum. Yet Irish theatre north of the border could not compete with the creativity of the Republic.

Conclusion

All history, no matter how well balanced, tends towards a uniformity that is contradicted by experience. In the 1990s, British theatre was not simply in-yer-face, nor flagship dominated nor newly commer-cialised, nor even a mix of all three. For those who went to the theatre, it was a time characterised – as all eras are – by exceptions and oddities as much as by safe and predictable experiences. In this decade, you might have been lucky to catch the work of directors such as Garry Hynes, Phyllida Lloyd or Annie Castledine, or that of Terry Hands, Michael Boyd or Lindsay Posner. You might have seen great performances by Simon Callow, John Hurt or Alan Rickman, or by Julie Walters, Frances Barber or Indira Varma. A theatregoer's experience might have included seeing Debbie Isitt's *The Woman Who Cooked Her Husband* on its first outing in 1991 or Alan Cumming in David Hirson's *La Bête* (1992), a verse drama which seemed to anticipate Crimp's more sophisticated adaptation of *The Misanthrope* later in the decade. They might have caught Prowse's breathtakingly lavish set design for *The White Devil* in the Olivier (1991), or comedians Rik Mayall and Adrian Edmondson in a genuinely funny *Waiting for Godot* in the West End (1991). They might have seen Rachel Weisz in David Farr's *Neville Southall's Washbag* at the Finborough (1992) or its West End transfer, renamed as *Elton John's Glasses*. They might have enjoyed the expressionistic high-tech set of Daldry's *Machinal* or seen Eileen Atkins in *The Night of the Iguana* (both at the National, 1993), or Pam Ferris playing Her Majesty in Sue Townsend's *The Queen and I* for Out of Joint (1994). Or talked about male rivalry after seeing Jonathan Lewis's *Our Boys* (1995).

They might have heard the gossip about Stephen Fry walking out of Gray's *Cell Mates* in the West End three days after its opening, and hiding out in Bruges after a case of stage fright in early 1995. They might have seen Paul Merton and Caroline Quentin in Arthur Smith's *Live Bed Show* (1995) or they might have roared at Alison Steadman in the West End transfer of *The Memory of Water*. They might have appreciated Judi Dench singing 'Send in the Clowns' in Sondheim's *A Little Night Music*, or watched the planets descend in Godfrey's *The Blue Ball* (both at the National, 1995). They might have seen Paul Scofield and Vanessa Redgrave in Eyre's *John Gabriel Borkman* (1996), or Marie Jones's *Women on the Verge of HRT* (1997). They might have goggled at Johnson's *Cleo, Camping, Emmanuelle and Dick* (1998), his tribute to *Carry On* films, or caught Roy Williams's magic-touched *Starstuck* (1998), or watched as the entire cast of Nick Grosso's *Real Classy Affair* (1998) listened in silence to Rod Stewart's 'I Don't Want to Talk About It'. They might have admired the radiant Janie Dee in Ayckbourn's *Comic Potential* (1999), or shuddered to the camp grotesquerie of the puppets and props in Improbable Theatre's *Shockheaded Peter* (1999). They might have witnessed a musical that flopped – such as Cliff Richard's *Heathcliff* (1997) – or one – such as Abba's *Mamma Mia!* or Disney's *The Lion King* (both 1999) – which then went on to run for more than a decade. This kind of complex account of shows seen, and shows missed, forms the texture of an individual's experience of British theatre in the 1990s. Depending on where you lived, and what else you did, this was a decade of many different memories. In an individual's personal experience, the exceptional and the odd is often more memorable than the usual accounts given in standard histories, which at best offer a general distillation of events.

CHAPTER 2
PLAYWRIGHTS AND PLAYS

PHILIP RIDLEY

Cosmo We kiss and it kills us. I've seen photographs of what happens to people when they fall in love. Their skin falls off. Like they've been in a nuclear war or something. It's terrible, Mr Chocolate.

— Philip Ridley, *The Pitchfork Disney*, 1991

Introduction

Most histories of new writing are written from the point of view of a new-writing theatre system led by the Royal Court, which in the mid-1990s saw itself as 'a major focus' for new play production, boasting that 'scores of plays first seen at the Royal Court are now part of the national and international dramatic repertoire'.[1] The theatre's proud heritage of producing John Osborne, Arnold Wesker, Edward Bond, David Hare and Caryl Churchill still contributes to its pre-eminence. In this optic, the history of 1990s British playwriting begins with Sarah Kane's shocking debut, *Blasted*, at the Royal Court in January 1995, and the continues with Jez Butterworth's *Mojo* (1995) and Mark Ravenhill's *Shopping and Fucking* (1996), both also at the Royal Court. Playwrights such as these are thus seen as part of a highly hyped brat-pack of young playwrights, including Martin McDonagh, Joe Penhall, Judy Upton, Nick Grosso and Rebecca Prichard, all of whom had successes at the Royal Court. Exceptions, such as Patrick Marber (whose work was staged by the National), are just that — exceptions. But even if the story of the 1990s includes a range of theatres, as it does in the account given in *In-Yer-Face Theatre*, for example, it is still seen as a narrative based on theatre buildings. It is the story of what happened at the Royal Court, the Traverse, the Bush, the Hampstead and the Soho. These big five specialist new writing theatres dominate the narrative, with occasional mentions of the National and a couple of London fringe venues such as the Finborough. But another way of telling the story is possible, one which shifts the focus to arts institutions of a different kind: the art gallery and the art college, the publisher and the film studio.

This is the story of polymath Philip Ridley, whose plays did so much to set the tone of 1990s new writing. At the age of thirteen, he began to explore the National Gallery and the National Portrait Gallery. Then, inspired by seeing 'The Sleeping Fool', a painting by Cecil Collins in the Tate Gallery, Ridley bluffed his way into this artist's drawing class at the Central Art School (now Central St Martins); he was fourteen years old. 'I'm sure,' says Ridley, 'he realised I wasn't eighteen, but he could see how desperately I needed the tuition.'[2] He began a foundation course at St Martins when he was sixteen and spent the early 1980s at art school. Not drama school. Over the rest of the decade, he disproved the advice of his school-teachers, who said that one 'can't be a painter and write stories'.[3] In his own words, 'visual art has always been an integral part of what I've done', so he painted, took photographs, created performance art pieces, and wrote poems and novels.[4] His 1980s novelist credits include *Crocodilia* (1988) and *In the Eyes of Mr Fury* (1989), along with children's books *Mercedes Ice* (1989) and *Dakota of the White Flats* (1989). Two short films, *Visiting Mr Beak* (1987) and *The Universe of Dermot Finn* (1988), were followed by radio plays and his highly acclaimed screenplay for *The Krays* (1990), whose East End setting foreshadows that of his early plays. He wrote and directed *The Reflecting Skin* (1991), an award-winning film remembered for its image of an exploding frog. In this context, his 1991 theatre debut, *The Pitchfork Disney*, was originally a minor tributary to his main creative output: 'One explanation for the originality of Ridley's imagi-nation is that, as far as theatre goes, he is an outsider.'[5]

Ridley is a pivotal figure in the history of 1990s playwriting because *The Pitchfork Disney* introduced a new sensibility into British theatre. Performed at the start of the decade, it was, in the words of Dominic Dromgoole, 'one of the first plays to signal the new direction for new writing', eschewing as it did naturalism, political ideology and social commentary.[6] It was an agenda-setting work: the era of in-yer-face theatre in London began with this play. Ridley's subsequent work, especially the controversial *The Fastest Clock in the Universe* (1992) and *Ghost from a Perfect Place* (1994), established his position as the exponent of a dark, hard-hitting style of drama which influenced many other writers. His own career, however, has developed outside the mainstream of Britain's new writing culture. His plays were ignored by the Royal Court while the National staged only plays such as *Sparkleshark* (1997) as part of the venue's annual *Connections* festival of work performed by young people. The companies that have championed his work, mainly the Hampstead Theatre – which also staged *Fairytaleheart* (1998), another play for young people – and later Paines Plough and the Soho, are part of the new writing system, but do not occupy its top rungs in the way that the Royal Court does. Likewise, the Royal Shakespeare Company has, in the 2000s, promoted new writing, but not by Ridley.

Neither has Ridley been much appreciated by the academy. Despite his centrality to the story of 1990s new writing (there is a section about him in *In-Yer-Face Theatre*), very few articles have discussed his work. For example, his name does not appear in the index of the magisterial *Cambridge History of British Theatre*.[7] There are exceptions to this silence: David Ian Rabey, for instance, has analysed the way that 'Ridley's anatomies of menace helped to define this 90s vogue' by using 'paradigms strongly reminiscent of early Pinter and Orton, with solipsistic but insecure characters responding violently to invasive threats, but ultimately contracting into regression'.[8] Such accounts, however, are marred by a preoccupation with Ridley's debts to Pinter.[9] On the other hand, the work of playwright academics, such as Ken Urban and Dan Rebellato, has been especially valuable. Urban has diagnosed Ridley's characters as 'sick with nostalgia', in a way that is reminiscent of 'nostalgia's origins as a physical affliction caused by an acute longing for home and the past'.[10] Even when, as in *Ghost from a Perfect Place*, change is seen as possible, it is nostalgia itself that helps the characters escape their condition, just as the 'gaze backward can on occasion be painfully turned towards the future'.[11] Rebellato, noting that Ridley was 'influenced as much by surrealist film-makers like Luis Buñuel and Jan Švankmajer or painters like Francis Bacon as by any playwright', and was a contemporary of Young British Artists such as Damien Hirst and Tracy Emin, sees him as fundamentally influential: 'The baroque violence of the first plays was taken up by playwrights like Anthony Neilson in *Penetrator* (1993), Sarah Kane in *Blasted* or Jez Butterworth in *Mojo* (both 1995).'[12] Building on these insights, and aware of the perception of many critics that Ridley's work is suffused with a sensibility that mixes pop culture with gothic traditions, it feels right to examine his early plays by using elements of theory derived from the study of the gothic, the grotesque and the apocalyptic.

The Pitchfork Disney

The Pitchfork Disney was first performed at the tiny Bush Theatre on 2 January 1991, in a production directed by Matthew Lloyd and featuring actor Rupert Graves. Dominic Dromgoole, artistic director of this venue, remembers that Ridley attended twenty-three of the play's twenty-four performances, 'with his trademark beret pulled defiantly down to his ears', and noted that 'his eyes stared and gleamed, luminous with excitement'.[13] With its deliberately provocative content, including the vomiting and cockroach-eating scenes, and its pop-culture names – Presley, Haley and Disney – this was a new kind of drama. In a '*dimly lit room in the East End of London*' (p. 11) we find Presley and Haley Stray, twenty-eight-year-old twins who live what Ridley calls 'a hermit-like existence'.[14] It emerges that they have been abandoned by their parents some ten years before, and they fantasise that they are the only survivors of a nuclear holocaust. Afraid of the outside world, they live on chocolate and tell each other stories about their childhood, but their isolated, nocturnal existence is shattered when Presley spots the beautiful teenager Cosmo Disney – who makes a living by eating live insects in pubs – and invites him in.

Shortly afterwards, Cormo's business partner, the sinister Pitchfork Cavalier, arrives. But while Presley is attracted to Cosmo, Cosmo is drawn to the vulnerable Haley. And so is the fearsome Pitchfork Cavalier. In the playtext, the preliminary epigraphs stress the idea of fear – especially Chazal's 'Extreme terror gives us back the gestures of our childhood' – and prepare us for a play about childhood night-mares in which parents are absent.[15] In performance, there's a sense of strangeness from the start. As in other gothic or science fiction narra-tives, the otherness of the situation is quickly established.

Presley and Haley are no ordinary youngsters. As they bicker about chocolate, biscuits and whose turn it is to go to the shops, they settle into storytelling mode, a characteristic of Ridley's playwriting style. In his work, stories are performances in which the act of telling them will have an ulterior effect. In the case of Haley's first story, a narrative of what happened the last time she did the shopping, Presley is clear: 'Tell me again. Go on. If it's good enough . . . I'll do all the shopping in future' (p. 17). This story, about Haley being chased by wild dogs, has been told before and, depending on Haley's performance, Presley offers to undertake the domestic chore of going shopping. Typical of the play, Haley's narrative combines elements of the gothic and the apocalyptic. Her first meeting with the animals carries a sexual conno-tation as one dog sniffs her; 'its nose was like an ice cube between my legs' (p. 17). The detail is gothic in its gross physicality: 'Big, filthy dogs. With maggots in their fur. Foam on their lips. Eyes like clots of blood' (p. 17). As she runs away from them, she falls on a dead cat: 'My hand went into its stomach. All mushy like rotten fruit' (p. 17). With the sound of the dogs' wolf-like howling in her ears, the dream-like pursuit, in which Haley is always ahead of the animals, ends up in a church. As they close in, attracted by her smell of fear, with their breath 'hot and reeking of vomit' (p. 18), she throws Bibles at them and climbs up a marble crucifix, with her 'chest' pressed 'against the chest of Christ' (p. 18). As the crucifix starts to crumble, she kisses Jesus' lips and begs for salvation. A priest appears and shoots the dogs. He then persuades her to enter the confessional and bullies her into telling him 'something that made [her] a naughty girl once' (p. 19). She can't think of any sins so she makes one up: 'I kissed the lips of Christ and they tasted of chocolate' (p. 19) – the priest refuses absolution and she leaves the church in hysterics. With its rabid dogs, wasteland cityscape, sexual suggestiveness, flirtation with blasphemy, mix of Protestant and Roman Catholic symbols, and final surrender to the feminine in her repeated refrain of 'Hysterical. Hysterical' (p. 19), this fantasy is a litany of the gothic and apocalyptic.

Likewise, both Presley and Haley are gothic figures. Their appearance is a giveaway – one critic of the original production noted that Rupert Graves's Presley had 'blackened teeth and hair that seems to have been cut with a chain saw' in what another called 'a grim and gothic fairy tale'.[16] When Cosmo meets Presley, he notices the latter's blackened teeth, bloodshot eyes, unhealthy skin, and tells him, 'Jesus, your breath reeks' (p. 40). According to this visitor, Presley has been in hibernation: he not only looks like a vampire, he acts like one, only going out after dark. But if he embodies the rottenness of the undead, he doesn't feast on the living. He vampirises himself, and his past. The same applies to Haley, who, like a satire on gothic heroines, spends much of the play in a sedative-induced sleep, vulnerable to the attentions of both Cosmo and his partner. Indeed, the terrifying figure of Pitchfork Cavalier, tall, shuffling, with a leather bondage mask concealing a hideous face that makes 'women faint and grown men vomit' (p. 92) is a parody of Frankenstein's monster. The play's cockroach eating, accounts of animals dying and its creepy sense of death feel like a modern horror story, whose excesses aim to both scare and titillate. As Cosmo says, listing the insects he eats, his audience loves being scared: 'That's why they pay' (p. 69). He even claims to eat live mice. Cosmo elaborates on this widespread desire to be scared: 'Man's need for the shivers. Afraid of blood, wanting blood. We all need our daily dose of disgust' (p. 75). Humankind loves the spectacle of fear: 'Public flogging, the Roman Coliseum, bear-baiting, torture, crucifixion, Bedlam, bull-fighting, hunting, snuff-movies, the atom bomb' (pp. 74–5).

But as well as having gothic elements, this is also a post-apocalyptic fantasy world. It is written, says one critic, in 'the apocalyptic punk-baroque style'.[17] Take Presley's recurring nightmare, which he tells in order to soothe his sister's fears, and which invariably begins by setting the post-apocalyptic scene: 'It's black. A sheet of dark cloud obscures everything. No heaven visible' (p. 23): 'the whole world' is a 'wasteland. Black sky. Black earth. Black nothing' (pp. 24–5).[18] Living in a metaphorical 'dark tower in the wasteland', the siblings are the only survivors (p. 25). In this post-apocalyptic existence, there is something unearthly about Cosmo: according to the stage directions, he has a *'menacing, angelic beauty'* (p. 35), an example perhaps of the genre's characteristic 'postmodern blurring of the distinction between the secular and the sacred'.[19] The play also exemplifies 'the problematic position of sex, and particularly of women's sexuality', often 'an enduring feature of apocalyptic discourse', with anxiety over sex a metaphor for anxiety over being.[20] All of the characters are anxious, uncertain or guilty about their sexuality. With its post-apocalyptic atmosphere, and repeated Beckettian refrain of 'no heaven visible' (p. 23), this is also, suggests Urban, a play about survival in a universe without God. Following Nietzsche, a godless world poses the problem of nihilism. 'In the face of nihilism,' argues Urban, Ridley suggests that 'we seek comfort in narratives', especially stories that view the past in a nostalgic light.[21] The present might be fraught, but the past is stable; the present has to be coped with, but the past can be contemplated from afar; the present is troubling, but the past soothes. In a world without parents, guardians or a deity, 'we invent an idealized past' because harsh reality is 'almost too much to bear'.[22] As Cosmo remarks, 'You like talking about the past, don't you?', to which Presley says, 'It's . . . comforting' (p. 64). As Urban says, the Strays are sick with nostalgia. But they are not the only ones. Pitchfork Cavalier also has, in Cosmo's words, 'a sense of nostalgia' (p. 99). He wants to touch Haley. But because he has no genitals, 'Pitchfork represents the castrated nostalgic, whose love of the past has been rendered harmless and inoffensive'.[23]

But as well as being sick with nostalgia, the twins are stuck in childhood. The reason Presley gives for their survival is that they 'were good children', praised and loved by their parents (p. 25). Urban emphasises the meaning of their surname: 'the twins never grew up, reverting instead to an infantile state. They have become perpetually lost children: strays.'[24] In the play, there are many references to childhood: Haley's dream about everything being 'made out of chocolate' (p. 28) and Cosmo calling Presley 'Mr Chocolate' (p. 39) suggest Willy Wonka, and Cosmo describes the twins, and their like, as 'Ancient children addicted to their chocolate' (p. 74). When Haley imagines losing Presley, she dreads having to do adult things, such as shopping, sweeping the pavement, talking to the postman or gasman, and paying the electricity bills (p. 32). The many references to childhood fears is a reminder of Frank Kermode's point about how fantasy works on the emotions: 'Who supposes that fantasies cannot be terrible? Terror does not depend upon an accurate estimate of the threat. That should be obvious to all who have experienced childhood fears.'[25] Given Ridley's interest in science fiction, there is also an alignment in the play between childhood and sci-fi elements. For example, Presley's childhood fantasy was to be an astronaut, floating out of gravity, longing for the 'oblivion' of space (p. 77). Likewise, Cosmo claims to have had no parents: 'I was hatched from an egg [. . .] I unzipped my old skin and threw it away' (p. 74). The darkness of some of the play's narratives also mirrors the darkness of the sci-fi imagination. As the science-fiction writer Robert Bloch explains: 'Those of us who direct our storytelling into darker channels do so because we were perhaps a bit more mindful than most regarding our childhood confusions of identity, our conflicts with unpleasant realities and our traumatic encounters with imaginative terrors.'[26] The infantilism of the twins is most evident in their sheltered attitudes to love and sex. When Haley asks, 'What do you think falling in love's like, Presley?', he answers 'Scary'.

Haley   More scary than being lost?

Presley   About the same. (pp. 28–9)

When Haley imagines the threat of 'foreigners', she says that they 'abuse children' and fears that, when she's asleep, 'they'll kiss me and cut me' (pp. 30–1). (In the revised unpublished text, this has been changed to 'marry children'.) Later, Presley tells Cosmo that he's never been in love and that he's a virgin (pp. 55–6). In Presley's long nightmarish monologue, he fantasises about kissing a serial killer, although admittedly, 'I've never had a stranger's tongue in my mouth before' (p. 84). Finally, when Cosmo tricks Presley into leaving him alone with Haley, he gets her to suck his finger in her sleep, disposing first of the childish dummy she has in her mouth. This oral sex act alludes to sexual awakening, although not for Haley – she remains unconscious. By contrast, Cosmo gets very excited and '*reaches orgasm*' (p. 104). When Presley finds out, he breaks Cosmo's finger – a symbolic castration. The sense that this protective act is motivated by jealousy also implies that the infantilism of the twins has an incestuous edge.

Drawing on the intense emotions of childhood, Ridley creates vivid visual and verbal images. As he says, 'I've always seen images as engines of emotion. I've always sought that one icon-like image that will convey a wordless meaning, an image-aria, if you like.'[27] Certainly, critics watching the first production were quick to see that 'images of horror and disgust abound'.[28] The visual appearance of the actors playing the twins, with their 'kiddie-type nightwear', evoked their mutual psychological dependency.[29] The objects in the room were symbolic: the chocolate which both sustains them and rots their bodies, the medicine bottle which links them with their parents, and the scorched frying pan that goes with the description of the frying of the snake (p. 27). There is also the image of Pitchfork Cavalier, wearing a bondage mask, part Cambridge Rapist and part Freddy Krueger from the 1980s *Nightmare on Elm Street* horror franchise.[30] There is also the image of Cosmo in his sparkling red sequinned jacket, a rock 'n' roll entertainer who eats insects, a deliberate challenge to the audience's feelings of disgust. The insect-eating scene, as Cosmo 'swallows' the dirty 'cockroach' (p. 69), breaks the taboo on distinguishing between what can and cannot be eaten. As anthropologist Mary Douglas points out, 'uncleanness is matter out of place' so Cosmo not only provokes disgust by violating taboo, he also challenges the order of society: what if it is okay, after all, to eat the forbidden?[31] Which suggests other forbidden desires, such as incest, or – in Cosmo's homophobic imagination – homosexuality. If the child-like Presley and Haley parody the world of the straight family, with its breadwinner male and passive female, Cosmo symbolises the heroic, taboo-busting but predatory male.

The play is called *The Pitchfork Disney* for a reason: there is something deeply uncanny in the Freudian sense about Presley's long fantasy in which he invents the figure of the handsome but murderous Pitchfork Disney – created out of both the names of his visitors, whose arrival has destabilised the ordered world of the Strays. In a story grounded in instinctual drives and psychological repressions, Presley's nightmarish narrative evokes an uncanny mood in which two strangers form into one monster, and in which he loses his own face in an accident and is then given the face of the murderer by means of plastic surgery: 'They've given me the face of the Pitchfork Disney' (p. 85). This leads to his being hounded as a killer. So an imaginary story which began with a symbolic loss of teeth climaxes with him destroying the world by unleashing a nuclear apocalypse, and ending up in invincible solitude: 'I am the sole survivor' (p. 87). Then the trauma victim, though his own self-narrative, becomes whole again: 'I rise from the ashes and I am perfect. I am a boy again' (p. 87). The adult returns to infancy as a place of inviolable safety. Here Ridley's highly literary imagination adds an imaginary reality to the strangeness of the encounter between his characters. Such writing, in Freud's words, 'is a much more fertile province than the uncanny in real life, for it contains the whole of the latter and something more besides, something that cannot be found in real life'.[32] The real-life uncanniness in the play is the recognisable aspect of repression and infantilism, and the 'something more besides' is the fantastical and flexible narratives which the characters use as a way of controlling an uncontrollable world (which has after all taken their parents away from them).

Critics have rightly seen *The Pitchfork Disney* as partly 'B-movie horror' and partly 'a gothic concoction'.[33] The gothic, as Clive Bloom says, is 'always linked to the desire of contemporary readers. At once escapist and conformist, the gothic speaks to the dark side of domestic fiction: erotic, violent, perverse, bizarre and occasionally connected with contemporary fears.'[34] So as well as being erotic, violent, perverse and bizarre, the play abounds in contemporary fears, from images of nuclear holocaust to those of environmental disaster, yet the play is never overtly political. It's not an issue play; instead, it creates a landscape of fear. After all, the last words of the play are both twins repeating 'I'm scared' (p. 108). But there are other fears. Cosmo's fear of being 'touched' and his hatred of homosexuals – 'they should be gassed' or 'herded' into a stadium (p. 57) – alludes to contemporary homophobia. Presley's fantasy about being sprayed with toxic waste sounds like a dystopic fantasy but his fear of being operated on while still conscious is based on reality. The play is also exemplary in having, in David Stevens's words, both 'a vividly dramatic sense of sensational action', and in portraying 'the link between the gothic and the experience of childhood' as 'an especially strong one'.[35] The play successfully mixes the gothic with the grotesque, the horror movie with sci-fi fantasy. If Roger Luckhurst is right to define science fiction as 'an adolescent and exuberantly kinetic genre', then the energy of youth is clearly on display here, and Ridley's mix of different genres gives the play its strangeness and its compelling power.[36]

The Fastest Clock in the Universe

The Fastest Clock in the Universe was first performed at the Hampstead Theatre on 14 May 1992, in a production directed by Matthew Lloyd and featuring actor Jude Law. Set in '*a dilapidated room above an abandoned factory in the East End*' (p. 119), which is full of stuffed birds, the play features, in the words of Rabey, some 'splendidly energetic monstrous characters, whose names combine the self-styled extravagance of graphic novel hero/villains with the suggestive but imperfectly definable resonances of Dickens'.[37] Thirty-year-old Cougar Glass and his older friend, Captain Tock, share the flat, whose most frequent visitor is Cheetah Bee, an eighty-year-old neighbour. Unable to face the reality of ageing, Cougar holds regular birthday parties during which he and the Captain pretend that he's just turned nineteen. On this occasion, Cougar has invited a young teenager, fifteen-year-old Foxtrot Darling, whom he has met at a local hospital, with the aim of seducing, or raping, the boy. But Foxtrot has his pregnant sixteen-year-old girlfriend, Sherbet Gravel, in tow. It emerges that Cougar has concocted an elaborate story about losing his wife, Savannah Glass, which matches Foxtrot's real loss of his older brother,

Sherbet's fiancé. But Sherbet sees through the deception. As one critic said of the original production, 'from the moment she takes charge, the play assumes a furious and hilarious momentum'.[38] At its climax she challenges Cougar, unmasking his pretence to be nineteen, and he responds violently, precipitating a fight that ends when he kicks her in the stomach, causing her to lose her baby. In the end, Cougar remains alone with the Captain.

This play is clearly linked to *The Pitchfork Disney*. One recurring motif is the idea of the perfect body. Like Cosmo (pp. 39–40), Cougar aspires to physical perfection, and can barely endure another person's touch. There are other continuities: 'Like Presley, Cougar is trapped in time; he wants to remain a perpetual teenager. Like Cosmo, he is an object of desire capable of extreme violence.'[39] Cougar also has similarities to Dorian Gray, protagonist of another gothic story: one critic called him 'a Dorian Gray for the 1990s'.[40] So, at one point, an old school acquaintance tells him, 'You look just the same as the day you were expelled' (p. 132), except that this time there is no ageing portrait in the attic, and Cougar relies on dyes and sun lamps to maintain the illusion of eternal youth. Like Cosmo, he is also the embodiment of cool, which is what attracts his sexual victims. With his sunglasses, quiff, white T-shirt and jeans, he looks like a rock 'n' roller from the past. His cool, like that of countless teenagers since the 1950s, is a complex mix. In the words of Dick Pountain and David Robins, it is 'profoundly hedonistic', but also 'flirts with death' and hides its defiance 'behind a wall of ironic detachment' – 'cool is a new mode of individualism'.[41] It is also a way of being in control. As Cougar says, 'Life's too short to have feelings for people' (p. 139). Being touched, physically or emotionally, unsettles him. Makes him lose control.

Despite this, both Cougar and Captain, who may or may not occasionally have sex, certainly are emotionally dependent on each other. They have their own private language, with its deliberately outmoded expressions 'have some larks', 'in a tizz' and 'on my pins' (pp. 129–30). There are elements of parodic exaggeration in their interactions: the Captain calls Cougar 'a fiend' (p. 126), and dubs his actions 'monstrous' and 'diabolical' (p. 149). Here, such gothic tags are both expressions of dismay and examples of Ridley's love of heightened language. Thus the following declaration by Cougar positively seethes with self-satisfied awareness of his own performance: 'We're all as bad as each other. All hungry little cannibals at our own cannibal party. So fuck the milk of human kindness and welcome to the abattoir!' (p. 150). Although the relationship between the two men is presented without comment, Nicholas de Jongh objected to the play's sexual politics, arguing that 'Ridley seems to accept the stereotypically gay notion of time as remorseless enemy and fantasy the magic bulwark against it' – he called the play's world 'this realm of the quirky fantastic'.[42]

The idea of a 'quirky fantastic' suggests science fiction and fantasy, and some of the metaphors of the play allude to this: for example, the image of Sherbet's baby on the hospital scanner, with its 'ancient meteors' (pp. 201–2), alludes to the sci-fi world of space and the planets. But, in general, the science-fiction elements of Ridley's previous play have been toned down, or rather developed into a fantasy world, a distinctive Ridleyland, a place which characteristically throws together the normal and the abnormal. One obvious example of this abnormality is the fact that simply mentioning Cougar's real age is enough to send him into a fit. Likewise, this is a fantasy world where he can be calmed only by Cheetah, who contrasts her age with his youth. Her incantations – what one critic called her 'tonic chant about time' – are central to the play's distinctive ritualistic character.[43] Similarly, the action is punctuated by other rituals. For example, the Captain has to ritualistically dust his stuffed birds, his 'babies' (p. 159), once a day, and scream out of the window, disturbing the birds outside, to relieve his tension (p. 140). Cougar's seduction of Foxtrot is also a ritual, with its elaborate preparations, and one that has clearly been enacted before. Rebellato's analysis of the play uses the idea of the grotesque to highlight its mixture of the ordinary and the extraordinary, the real and fantastic. If, in Wolfgang Kayser's words, 'the grotesque is the estranged world', then *The Fastest Clock in the Universe* dwells deeply within that sense of the strange, the odd and the alarming.[44]

The play is also full of images that evoke both Jacobean tragedy and gothic horror. The ambiance, one reviewer noted, is 'East End gothic'.[45] Examples of this mix of gothic and Jacobean include the stuffed birds that dominate the set, Cougar's 'gut full of maggots' speech (p. 132), Captain's leaking, gnawed fingers, and his troubling account of the death of a trapped bird as well as his contrasting comic image of the 'rotten magpie on my head', although his plan to 'exterminate' the birds (p. 131) evokes *Dr Who* as much as genocide. If the incident of the bird flying into the window pane recalls Hitchcock's 1963 film *The Birds* (p. 141), the story of Cougar's first 'electric current' orgasm is like something out of *Weird Tales* (p. 143). Similarly, Cheetah's tale of the television programme about the boy 'born without a face' mixes shock television with the gothic horror figure of a 'surgeon who performs endless operations on him' (p. 158), a Dr Frankenstein for our time. Foxtrot says that the world of Cougar and Captain feels 'like living inside a huge cracked egg' (p. 159), and his tale of journeying into the Underworld (pp. 162–4) is as gothic as Captain's stories of the birds' eyes that glint like stars and the hidden 'torture chamber' where minks are kept (p. 182). Cheetah's account of the mink being skinned alive, which Ridley expanded in the 2009 edition of the playtext, is pure horror.[46] When Sherbet arrives, the gothic atmosphere intensifies: '*Lights flicker off and on./ Sound of crackling electricity*' (p. 168). Often such images are described through extended riffs or allegorical narratives. Frequently, the language is allusive. Beyond the play's cosy indoors, you can detect the howling of vampires, cannibal salivations and the fluttering and scurrying of sinister animals. As Clive Bloom says, 'The gothic sensibility takes pleasure in the bizarre and the wild, the magical and the arabesque [. . .] it is fascinated with the abnormal and the hallucinatory – drug abuse, torture, terrorization, the fear of the victim – the pleasures of being insane!'[47]

Again, as in Jacobean tragedy, the play revels in its own extremism, with heightened language and grotesque action. It is also firmly rooted in the human body, in our corporeality. Cougar is clearly obsessed with his body, trying to stop its inevitable ageing and its slow loss of freshness. His attempt to keep his body a temple of youthfulness is partly a wilful denial of reality, partly a psychological fixation on a moment in his life when the world looked almost preternaturally bright and hopeful: his first orgasm, on a rooftop, throbbing with electric vibes. It's the first time he felt truly alive and it's an experience which he seeks to repeat, tragically with less and less success. Led by this memory of violent pleasure, he's forever chasing a buzz. And, as he gets older, his prey gets younger. Ridley's play is both a social study of narcissism and a mythic account of the fear of nature and of its whispers of mortality. As ever, it's the clear-sighted Sherbet who suggests, 'We'll all wear masks. Our faces will be hidden. Who knows what we're thinking? Or what we might do?' (p. 189). In this case, the party masks are a metaphor for Cougar's desire to change the laws of nature by concealing the truth about both his age and his desires.

In the published playtext, one of Ridley's epigraphs is from French poet Paul Valéry: 'Your ideas are shocking and your hearts are faint. Your acts of pity and cruelty are absurd, committed casually, as if they were irresistible. Finally, you fear blood more and more. Blood and time' (p. 113). This sums up perfectly the cathartic nature of the play, with its furious chants of 'Blood! Blood! Blood! Blood!' (p. 208) in the climactic scene. At the pumping heart of the drama, there is the liquid of life. But also a primal fear of blood. At one point, Cougar is afraid that the Captain will leak all over him. This both echoes the fear of AIDS and is a twisted fear of women, and of their bodies. Blood symbolism also restates the play's gothic character. But Ridley has a wider sense of the clash between humans and the natural. He has an artist's understanding of animals as symbols, and his stuffed birds and tales of mink skinning come from the same corner of the contemporary imagination as Damien Hirst's shark in formaldehyde. In English culture, there is also a peculiar sensitivity to animal cruelty, which sometimes distorts moral values. During the original production, audience outrage was fixated on the abuse of animals, while the fact that a sixteen-year-old schoolboy was about to be seduced by a man almost twice his age excited no comment.

Ridley writes with the exultation of someone who is creating a new world, similar to many aspects of the real world, but also distinct and different. His pleasure in the act of playwriting is evident in many of the more elaborate passages. The mix of the gothic, the surreal and the grotesque is beguiling. As is the studied ambiguity of his characters.

What exactly is the nature of the relationship between Cougar and the Captain? Are Foxtrot and Sherbet lovers? Whose baby is she carrying? In the symbiosis between the Captain and Cougar, there's all the love and hate that any couple might experience. In their power play, there is psychological truth and emotional honesty. But their relationship is perverse, maintaining the fiction of eternal youth by repeated denials of the world beyond their rooms: in Urban's words, 'Cougar is a paedophile with a quasi-genocidal streak, and the Captain, his somewhat willing accomplice.'[48] Cougar's inability to face ageing is never explained but might be the result of trauma; if so, the trauma has resulted in his internalising the nihilism of total destruction, a reminder that you can 'link the idea of apocalypse with the psychoanalytical concept of trauma'.[49] Similarly, in Sherbet's switching of her attention from her dead lover to his younger brother (who hero-worshipped him) there is a suggestion of an incestuous inability to break out of a family that mirrors the dependence of Cougar on the Captain. But Sherbet's chief asset is her fecundity, the fact that she bears her lover's child, the aptly named 'Future One'. Obsessively, Sherbet and Foxtrot call each other Babe. Sherbet is a year older than Foxtrot; like Cougar, she has designs on him. But whereas Cougar wants to have sex and discard Foxtrot, Sherbet wants the opposite: to improve him. Anyway, there is something morbid here about her relationship with both brothers. Likewise, Cougar's invention of Savannah Glass, the fictitious wife who dies at the same time as Foxtrot's brother, is both cunning and implies a fascination with death. Since, in his invented reality, Savannah dies on the same day as Foxtrot's real brother, this an example of an uncanny coincidence whose weirdness is articulated through language that echoes itself: 'My poor dying wife who was in the same hospital as his poor dying brother', says Cougar mockingly (p. 148), while Foxtrot naively says 'a coincidence like that must mean something' (p. 160). Uncannily, Foxtrot identifies Cougar with his own dead brother, and imitates Cougar's hairstyle. After his brother's death, Foxtrot experiences the uncanny feeling of floating (p. 164). Here identities are fluid.

In the final showdown, in her struggle with Cougar, Sherbet fights fantasy with fantasy. Calling his bluff, she claims that she has met the imaginary Savannah Glass in the hospital. She says that Savannah told her 'a lot of things', including Cougar's real age (pp. 205–6). As the electricity in the room goes mad, and with *'Everything exaggerated to the extreme'* (p. 207), Cougar hits Sherbet and causes her to miscarry. This is not only the result of his desire for Foxtrot being frustrated, but also represents his attack on both the female and the future. He cannot stand either women or babies, neither fertility nor new life. Urban concludes that 'in Cougar and Sherbet, Ridley presents two models of nostalgia united by a principle of cruelty', and that Cougar's attack on Sherbet is a 'sadistic act', 'the price the female body must pay for attempting to castrate the narcissistic and nostalgic male'.[50] In the final fairy tale about the fastest clock in the universe, love is time-less, love is blind. But only in the realms of fiction: in the real world, a woman has lost her child. Perverse, morbid, nostalgic, grotesque – Ridley's work is also an attack on bog-standard naturalism.

Ghost from a Perfect Place

Ghost from a Perfect Place was first performed at the Hampstead Theatre on 7 April 1994, in a production directed by Matthew Lloyd and featuring actor John Wood. It begins with the return of a 1960s gangster, Travis Flood, to his old stomping ground in Bethnal Green. He pays a call on Rio, a tart he's met in a grave-yard, but finds only Torchie, her grandmother, at home. Both reminisce about the past, but while the gangster's vision is nostalgic, Torchie's is full of pain: her daughter Donna was raped at the age of fourteen, and then died in childbirth. Rio, Donna's twentysome-thing daughter, arrives, but Travis is no longer in the mood for sex. When he tries to leave, however, Rio knocks him down and ties him up. She then summons her girl-gang, a trio called the Cheerleaders, and they torture him. To stop the pain, he confesses the worst thing he ever did, which was to rape Rio's mother. Realising that he's her father, Rio dismisses the gang and releases him. One critic summed up the feel of the original production: 'East End gothic horrors, sex, violence and cruelty to animals.'[51]

An East End gothic atmosphere and eldritch lyricism locates the play instantly in Ridleyland. With its Victorian plot about a daughter discovering her long-lost father, *Ghost from a Perfect Place* owes something to Dickens, and with its evocation of a gangster past something to the 1960s London of Ridley's *The Krays*. The set, a burnt-out flat, has a post-apocalyptic feel; the girl-gang gothically haunts the local graveyard, where Travis meets Rio. He sees the urban landscape as decayed and destroyed: 'Everything smashed and broken. No order. It's like a wasteland' (p. 228). The local kids are 'pale as ghosts. Zombies' (p. 228, cf p. 266). As in a classic gothic story, Torchie's husband goes 'mad with grief' at his daughter's death and a suicide attempt leaves him a human 'vegetable', 'like a child now' (pp. 248–50). 'Was I cursed?' asks Torchie. At another point, she evokes the ghost of Donna, and feels a 'chill' in the room (p. 262). But although the play's ending differs significantly from the endings of Ridley's earlier plays, there is also evidence of continuity: for example, one critic spotted 'the theme of dangerous nostalgia', while the image of the Cheerleaders in gold-sequinned miniskirts recalls Cosmo's shiny jacket, and the image aria of the open scissors wielded by Rio who threatens to castrate or blind Travis, recalls Cosmo's symbolic castration.[52] The images of the hanging cow carcass and the story of shark fishing (pp. 245, 255) align the play with the conceptual art of Hirst.[53] In one passage of vivid intensity, a bed burns (p. 232) and later a birth is described as a bloodbath (p. 273). Likewise, after poisoning a litter of baby rats, the child Rio can't sleep because 'she imagines a rat coming to kill her' and 'eat [her] guts' (pp. 275–6). Very Jacobean. In the eyes of the girl-gang, Donna is a gothic 'Saint of All the Damaged Girls Living in the Ruins' (p. 279), and her cult is a parody of Roman Catholic commandments and prayers. The girl-gang with 'their space-mutant make-up' contribute, in the words of another critic, to 'the post-apocalyptic feel of these whores with hearts of ice'.[54] Like his other plays, there is a fairy-tale element: Travis's book starts 'like a fairy-tale' (p. 245) while Rio's life story is 'a fairy-tale with spikes and acid' (p. 273). As Rebellato says,

This reflects the proximity of Ridley's story-worlds to fairytales, which are filled with parents losing or abandoning their children, children sent to wicked stepmothers and cruel stepfathers, lured by wolves and witches, imprisoned in cottages and castles. This parental absence is not always an unambiguous disaster; in many of the plays, they present an opportunity for young people to free their imaginations beyond the boring constraints of adult society.[55]

The play is also a good example of Rabey's insight that 'Ridley also demonstrates a Beckettian sense of the power (and fragility) of the narrative of displacement, whereby a character attempts to (re-)order their past through a repeated activity of storytelling which wilfully obscures any reliable boundaries between truth and fiction'.[56] The narratives are used by the characters in different ways, and are often fluid: in his moment of truth, Travis says, 'Everywhere I go I change my name. Invent new stories about myself [. . .] I begin to forget who I am' (p. 290). And in the climactic acting out of Donna's rape, by her daughter, Rio's imagined version is corrected by Travis, the perpetrator who has not forgotten his crime: so when she says 'I'm hysterical', he corrects her: 'You're very calm' (p. 289). Crucially, the telling of such stories is a performance. As one critic correctly spotted, 'Travis, Torchie and Rio each re-enact crucial adventures from long ago, and each persuades the other person to play some role in it.'[57] So Torchie performs her story and asks Travis to judge her; Rio plays out the story of her mother and achieves a kind of catharsis. As Wyllie sums up, 'a masculine mythology of the gentleman criminal is destroyed, first by Torchie's exposure of female suffering and then by Travis's own admission of his poverty and inadequacy'.[58]

Ridleyland is richly symbolic, and is open to a richness of possible interpretation. So, for example, within the post-apocalyptic atmosphere of the play, there is also a sense of deep trauma. James Berger argues that 'a post-apocalyptic theory of trauma' concerns not just disastrous events but the way that the effects of catastrophe 'may be dispersed and manifested in many forms', and 'produce its full impact only years later'.[59] In this perspective, Ridley's East End of the 1960s is, to quote the play's title, the perfect place of a mythologised past, whose actuality has been torn apart by decades of economic and social change. Here the reality of change is a catastrophic rupture of the wholeness of a fantasy past, leaving its survivors to cope with the psychological trauma not only of change, but also of facing the truth. In the play, not only do individuals have to choose whether to heal themselves, but the trauma of an East End that has changed beyond recognition has to be acknowledged. By abandoning the heydays of his youth, and going to America, Travis has suffered a personal catastrophe which he covers up by telling mythological stories. On his return, he realises that the place he so fondly remembers has also been subject to social catastrophe. By the end of the play, this social trauma remains repressed as the focus falls solely on the three individuals at the heart of the story. Thus Ridley articulates the postmodern gothic sense of how the breakdown of modernity's metanarratives leads to 'a horror that identity, reality, truth and meaning are not only effects of narratives but subject to a dispersion and multiplication of meanings, realities and identities that obliterates the possibility of imagining any human order and unity'.[60] Not only is the myth of an idealised Bethnal Green shattered, but the three main characters remain disunited and disordered.

As with *The Fastest Clock in the Universe*, there is also a hidden skeleton of tragedy in the play. The psychodrama played out between the ignorant witness, Torchie, who inadvertently tells the protagonist, Travis, the truth about the past, and then the confrontation between the daughter of the victim, Rio, and the perpetrator, Travis, has the texture of Greek tragedy. Donna's sacrifice of herself to protect her father is echoed by Travis's symbolic self-sacrifice, a ritual cleansing, at the hands of Rio. At the end of the play, the mutual recognition of father and daughter carries a faint suggestion of incest – after all, the reason for their meeting was to have sex. As in tragedy, only an act of violence can shatter the stalemate, only violence can uncover the truth. Violence, of course, gave the play's original production its notoriety. But the brutality administered by the perpetrators is less interesting than the violence craved by the victim. After all, Travis provokes his assailants because, however unconsciously, he understands his own need to suffer retribution, craving redemption. He is more in control than his torturers. Brutality is not only used as a way of showing Travis's almost religious sense of guilt, but also as a criticism of nostalgia.

What makes *Ghost from a Perfect Place* Ridley's best early work is the tension between its vivid gothic images and its deeply felt emotional subtext of love, loss and sacrifice. Under torture, Travis confesses that he is Rio's father and that he raped her mother, Donna. The idea of a child protecting her parents is complicated because the figure on stage, Rio, is playing the role of her long-dead mother, and acts out the trauma of her own conception. Psychologically, this is not only an adolescent fantasy (saving your parents), but also a reminder of the strength of youthful feelings, and of their idealism. The confession exposes Travis's self-aggrandising myth-making as a lie. Through confession, in an almost Roman Catholic manner, comes self-knowledge. His self-loathing leads him through pain and suffering to self-knowledge: 'Now I know who I am' (p. 290). In Urban's interpretation, *Ghost from a Perfect Place* reverses the retreat into nostalgia of the previous two plays. During its confessional ending, 'Travis is cured of his nostalgia, and as a result he is able to recognize himself for the first time.'[61] And the climactic re-enactment of Donna's rape, this time desired by her daughter Rio and involving her previously unknown father, 'demonstrates how terror unveils memory and cures nostalgic impulses'.[62] The resulting self-reflection and self-knowledge may not apply to Torchie, but both Travis and Rio finish the play in a different place to where they started it. The characters began, in the words of one critic, by 'fictionalising their past and fantasising their present', but they end in different, and imperfect, places.[63] Ridley's storytelling has the force of a cautionary tale: the play shows what happens when people are so obsessed about fabricating their own stories that they forget to listen to other people's. Travis realises this; Torchie doesn't. Rio experiences it as a revelation that will change her life. At the end, two people are left on stage: Rio and Torchie. One knows the truth, the other doesn't. 'Who's better off?' asks Ridley. [64]

Conclusion

In his first three plays, Ridley is not only the master of East End gothic, a geographic locale that mixes fantasy with reality, but also demonstrates a heightened playwriting style. His plays are distinguished by their evocation of basic gothic fears: the fear of the other, the fear of nature and the fear of psychic invasion. His best work tells powerful stories using a kind of symbolist discourse, akin to poetry – his words take flight. Here, as in any histrionic horror movie, there is both the evocation of, in the words of Mark Gatiss, a 'different realm' but also the 'knowing excess' of camp and the deliberate 'blurring of fantasy and reality'.[65] There is also a dynamic atmosphere of psycho-sexual tension, where desire is mediated by various inhibitions, repressions and anxieties, or directed at unsuitable objects. For example, *The Pitchfork Disney*, in Ridley's words, is 'about the sexual interplay between these three characters'.[66] Yet there is also, as Wyllie points out, something 'sadomasochistic' in the play's eroticism, where sex is both desired and rejected.[67] At the same time, Ridley's characters carry no sexual labels: we don't know what their sexuality is exactly, and this ambiguity creates its own dramatic tension. Male narcissism pervades the air of his claustrophobic rooms. Fathers are notable by their absence. Some adults are still kids.

Ridley is a polymath whose plays are extremely writerly: in his *Plays One*, for example, not only are the dialogues of the plays extremely polished but Ridley's 'Introduction' is a series of vignettes in which he creates literary accounts of his life, some of which find echoes in the plays. Here autobiography is refracted through a heightened but evocative gauze of words. There is also a postmodern sense in which the work seems to allude to a personal mythology, which is by definition beyond the grasp of the audience. Experiencing his plays involves both a thrilling feeling of the sensational and a more subtle awareness of obscure shadows lurking behind the visible. This sometimes feels like what Steven Connor means when he paraphrases Charles Jencks's idea of 'a postmodern style of allegory', which 'does not allow us to be sure of what the main story is, nor what the underlying myth may be that it alludes to'.[68] If this kind of 'postmodern gothic' is characterised by a 'playfulness and duplicity' then so is Ridley's.[69] Likewise, 'it questions the notion that one inhabits a coherent or otherwise abstractly rational world', and his work, in common with much gothic, 'often trades in tabooed representations of desire'.[70] Yet one constant is his passionate concern with the need to tell stories to make sense of experience.

The critical contempt that greeted Ridley's *The Pitchfork Disney* indicates how ahead of the game he was. Kenneth Hurren, for example, wrote: 'It struck me that the author was in need less of an audience than a psychiatrist', a sentiment later echoed by Charles Spencer in his dismissal of Kane: 'It's not a theatre critic that's required here, it's a psychiatrist.'[71] One reason for this is that Ridley's work sits more comfortably in the context of the visual arts than of the theatre most critics were familiar with at the start of the decade. For example, his debut play has obvious affinities in terms of shock with controversial art such as Rick Gibson's foetus earrings, Rebecca Scott's painting of a young man with an erection and war artist John Keane's image of a Mickey Mouse figure in a Gulf War painting, all of which provoked controversy in 1989–92.[72] Likewise, his kinship with the Young British Artists is reflected not only in his stage imagery but also in his symbolic use of animal, bird and insect life. His taboo-busting attitude to what disgusts humans is present in every play. So you can see his point when he says that 'the theatrical world is about fifteen years behind every other art form', and the truth of his explanation that 'the violence towards animals, for example, is just a device, often used in fine art, to question mortality in a godless world'.[73]

But, however misunderstood at first, Ridley's work soon began to attract revivals. By the end of the decade, *The Pitchfork Disney* and *The Fastest Clock in the Universe* had had New York premieres, *Ghost from a Perfect Place* enjoyed a London fringe revival, plus there were productions at the Bolton Octagon of *The Fastest Clock in the Universe* (1994) and *The Pitchfork Disney* (1997).[74] The playwright was exciting interest, and he was pioneering a new sensibility: what Clive Bloom says of the gothic applies to Ridley's stage language; it was 'not merely a playground for the imaginative, it was also the very foundation of a new sense of the imagination'.[75] Certainly, his work has proved influential: the stage image of a young man entering a room and immediately vomiting, as Cosmo does (p. 36), was echoed in the first scene of Ravenhill's *Shopping and Fucking* (p. 3), and indeed Ridley's hothouse world of young people abandoned by their parents is echoed by Ravenhill's flat-sharers, who also tell each other stories to make sense of their world.[76] Similarly Cosmo's speech that 'Money is confidence' (p. 65) is echoed by Ravenhill's 'Money is civilisation' (p. 87). Equally, Cosmo's 'bobby-dazzler' (p. 43), his red sequin jacket, is echoed by Jez Butterworth's figure of Silver Johnny in *Mojo*; and Sherbet's bleeding (p. 208) by Cate's in Kane's *Blasted* (p. 60).

In the context of new writing, where the hegemonic style is that of social realism and naturalism, Ridley's work was innovative because it opposed this aesthetic. Because of his background in the visual arts, he was free of the baggage that any writer's workshop might have imposed on him, and he used this freedom to explore his own imagination. In the process, he not only became a pioneer of in-yer-face theatre, but also a master of the uncanny. Especially if you define the uncanny as that which turns rationality into the irrational, familiar into unfamiliar, certainty into uncertainty, real into unreal, life into literary words, where the literary – words as spoken on stage as much as the playtext – is odder, more disturbing, than life. His work is an example of what Andrew Smith describes when he says, 'uncanny tales should be read not solely for their hidden psychological meaning but also for how their literary qualities generate new forms of uncanniness'.[77] Ridley is the poet of the uncanny, whose work spawns new images of the strange, the weird and the wonderful. A terrified girl clings to a statue of Jesus, a wizard changes a prince's face into that of a vulture, a girl-gang makes a religious cult out of a dead mother. At once magical and menacing, it's a place where you might be dazzled by sunlight on razor blades or beguiled by blood on gold sequins. Ridley's plays are experiences of the uncanny.

SARAH KANE
By Catherine Rees

> **Ian** I write . . . stories. That's all. This isn't a story anyone wants to hear.
>
> – Sarah Kane, *Blasted*, 1995

Introduction

Sarah Kane is the most famous and infamous playwright of the 1990s. Her theatrical legacy has become crystallised in five plays and one film, and her untimely death in February 1999 has accelerated the process whereby her work has become canonised. Her brief career is most succinctly illustrated by the title of her one-volume collected work, *Sarah Kane Complete Plays*, which feels, as David Greig put it, like 'the sound of a door shutting'.[1] Because we know that Kane can never produce any further plays, or add any additional commentary to her work, there is a temptation to see these plays as a summation of her life. Furthermore, the truth about Kane's somewhat troubled early theatrical career, the terrible reviews and controversy surrounding her debut *Blasted* (1995), for example, become subsumed by her suicide, which seems to validate her work, suggesting that she 'really meant it, whatever that "it" was'.[2] Clearly, her death has created a critical climate in which the details of her life become the lens through which to view and discuss the plays she left behind. Frequently, this tendency is associated with her gender identity, for, as Mary Luckhurst argues, it is 'common for female suicides to be represented as tragic icons'.[3] Kane's work is also recurrently categorised: the influence of Sierz's *In-Yer-Face Theatre* (2001) and Graham Saunders's *'Love Me or Kill Me'* (2002) encourages her work to be read within the confines of the so-called in-yer-face sensibility. Indeed, when reflecting on this period of British playwriting, Sierz suggests that 'the renaissance in new writing [. . .] began in the early 1990s, became a public scandal with the staging of *Blasted* in 1995, and more or less ran out of steam by the end of 1999, the year of Kane's suicide', effectively framing the entire resurgence of new British plays by Kane's life and career.[4] It is time to reassess Kane's role as an in-yer-face playwright by discussing other ways of theorising her work, using the concepts of postdramatic theatre, trauma theory and theories of bodies, power, violence and institutions. Similarly, Kane's position as a female playwright needs further exploring: has her gender caused her work to be seen differently to that of male writers? And how does her suicide affect readings of her plays in the decades following their first performances, and of her death?

One problem with viewing Kane primarily as an in-yer-face playwright is that although her work does seem to fit with this sensibility in some ways, it rejects it in others. For example, in-yer-face theatre is described by Sierz as 'deliberately relentless [with] ruthless commitment to extremes' as well as being defined as plays in which 'the language is usually filthy, characters talk about unmentionable subjects, take their clothes off, have sex, humiliate each other, experience unpleasant emotions, become suddenly violent'.[5] Evidently, Kane's work, particularly her first three plays – *Blasted, Phaedra's Love* (1996) and *Cleansed* (1998) – fit very well into this description. However, she also demonstrates a commitment to original and challenging theatrical form. So although *Blasted* may feel like a conventional play in its first act, in which characters exist in recognisable social situations, have conventional conversations and talk about everyday things such as football matches, room service and newspapers, the second act undermines this naturalistic setting and the action from then on is underpinned with more shocking, unusual and difficult images. Laurens De Vos and Saunders suggest that in-yer-face theatre has a 'territory of social realism', indicating that plays within that genre tend to rely on recognisable social images and political 'issues' to structure their plays.[6] Many critics have argued that Kane's work rejects this aesthetic, and instead explores a more flexible and alienating form of theatre, often called postdramatic theatre. Although Kane's work remains textual (in that an unnegotiable text is used for performances) and the action she describes is still representational, she does seek to challenge the boundaries of socially realistic drama by refusing to provide the audience with political contexts or explanations for the violence she represents. For example, *Blasted* has been criticised by critics precisely because of Kane's refusal to pin down the specifics of her action. Christopher Innes argues that *Blasted* has 'no believable social context' and Michael Billington asserted that the play wasn't logically structured because she refused to provide an answer to the question 'Who exactly is meant to be fighting whom out on the street?'[7] In this way, she rejects the simplistic associations between cause and effect in representational violent action – it is frequently shocking, inexplicable and sudden, much like violence outside of the theatre. By refusing to provide audiences with easy answers and contexts, she encouraged them to reflect more on the nature of violence itself, and also to ask questions about violence in their own lives and social environment.

Kane's later plays *Crave* (1998) and *4.48 Psychosis* (2000) go even further in fracturing the tentative social structure suggested in the early plays: they have no recognisable location, or context, nor do they offer recognisable social explanation or commentary. The concept of character is also beginning to disintegrate; in *Crave* the characters are distinguished only by letters and in most of *4.48 Psychosis* there is no attempt to break the text up into conventional dialogue. In applying the tenets of postdramatic theatre to her later plays, Eckart Voigts-Virchow suggests that 'it is less of a risk to call one's play *Shopping and Fucking*, simulate adventurous forms of sexuality and spill blood over the stage than to abandon "as-if" representation, character or story'.[8] Given the press reaction to *Blasted* this may well be the case.

Blasted

The critical response to *Blasted*'s first production in January 1995 is now legendary, and recounted at length by both Sierz and Saunders. As Sierz says, it quickly became 'the most talked about play for years [and] the most notorious play of the decade'.[9] The scandal included vitriolic newspaper reviews, discussion on late-night television shows, letters to newspapers and nationwide coverage. The most notorious headlines – the *Daily Mail*'s 'This Disgusting Feast of Filth' and the

Daily Express's 'Rape Play Girl Goes into Hiding' – encapsulate the hyperbole surrounding this event. However dramatic the media response, the plot of *Blasted* is relatively simple: Ian, a forty-five-year-old tabloid journalist suffering from lung cancer, and Cate, a naive twenty-one-year-old, walk into an extremely expensive hotel room in Leeds.[10] They evidently once had a sexual relationship and Ian tries to initiate sex but she rejects him, although, when she is unconscious, he simulates sex with her, and then rapes her during the night. There is a knock at the door and an unnamed soldier appears. Cate escapes, but the soldier subjects Ian to a series of horrifying stories involving the rape and torture of women and children that he has either endured or participated in himself. He rapes Ian and then sucks out and eats both his eyeballs. He then shoots himself. Cate returns with a baby she has been given to take care of. It dies and Cate buries it, leaving Ian alone again to suffer a series of crises. Eventually, he exhumes the body of the baby and eats it. Cate returns once more with food, and feeds herself and Ian. The play ends with his words: 'Thank you' (p. 61).

Although this catalogue of catastrophe may sound horrific, the structure of *Blasted* is at first fairly naturalistic and conventional. The setting is specified as a hotel room '*so expensive it could be anywhere in the world*', complete with '*bed, mini-bar, telephone, large bouquet of flowers and two doors*' (p. 3). This is instantly recognisable and places the play well within the familiar world of social realism. Similarly, the characters are introduced as naturalistic creations: Kane gives descriptions of their age, appearance and personality. If we approach *Blasted* in this way, its horrors seem particularly bleak. Many reviewers in 1995 merely listed the events and, as Innes points out, 'With such contraction, the overwhelming catalogue of atrocities becomes numbing.'[11] Indeed, the listing of them can alienate and confuse; it is certainly difficult to imagine enjoying a play in which these atrocious events take place. Paradoxically, Luckhurst's attempt to explore the play begins with her claim that it 'is best summarised as a series of actions' (which do help evoke its fragmentary structure), but then goes on to quote Kane's own defence of her play: 'A list of contents is not a review.'[12]

Certainly if we approach the play from the familiar territory of social realism and naturalistic theatre, these events seem brutal and gratuitous, but there are moments when the realist framework breaks down. The moment at which the soldier enters the room is also the moment where the play turns from naturalistic to chaotic: '*there is a blinding light, then a huge explosion*' and we are told that '*The hotel has been blasted by a mortar bomb. There is a large hole in one of the walls and everything is covered in a dust*' (p. 39). Similarly, and interestingly, this is often only apparent in the text alone; Kane includes the stage direction '[Ian] *dies with relief*' (p. 60) on the penultimate page, and yet he continues to speak and interact with Cate. These moments seem impossible to explain within the confines of social realist drama, and also complicate the categorisation of *Blasted* simply as an in-yer-face play. Structurally, it has little in common with other plays of this genre, and, as Steve Waters points out, many other in-yer-face playwrights produce plays which 'bear little resemblance to the ambitions and formal violations that Kane's work proposes'.[13] Kane herself suggested that in *Blasted* we see 'form and content attempt[ing] to be one' – the effect of sudden violence experienced through a corresponding jolt of the form, with traditional theatrical structure also collapsing.[14] This is a crucial concept in approaching her work.

This break with naturalism compromises the categorisation of *Blasted* simply as an in-yer-face play. While other writers associated with this genre also employ shockingly violent or sexually explicit images they are often contained within realistic social settings. In Kane's play, despite the fact that it begins with the highly conventional hotel room and discourse between Cate and Ian, this veneer of realism is overthrown when the room is blasted and the naturalistic structure literally blown away. However, while Kane rejects the form of realist theatre, her play does remain rooted in realistic situations. It is often mentioned that her inspiration was the Srebrenica siege during the Bosnian war, in which thousands of Muslims were killed, and that she deliberately related the 'domestic' rape of Cate to the atrocities in Bosnia: these events, which she refers to as 'one [as] the seed and the other [. . .] the tree' explicitly politicise the play, and pull it back into the realm of the real, creating an unsettling scenario in which it feels both expressionistic and nightmarishly unreal, but also brutally truthful and grounded in recognisable political contexts.[15] So although Kane is at pains to reject – in the second act – the naturalistic setting of social realism, she does not allow the play to fall away from the cruel reality of violence and war. This seeming contradiction means many commentators feel uneasy about the play. Billington, for example, argues that Kane needs to 'establish an iron-clad connection between personal abuse and the larger image of civic chaos; and I'm not sure she does'.[16] However, Kane's insistence that the form of her play should mirror the content helps us understand the immensely shocking nature of all violence. In many ways it is less interesting whether or not the connection is valid or if the play is naturalistic or otherwise; the real question is whether Kane addresses and adequately portrays the visceral nature of physical violence through theatrical form and imagery.

For many writers, Kane's refusal to explain the play in terms of gender conflict also makes *Blasted* a troubling play. Kane refused to accept that she was a 'woman writer', arguing that 'I don't believe there's such a thing'.[17] However, not everyone agrees about this. Elaine Aston, for example, insists on viewing *Blasted* as 'as a gendered, feminist' text.[18] Certainly Kane does deal with gender identity and politics in this play, but she complicates this by declining to assign simple binary positions to gender roles. Kane herself argued that 'I don't see the world being divided up into men and women, victims and perpetrators. I don't think those are constructive divisions to make, and they make for very poor writing.'[19] This argument raises a crucial point: do men and women behave as simple victims or perpetrators in the play, and does the play make attempts to disrupt such easy associations? While it is true that Cate is victimised, and suffers at the hands of Ian, she is also to some extent both complicit in this and aggressive in return; she bites his penis, and remains in the hotel room after her rape. Similarly, although we may see Ian as the perpetrator of violence against Cate, he is also a victim of the soldier, who is, in turn, both an aggressor towards Ian but again a victim of the violence he has suffered through the loss of his girlfriend Col. Kane's refusal to adapt *Blasted* to the mould of '"politically correct" victim drama' disturbs the simple associations between female as victim and male as aggressor.[20] Aston argues that Kane rejects these boundaries by reversing them, that once Ian is left blinded and abject he is 'in the position of the "feminine" previously occupied by Cate'.[21] But surely this view merely reinforces the binaries that Kane has rejected, and encourages us to see *Blasted* in a simplistic binary form – those who are violently subjugated must be associated with the feminine. More worryingly, Aston seems not to recognise the trauma experienced by Ian. While she discusses rape as an 'act of male-authored violence against women' – and suggests that Kane included Cate's rape by Ian to mark her association with other feminist playwrights – she does not discuss the rape suffered by Ian at the hands of the soldier as a similarly sexual trauma, referring to the moment Ian is raped by the soldier as 'Ian [being] penetrated by his own "filth"'.[22]

Aston's attempt to claim victim status only for Cate, to suggest that rape can only be suffered by women, and to assert an explicit feminist agenda on her behalf, is startlingly at odds with Kane's own claim that the division between victim and aggressor is blurred. However, Sierz's suggestion that in-yer-face theatre 'chip[s] away at [. . .] binary oppositions' does not go far enough; in the play, binary identity is held to such account that any essentialist behaviour associated with either gender is impossible.[23] Furthermore, Kane's focus is not solely on gender identity, however much Aston seeks to understand it in those terms. She seems more interested in the depiction of violence and victimhood, regardless of the gender of the sufferer or perpetrator. So although binaries are undermined, the distinctions between people and their actions are in some respects completely obliterated. We never know whom to sympathise with, or who has committed a crime we should condemn, as characters are frequently presented as both the sufferer and the torturer. A discussion of the theorisation of trauma may help us see the play more clearly.

Elaine Scarry's *The Body in Pain* (1985) suggests ways of viewing human identity not through a gendered lens but through the universalising experience of pain and trauma. While several critics have used Scarry to discuss Kane's work, the detail of her focus on the infliction of extreme pain or torture resonates with *Blasted* on many levels, and is worth drawing out in further detail.[24] Scarry describes the process of torture itself as 'a grotesque piece of [. . .] theatre', making reference to the highly performative nature of inflicting pain, taking a personal and private feeling and making it visible on the sufferer's body.[25] Scarry also mentions the significance of the room in which pain is inflicted: the everyday objects that are used to create pain but their association with the mundane is shattered when used to this effect.[26] An example of this in the play would be the newspaper and flowers. This makes us think of the familiar hotel room made alien and terrible by the arrival of the soldier. Furthermore, Scarry describes her room as 'a magnification of the body', in which the walls disintegrate along with the prisoner's sense of self and security.[27] This has clear resonances with the way the structure of the room collapses in *Blasted*. Scarry also explains that the 'prisoner is forced to attend to the most intimate and interior facts of his body (pain, hunger, nausea, sexuality, excretion) at a time when there is no benign privacy'.[28] This description recalls Ian's actions once he is alone, when he defecates, masturbates and is overcome with hunger. These usually private moments have become public. Although Ian is alone, he is constantly watched by the audience, underlining the visibility of his pain and trauma. The performative nature of this pain, in which the audience is asked to witness these extreme moments of human abjection and frailty, are extremely uncomfortable precisely because they are usually associated with privacy.

Finally, Scarry comments that there is a huge distance between the perpetrator and the victim. She argues that 'the distance between their two physical realities is colossal, for the prisoner is in overwhelming physical pain while the torturer is utterly without pain'.[29] This may seem like a fair assessment, but Kane refuses to allow this distance to be maintained: she does not exclude the soldier from the role of victim. Although he is arguably free from physical pain while he tortures Ian, he is clearly suffering from trauma. When he rapes Ian, he is described as *crying his eyes out* (p. 49). When attempting to apply trauma theory to the play, Peter Buse discovers that *Blasted* 'chooses to blur the distinction between perpetrator and victim by giving the soldier an originary trauma' – the rape and murder of his girlfriend Col.[30] There is also the suggestion that while we can see this event as the source of his trauma, we can also infer that although the soldier has committed many atrocities himself, he is also still traumatised by these events, and that the perpetrator can suffer as a result of their own actions. He appears anxious to tell Ian what he has done, asking him to bear witness to these crimes and asks Ian 'Would you?' commit similar crimes (p. 45), apparently genuinely wanting to know. He wonders if 'In the line of duty. For your country' (p. 45) other people may behave in similar ways, suggesting that he has been partly coerced. He also claims he'd be 'lonely' (p. 44) without Ian and advises Ian to 'stay in the dark' (p. 46) and not experience the killings he has witnessed, presumably because they are too traumatic. This conclusion suggests that Kane's consideration of the roles of victim and perpetrator are far from straightforward and cannot slip simply into gender binaries or polarised descriptions of trauma and suffering.

Peter Buse, whose analysis of *Blasted* by means of the theory of trauma provides some interesting observations, suggests that traditional understanding of trauma (in the writings of Cathy Caruth and Dori Laub) only concerns itself with the narrative of the victim. This is problematic when applied to Kane's play because its structure gives considerable emphasis to the stories of abuse the solider has perpetrated, not suffered. Buse suggests that Kane 'has produced a sort of melodrama (or even *grand guignol*) of traumatic memories – one that, if not glamorising the violence of the perpetrator, at least privileges it because so fascinated by it'.[31] The question here is framed as an ethical one; should Kane have given so much time in the text over to the harrowing memories of the soldier? While the soldier loses his life and seems truly traumatised by his own actions, perhaps we should ask why Kane has privileged his story above Cate's in the narrative of the play. Buse points out that physical and emotional trauma does not just destroy the individual; it also causes there to be a crisis in representation and narrative. This is due to the impossibility of describing horrific events directly; the magnitude of some events (the Holocaust is the most obvious example) creates the situation whereby it becomes possible to question all existing forms of language and testimony.[32] Scarry also argues that pain is 'resistant to language', leading to a 'shattering of language' and that extreme pain 'causes a reversion to the pre-language of cries and groans'.[33] This is why *Blasted* is such a challenging play – Kane makes it clear that actually we can discuss traumatic events, and they are recounted in chilling detail. The soldier has a number of monologues in which language very effectively conveys the trauma of the events he has participated in and witnessed.

Perhaps a more useful way of thinking about the trauma in *Blasted* is to reject categorisation and binaries altogether. Indeed, binaries can only be reversed or undermined if we accept certain assumptions about gender and victim identity in the first place, and I have argued that Kane has not actively engaged with those terms. Ken Urban argues that *Blasted* does not seek to represent the 'real life' events of Bosnia, or indeed any other historical moment. He argues that it 'does not seek to represent incidents, but reference them. The play and the production dramatise the logic that allows such events to occur in the first place.'[34] Interestingly, we also know that in the writing process Kane made a number of changes and 'systemically took out [specific] references and replaced them with more general ones: she wanted to universalise the play and generalise its politics'.[35] These changes include removing the name of the soldier (originally Vladek) and references to Serbia and Croatia. As Sierz rightly suggests, this universalises the play, but it also creates a collage effect, whereby events are not slavishly recounted, but instead used in a more ambivalent, referential way. Kane cites Bosnia but does not seek to create a piece of drama which discusses the specifics; there is a postmodern iteration of Bosnia, in which traumatic events like those suffered in the real conflict are mentioned, but other traumatic events are also thrown into the mix and there is no attempt to be historically accurate or ask the audience to make ethical judgements based on the evidence. In this way, *Blasted* does not set up or break traditional binaries; it simply recounts a series of traumatic events and asks the audience to experience the telling and depiction of these rather than to form opinions or relate the play to specific political contexts. This fragmentary approach is fundamentally postmodern as it removes a consistent narrative for the play and makes use of a series of intertextual images (such as those from news coverage of war zones) without providing a framework to understand these images solely in terms of male/female, victim/aggressor.

Cleansed

Although Kane's third play, *Cleansed*, is frequently discussed in terms of the gender politics it suggests, and its exploration of love and desire, the following analysis will focus more on the structural features of the play, and the depiction of violence in terms of trauma and punishment/incarceration theory. Ostensibly set in a university but actually in a more sinister institution, *Cleansed* focuses on the story of Grace, who is searching for her brother Graham, who in turn has been killed by the mysterious and sinister jailer/doctor figure Tinker. Grace starts to dress in Graham's clothes, makes love to his spirit and eventually 'becomes' him after his genitals are grafted on to her own. In the same institution, two lovers, Carl and Rod, discuss the meaning of love and obsession but when Carl is subjected to horrifying torture at the hands of Tinker he eventually betrays Rod. Further subplots involve Robin, a young man, who falls in love with Grace when she teaches him to read, and finally we also see the orchestrator of all the events, Tinker, regularly visit a strip club where an unnamed dancer performs for Tinker when he deposits a coin in a box. The play ends with Grace 'becoming' Graham, Robin hanging himself when he realises how long he has yet to spend in the institution and Carl, having been largely dismembered, sitting with Grace/Graham while the sun blazes and the stage is overrun with rats.

Clearly *Cleansed* is extremely challenging to perform: the list of unlikely stage directions include '*a sunflower bursts through the floor and grows above their heads*' (p. 120), '*The rats carry away Carl's feet*' (p. 136) and '*Grace is raped by one of the voices*' (p. 132). Despite this, or perhaps because of it, Kane argued that the play can only ever be produced as theatre, and 'never be turned into a film, or short for television, turned into a novel' – she also claimed that the play is a reaction against 'all of this naturalistic rubbish', suggesting that she had consciously turned her back on the well-made play structure she had employed in *Blasted*.[36] Although Kane argues that this play can only ever be a theatrical event, it is also possible to imagine it in prose form. Indeed, the experience of reading the play is both shocking and beautiful as the stark but also poetic images can be realised in the mind perhaps more effectively than on the stage. This suggestion is at odds with Kane's own argument that to stage the play naturalistically would result in 'half the audience [dying] from sheer grief'.[37] However, Urban suggests that the play is best considered as 'a series of twenty episodes that could be played in a variety of orders and which could exist almost independently'.[38] This recalls Martin Crimp's influential *Attempts on Her Life* (1997) in which the action is split into seventeen 'Scenarios for the Theatre'. However, the fragmentation of the action in *Cleansed* also feels distinctly textual, as if a narrative, or an attempt to create a linear structure with a naturalistic plot and through-line, has been fractured and distorted. Urban quotes Mel Kenyon, Kane's agent, discussing the political implications of this structure: 'The strong Right is full of certainties, certainties which are abhorrent. The Left was full of certainties, certainties which proved to be bogus. So to write these big political plays full of certainties and resolution is completely nonsensical in a time of fragmentation.'[39] Most obviously, this comment recalls Ravenhill's *Shopping and Fucking*, in which a character explains:

> I think we all need stories, we make up stories so that we can get by. And I think a long time ago there were big stories. Stories so big you could live your whole life by them. The Powerful Hands of the Gods and Fate. The journey to Enlightenment. The March of Socialism. But they all died or the world grew up or grew senile or forgot them, so now we're all making up our own stories. Little stories. It comes out in different ways. But we've each got one.[40]

This focus on 'stories' and 'narrative' recalls the comments made about *Blasted*'s use of victim and survivor testimony. Scarry's suggestion that in moments of extreme trauma language is destroyed seems to resonate with the way in which *Cleansed*'s structure is illogical, disparate and free-floating. Any attempt to make sense of the play within the confines of naturalistic playwriting, in which events are logical and structured, in the same way that language usually is, is indeed deeply problematic. Scarry describes the ostensible purpose of torture as the attempt to encourage confession: the '"it" in "get it out of him" refers not just to a piece of information but to the capacity for speech itself'.[41] This means that the torturer will attempt to take ownership of the prisoner's ability and control of their own voice and language; they will not be able to control what they say and the regime responsible for the torture will then take ownership of the words and narratives produced. This idea is played out in Kane's plays: the narrative of *Blasted* does not give space to the voice of the victims of the soldier's abuse; instead we are only confronted with the soldier's own response to the events he is responsible for. Similarly, in *Cleansed*, Tinker tortures Carl in order to make him betray his lover Rod. Tinker asks him a series of questions, 'What is your boyfriend's name?' and 'Can you describe his genitals?' (p. 117) until Carl is forced to confess, 'Please not me, don't kill me, Rod not me, don't kill me' (p. 117). In a final act of silencing, and, in Scarry's terms, removing the act of speech from the prisoner, Tinker then '*produces a large pair of scissors and cuts off Carl's tongue*' (p. 118), an act of literal and final removal of the capacity to create and manage one's own narrative.

The way we view people and institutions of power is also disturbed in this play. The play supposedly takes place in a university but it is clearly now being used for more sinister purposes. In fact, Kane once said that she was influenced by Roland Barthes's offhand statement that the situation of a rejected lover is not unlike that of a prisoner in Dachau, thus adding to the sense that this is some kind of death camp. The instigator of the terrible events of the play is the enigmatic Tinker, who initially claims to be 'a dealer not a doctor' (p. 107), but is frequently referred to as 'doctor' by a number of the characters and also describes himself in those terms when talking to the stripper (p. 122). Scarry describes the presence of medical doctors in the process of torture and discusses the ways in which medicine and the imagery of 'treatment' commonly underpin acts of torture. Clearly in such examples the image of the doctor as a caring agent or healer is horribly subverted, and 'the institution of medicine [. . .] is deconstructed'.[42]

Michel Foucault also considered the role of hospitals and medical institutions in his analysis of punishment and incarceration, *Discipline and Punish* (1975). He gives a series of historical accounts of torture and execution, and points out that, even when writing in the 1970s, 'a doctor must watch over those condemned to death [. . .] thus juxtaposing himself as the agent of welfare, as the alleviator of pain, with the official whose task it is to end life'.[43] This blurring of roles, and the sinister subversion of the widely accepted concept of a doctor figure bringing relief, is developed by Foucault to include the way in which prisoners regulate their own behaviour, because if they know they are being watched they will 'assume responsibility for the constraints of power' and 'simultaneously play both roles; he [the prisoner] becomes the principle of his own subjection'.[44] Foucault also argues that hospitals have much in common with prisons in the way they are structured – both depend upon constant observation and both have discipline at their core; both prisoners and patients need to be constantly monitored and subjected to treatment or punishment. Clearly these observations can be applied to *Cleansed*. Despite Tinker's many atrocities Grace still appeals to him to 'treat me like a patient' (p. 114) and the dancing woman says, 'You're a doctor. Help me' (p. 138). Foucault's theories of the power of the institution, be it medical or penal, suggest that observation is a key factor. He argues that surveillance 'becomes a decisive [. . .] operator [. . .] as a specific mechanism in the disciplinary power'.[45] He also compares prison cells to 'small theatres, in which each actor is alone, perfectly individualised and constantly visible', an image which recalls the dancing woman who performs in a booth converted from the university's showers.[46] Tinker puts money into a slot and a flap opens whereby he can watch the woman dancing. Tinker observes the woman and objectifies her body; in this process of surveillance he is dominant and the act of observation creates a theatre for him in which he can access the woman and her body whenever he chooses. Foucault also argues that the physical body is crucially significant in punishment: 'the body is directly involved in a political field: power relations have an immediate hold upon it; they invest it, mark it, train it, torture it, force it to carry out tasks, to perform ceremonies'.[47] All of these actions are encountered in *Cleansed*, from Tinker's beating of Grace, the cruel task in which he makes Robin eat an entire box of chocolates, the constant maiming and marking of the body and the commanding of the woman to dance. The way in which the body is altered or controlled is taken to the extreme; we see Graham's body being grafted on to Grace's and the mutilation of Carl is a frequent horror punctuating the whole play. As Judith Butler argues, 'The body implies mortality, vulnerability, agency: the skin and the flesh expose us to the gaze of others, but also to touch, to violence, and bodies put us at risk of becoming the agency and instrument of all these as well.'[48]

Both Butler and Foucault see the use, constraint and abuse of bodies in this way as broadly political; Butler goes on to describe the process whereby grief at the loss of a loved one is a profoundly political experience because it brings 'to the fore the relational ties that have implications for theorising [. . .] ethical responsibility', while Foucault's analysis of the prison system is rooted in the implications of institutional power and responsibility.[49] But not everyone agrees that Kane's work fits into this context. For example, Sanja Nikcevic argues that in writing *Cleansed* Kane 'showed no interest in wider political situations of violence' and that 'the characters have no connection with world atrocities'.[50] While it is true that no obvious newsworthy 'world atrocities' are mentioned, and the political context is not as clear as it is in *Blasted*, given Kane's preoccupation with institutional violence and abuse in this play, is this a fair comment?

The argument that there is little of 'wider political situations' in *Cleansed* is undermined in the dedication of the play, which reads 'For the patients and staff of ES3' (p. 105), presumably referring to the Eileen Skellern 3 ward (known as ES3) in the Maudsley Hospital, at which Kane spent time. Although autobiographical readings of her work are ultimately fruitless, this dedication suggests that we cannot discount her personal response to institutions. Further evidence for the locating of political context for this play is provided by Hillary Chute, who argues that Kane makes use of historical images in the play in order to remind the audience 'that history hurts [. . .] and we cannot distance ourselves from its cruelty'.[51] Chute argues that *Cleansed* does make use of several 'real world' events, including basing Robin's suicide on the story of a prisoner on Robben Island and Carl's impalement on a Serb method of execution. This particular historical link makes explicit connections to the political context of *Blasted* as well. However, even those who argue that political theatre cannot simply rely on replicating political content may still have an interest in Kane's work. There has been a growing tendency to view her work in the postdramatic sense, that is, as theatre based on experiential emotions rather than traditional text. The proponent of postdramatic theatre, Hans-Thies Lehmann, argues that 'politically oppressed people shown on stage does not make theatre political [. . .] It is not through the direct thematisation of the political that theatre becomes political but through the implicit substance and critical value of its *mode of representation*.'[52] Lehmann is arguing that the creation of political narratives, or stories, on the stage, for example the re-creation of the Robben Island story, is not sufficient for theatre to be political. He suggests that the form of that theatre must be radical also; that it must 'hurt feeling [and] produce shock and disorientation'.[53] Although the application of postdramatic theatre theory to Kane's work is problematic, Lehmann's argument that form and content must be mirrored is consistent with Kane's own suggestion that in *Blasted* 'the form and content attempt to be one – the form is the meaning'.[54] This means that for Lehmann and for Kane theatre must be more than an intellectual discussion of shocking images or historical events – it must also be physically and emotionally shocking in itself, so that the act of watching the play must be challenging and disorientating for an audience. This is evidently the case for both *Cleansed* and *Blasted*, but we must not forget that Lehmann advocates the complete rejection of scripted theatre and argues that naturalistic staging is limited and politically impotent. We have already seen that *Blasted* has a troubled relationship with naturalistic theatre; it is both reminiscent of social realism yet also rejects naturalism in its form. However, both *Blasted* and *Cleansed* are still recognisable pieces of dramatic text – they have settings, characters, action and dialogue. In Kane's last piece of theatre, *4.48 Psychosis*, these recognisable structures have completely fallen away, and postdramatic theatre may be more relevant to discussing this work.

4.48 Psychosis

Kane's final play will always have the dubious honour of carrying the legacy of her life and, inevitably, her death. Kane's suicide in February 1999 pre-empted the premiere of this play and when it was staged posthumously eighteen months later it seemed unavoidable that connections would be made between this play and the playwright's own life and death. Indeed, *4.48 Psychosis* has been described as 'a 75-minute suicide note'.[55] Such an assessment, however, ignores the pitfalls associated with directly comparing the play to the author. It also fails to take account of the complex structure of the play, which many have discussed in relation to Lehmann's analysis of postdramatic theatre. It also overlooks the more playful or ironic aspects of a fiction in which Kane nevertheless critically assesses the way mentally ill patients are treated by the NHS. The play has little plot or structure. Apart from a more or less consistent authorial voice, there are few identifiable characters, and dialogue – usually between an unidentified doctor and patient – is suggested by the structure of a conversation punctuated with dashes to indicate a new speaker. Similarly, scenes are not indicated, but various dashes appear across the page to designate a break in the narrative structure. Most interestingly, the layout of words on the page is highly poetic – seemingly random and meaningless letters and numbers appear at intervals, giving the play a highly textual quality, as there is little suggestion of how this would be realised in performance. Although no location or setting is indicated, the play clearly addresses the struggle with mental illness one, or more characters, is currently facing. For example, at various stages there is clearly a conversation between a female/male patient and his/her psychiatrist or doctor. It is difficult to know how to stage the play in terms of character. Depending upon the interpretation of the individual director, *4.48 Psychosis* has been staged as a solo piece and with several actors. Equally ambivalent is the question of gender in the play. Although many automatically see the patient as female (presumably by making connections with Kane's own struggle with depression), there is no certainty about the gender of the protagonist and any of the roles within the text could be equally well portrayed by a male or female actor.

The main problem critics face when exploring this text is the centrality of Kane's own presence. Knowing about Kane's personal experience of mental illness and her eventual death inevitably flavours the work, and imbues it with signification. Clearly *4.48 Psychosis* explores issues and emotions surrounding mental illnesses, but to say the play is solely about those topics limits the possible readings of a very open-ended text. As Sarah Gorman argues, 'The authority of Kane's voice limits the generation of alternative meanings, which would otherwise appear to be encouraged by the play's open structure.'[56] Gorman points out that such readings privilege a view of the author as the final authenticator of a play's reading, reluctantly concluding that it is 'naïve to imagine that [. . .] the author's "version" of events will not be upheld as definitive'.[57] These debates are framed by wider analysis of the place of the author in respect of the meaning of literary texts. Initially termed the intentional fallacy, arguments about the centrality of the author's voice in the interpretation of the text remain significant literary questions. Critics of the intentional fallacy maintain that the author's intentions can never be relied upon for a definitive reading of the text, and indeed any desire to secure a definitive reading is, in itself, self-defeating, as texts are endlessly open to different interpretations. This is clearly demonstrated in *4.48 Psychosis* as, for example, Kane provided no indication of the number of actors required. While the original Royal Court Theatre Upstairs production used three actors, other choices are equally possible and valid, opening up the interpretation of the play.

Interestingly, Ehren Fordyce reads *4.48 Psychosis* as a play devoid of readings centred around Kane's own biography, which is a view many others feel is unrealistic.[58] He suggests that it 'constitutes a "death-of-the-author" play in that it does away with setting, authorial voice, narrative voice and character voice'.[59] Fordyce is of course referring to Roland Barthes's 1968 essay 'The Death of the Author', which argues for the independence of the text from authorial intention or influence. Barthes thought that the reader has endless power to interpret the text for themselves and that any attempt to reach a definitive reading of the work is fruitless. This argument fits into poststructuralist readings of text, which maintain that all texts are in a state of constant interpretation and no final reading can ever be established. Alicia Tycer applies these ideas to *4.48 Psychosis* by arguing that 'the play forces one to recognise the ambiguity of the author as bearer of meaning, and of the perception of the protagonist, or self, as a unified whole [. . .] That "I" that she claims [the "I" figure in the text of the play] clearly exceeds autobiographical dimensions.'[60] In making this argument, Tycer is suggesting that not only does the text make readings that focus on Kane's own life problematic, but that we should also be wary of assigning any particular character to the protagonist of the text. Indeed, the text resists such interpretation and remains open to multiple readings.

We saw in the analysis of *Cleansed* how some critics have suggested that the play was fragmented because that structure best resonates with postmodern times. Elizabeth Kuti goes on to argue that postdramatic theatre is 'the only proper response by art to the postmodern condition [because] we are living [. . .] in plotless times'.[61] As we have seen, postdramatic theatre refers to a piece of theatre that exists independently of text and does not attempt to locate itself within a specific location, social theme or display any concern for mimesis. Lehmann defines postdramatic theatre by its rejection of text-based drama which 'clings to the presentation of a fictive and simulated text-cosmos [. . .] while postdramatic theatre no longer does so'.[62] David Barnett argues that *4.48 Psychosis* is a good example of a postdramatic play, and others have sought to do the same.[63] Many point to the fractured structure and lack of identifiable characters as evidence of this, as well as the decentred protagonist and sudden outbreaks of unpredictable violence. Kane's ambivalent relationship with the naturalistic structure of social realism also encourages many to see her as a postdramatic playwright. Lehmann argues that the social implications of social realism include the 'importance of the hero, of the individual', which is another convention we have seen Kane reject, or at least problematise.[64] However, those who seek to align Kane with postdramatic theatre have overlooked two key problems: Kane is still writing within the conventions of mimesis, however much she fragments and fractures the structure of her plays, and her work is highly textual, almost poetic.

Postdramatic theatre rejects the theatrical convention of suspension of disbelief. Many performance or live artists and performers, for example, mutilate their own bodies on stage. If they do not engage with physical suffering, often their performance is based on real things happening to them in real time, be it simply washing their hair, painting their skin or displaying their naked bodies without the structure of a playtext or fictional plot. However, while we can argue that Kane's plays make huge demands on actors in terms of nudity and extreme emotional experience, in no way do they require actors to either physically harm themselves or to exhibit their bodies without the dramatic framework of plot, character and setting. So although the actor playing Ian in *Blasted* may be naked on stage, he is never exposed as himself and is only naked within the context of his imaginary interaction with Cate. Similarly, there may be intense physical demands put on the actor playing Carl in *Cleansed*, but he is never actually mutilated or injured himself in any way. Indeed, it is the point of postdramatic theatre that the performer's body is really interacting with the audience without the presence of plot of other characters. Lehmann argues that 'the dramatic process occurred *between* bodies; the postdramatic process occurs *with/on/to* the body'.[65] By this he means that traditional plays dramatise moments between characters who may be experiencing extreme physical violence or sexuality, but the interaction between the actors in role prevents these moments from being postdramatic. No matter how realistic the production, we do not believe that Tinker really mutilates Carl, neither do we believe that actors performing in *4.48 Psychosis* are really suffering from depression, or psychosis, and nor is such a belief necessary to appreciate the performance, as it would be in postdramatic theatre.

Another factor that critics who argue Kane is postdramatic overlook is the centrality of text within her plays. Urban describes *4.48*

Psychosis as 'textual collage' in that it cites and parodies a number of other sources and textual structures.[66] The truth is that the play looks extremely textual, and frequently sections appear to be structured on the page visually rather than linguistically, for example the random spread of numbers (pp. 208, 232). Furthermore, various sections are laid out like poetic verse, suggesting a lyrical quality to both the performance and reading of the text:

> I don't imagine
> (clearly)
> that a single soul
> could
> would
> should
> or will (p. 222)

And:

> the capture
> the rapture
> the rupture
> of a soul (p. 242)

Towards the end of the play, the text becomes increasingly sporadic, with whole pages left almost entirely empty. The fracturing on the page mirrors the fracture of the protagonist's mind: 'And my mind is the subject of these bewildering fragments' (p. 210). While undeniably powerful in performance, the effect of reading *4.48 Psychosis* is also strong: its poetic qualities and lyrical structure lend the play a rhythmic value which can be appreciated as one would read poetry – as words on the page. David Barnett argues that text is not important for postdramatic theatre and that 'the words themselves [. . .] become just another element in a theatrical mode'.[67] This claim is undermined by Kane's highly textual structuring of *4.48 Psychosis*. Indeed, at one point Kane writes, 'A glut of exclamation marks spell impending nervous breakdown / Just a word on the page and there is the drama'

(p. 213). This section is highly significant; it suggests that Kane has crafted the play specifically to mirror the mental collapse of the speaker, as already suggested, and that exclamation marks on the page communicate the intensity of that experience. She could also be suggesting that drama is constructed through the words provided on the page – that the experience of reading or performing them creates the theatrical event. This play is highly, and self-consciously, textual.

Kane also uses language in *4.48 Psychosis* to ironically critique the social structures dedicated to treating mental illness. Although the play can hardly be classed as a comedy, there are moments of deeply ironic humour. For example, 'I dreamt I went to the doctor's and she gave me eight minutes to live. I'd been sitting in the fucking waiting room half an hour' (p. 221). The speaker also refers to 'my gallows humour' (p. 209). Both Voigts-Virchow and Gritzner argue that Kane's work is 'free of irony' and 'devoid of postmodern irony', but these claims seem to take little account of the clear ironic playfulness of the text.[68] *4.48 Psychosis* uses contrasting forms of narrative to humorously undermine the structures of health care, comparing the formal and rigid form of medical notes with the chaotic and disordered experience of a suicide attempt:

Venlafaxine, 75mg, increased to 150mg, then 225mg. Dizziness, low blood pressure, headaches. No other reaction. Discontinued . . .

100 aspirin and one bottle of Bulgarian Cabernet Sauvignon, 1986. Patient woke in pool of vomit . . . Severe stomach pain. No other reaction. (p. 225)

She also adds, as part of her parody of medical notes, again ironically, 'paranoid thoughts – believes hospital staff are trying to poison her' (p. 224) after a long list of drugs administered to the patient. These moments in the text are highly ironic and, rather than rejecting text, suggest that text is highly significant in *4.48 Psychosis*. Indeed, these moments are intertextual in that they make parodic use of one narrative form to create humour and irony when applied to incongruous situations.

Although Kane once said that she was 'finding performance much more interesting than acting; theatre more compelling than plays', there is little evidence that she was about to turn her back on textual writing and the production of dramatic plays.[69] Although *4.48 Psychosis* rejects traditional characterisation and plot, it is highly poetic and relies on specific linguistic structures to help create its effects. Although some commentators and academics might discuss her plays within the context of the postdramatic, and indeed this is an interesting exercise, it is clear that she was not a performance artist and that her plays are tightly woven and textually specific pieces of theatre. Attempts to suggest otherwise seem to overlook her ambivalence towards the relationship between mimesis and the real, and yet again to force her into categorisations that her plays seem to resist.

Conclusion

Kane's work can be explored from a variety of new perspectives, ones which question the established approaches to the appreciation of her work. Until recently, she was most commonly associated with the genre of in-yer-face theatre, as argued by Sierz and as used by other commentators. To apply this label to her work is not unreasonable as many of her plays contain elements commonly associated with this sensibility. However, Kane herself either distanced herself from any label, or at best seemed uninterested in it: when asked by Sierz about the term and its application to her work, she responded, 'That's your problem mate, not mine.'[70] While there was an attempt by some 1990s playwrights to 'write work which doesn't finish with a climax in the "right" place, doesn't have a clear message, and doesn't obey the dictates of naturalism', it is also clear that many so-called in-yer-face dramatists wrote within the confines of naturalistic theatre, and were driven by the structures of social realist drama.[71] By contrast, Kane attempted to blow apart the naturalistic frame while writing *Blasted*, and in her later plays – *Crave* and *4.48 Psychosis* – she almost entirely rejected the traditional structures of character and narrative. More recently, some critics have sought to claim Kane as a postdramatic playwright. This phenomenon has great currency in Germany, and Kane's success in Europe, often at the expense of popularity in Britain, has been explained by an association with postdramatic theatre.[72] The connections in Kane's work to postdramatic theatre are evident: fragmented narrative, lack of distinct characters and rejection of social realist structures. However, this narrative of Kane's success in Germany is not without its complications; Kane herself described her anger at a German production of *Blasted* which she 'hated' and made her 'heart just [break]'.[73] Furthermore, Kane's plays are not pieces of performance art; they do still hang on to structures of representation and mimesis (albeit without regard for traditional conventions of naturalism), and as such are not truly postdramatic. Attempts to describe her plays in this context thus seem problematic.

Finally, some critics have attempted to align her plays with a feminist agenda. David Ian Rabey suggests that her work can be compared to Sarah Daniels's, in particular her 1983 play *Masterpieces*, which Rabey argues 'importantly anticipates [. . .] *Blasted*'.[74] If this is true, perhaps it is only in form rather than content; Daniels's play is a brutal and shocking exploration of pornography and snuff films, but her examination of gender is highly polarised: men are violent and aggressive consumers of damaging pornography, and women are victims. This binary approach is strongly criticised by Kane, particularly in *Blasted*, in which male and female characters are shown to be equal victims of the horrors of civil war. Rabey points out that Daniels's plays 'centralise women', suggesting that female experience can be isolated and examined as different and separate from that of men.[75] Surely this essentialising approach is precisely what Kane was rejecting when she argued that there was no such thing as a female playwright. Her assertion that she cannot be judged according to her femininity is at odds with old-school feminist plays of the 1970s and 1980s, which tended to cast the woman as central and focus on their experience as something special and unique. Sierz also argues that plays from this era tended to offer 'easy answers and rather easy emotional trajectories', something Kane can certainly not be accused of doing.[76] While sexual politics are clearly a concern in her plays, she evidently rejected any easy associations between gender roles and victimisation; men are as damaged by violence and terror as women, even if they are also the perpetrators, and Kane rejects easy social contexts for her work. It is impossible to imagine Kane writing a play like *Masterpieces*, which criticises pornography without much subtle argument or any attempt to complicate the relationship between the sexes. Kane admitted to being horrified by the work of American feminist Andrea Dworkin, and argued that consumers of pornography are 'intelligent enough to know the difference between fantasy and reality'.[77] Kane's acknowledgement that people are not easily divided into victims and aggressors, and can indeed be exposed to sexual images without becoming violent, also recognises the fact that women can consume pornography as well as men. Her plays certainly reject the simplistic connection between pornography and male violence, as much as they reject simplistic connections based on any assumed gender role, and so the argument that she is a playwright heavily influenced by feminist dramatists of the 1970s and 1980s is insubstantial.

In the wake of her death, commentators and critics have been quick to try and categorise Kane. From the enfant terrible of the theatrical scene she has become accepted and lionised by the theatrical establishment. Critics, most notably Michael Billington, have come out and apologised for their initial responses to her plays, and both universities and schools have been quick to add her plays to their syllabuses.[78] This sudden acceptance and celebration of her work partly conceals the difficult questions her plays pose and ignores the challenges associated with discussing her work without relying on easy existing genres or labels. Kuti correctly argues that we must view Kane beyond mere labels and try to avoid the 'consequent misleading categorisation of plays into political versus non-political, public versus private, big versus little stories'.[79] The terms used here by Kuti describe the sorts of plays being produced in the 1980s and early 1990s, plays which were much more politically motivated and examined the relationships between personal characters and political, public events. Kane's use of imagery and narrative from Bosnia in *Blasted*, Dachau in *Cleansed* and the NHS in *4.48 Psychosis* seems to encourage us to try and locate the worlds of her plays within recognisable political situations. However, the intensity of her writing and the complex moral and ethical positions discussed within the plays make such associations problematic. We must also be wary of searching for any one category with which to approach her plays. From the very beginning, *Blasted* deliberately destabilised genre conventions by playing with naturalistic form and then fracturing it shockingly and violently. Kane deliberately refused to give a context to the violence in this play: we are never told who is fighting whom and, most crucially, we are never told whose side to take and whose to condemn. The challenge is to find new ways to read Kane's work, ways which more honestly approach the plays and do not attempt to fit her into any category, be it feminist, political or in-yer-face. If her plays teach us anything, it is that labels are only meaningful when they are rejected, reversed or suspended.

ANTHONY NEILSON
By Trish Reid

Kurten   You choose to believe that I am insane because you choose not to believe in evil.
– Anthony Neilson, Normal, 1991

Introduction

Anthony Neilson is among the most innovative and provocative Scottish theatre artists of his generation. It was principally via the dark and troubling subject matter that defined his most successful plays of the 1990s – *Normal* (1991), *Penetrator* (1993) and *The Censor* (1997) – that his reputation and his power to shock were established. The earliest of these works, *Normal*, is more than twenty years old and a reassessment of Neilson's 1990s output now seems timely. In what follows I intend to achieve this both by complicating and extending existing critical accounts of the earlier plays, and by re-examining them through the lens of his more recent work. In the first instance, it is worth noting that although he was born and grew up in Edinburgh, the son of two Scottish actors, Scotland's culture and its theatrical traditions have only recently been considered a factor in shaping his work. Writing before the launch of the National Theatre of Scotland (NTS) in 2006, the Scottish critic Adrienne Scullion emphasised the 'metropolitan' flavour of his work, describing him as the only Scottish playwright to 'fit neatly' into the 'London cultural milieu'.[1] For Scullion, Neilson remained an 'imponderable figure in Scottish Theatre in the 1990s'.[2] Given his connection to the NTS – where he is currently an Artistic Associate and for whom he created one of its inaugural shows, *Home Edinburgh* (2006), as well as *Realism* (2006), and which revived his *The Wonderful World of Dissocia* (2004) – this assessment was bound to change. In light of the repositioning of Neilson as a twenty-first-century Scottish artist, to which Scullion has contributed, it seems pertinent to consider how far his Scottishness can be considered a factor in shaping his early work.[3]

The most substantial critical discussion of Neilson's work in the 1990s appears in Aleks Sierz's *In-Yer-Face Theatre* (2001). For better or worse, Neilson's inclusion in this volume has meant that subsequent references to his early work have tended to reproduce Sierz's London-centric perspective and point to elements of the plays that conform to his definition of in-yer-face theatre: 'Often such drama employs shock tactics, or is shocking because it is new in tone or structure, or because it is bolder and more experimental than audiences are used to. Questioning moral norms, it affronts the ruling ideas of what can or should be shown onstage.'[4] Each of Neilson's major 1990s plays can meaningfully be described as shocking, taboo breaking and bold – involving as they do scenes of explicit violence, masturbation and defecation – and as such they fit rather neatly into Sierz's definition. Subsequently, the label has been applied to Neilson in a number of contexts. In an interview in 2007, for instance, Stephen Daldry, while acknowledging that the genuine controversy surrounding British playwriting in the mid-1990s centred around Sarah Kane's *Blasted* (1995), notes that the 'Royal Court had been putting on "in-yer-face" plays' for some time before then, citing 'Anthony Neilson's *Penetrator* at the Theatre Upstairs' as an example.[5]

Similarly, in their introduction to *Cool Britannia?* (2008), Rebecca D'Monté and Graham Saunders identify Neilson as one of a group of 'young in-yer-face dramatists' that includes playwrights such as Jez Butterworth and Martin McDonagh.[6] More recently, David Lane includes Neilson in his discussion of writers employing 'aggressive and eye-catching tactics' in the mid-1990s without mentioning that he is Scottish.[7]

In the event, the term in-yer-face has been refracted through so many critical lenses since its first appearance that its meaning has become somewhat obscured. Before reconsidering the utility of the label in relation to *Normal, Penetrator* and *The Censor*, and extending and complicating it, it is worth returning briefly to Sierz, who recently offered a welcome clarification in a lecture for the Society for Theatre Research:

> In-yer-face theatre is both a sensibility and a series of theatrical techniques. As a sensibility, it involved an acuteness of feeling and a keen intellectual perception of the spirit of the age. As a series of theatrical techniques, it is an example of experiential theatre, and its techniques include a stage language that empha-sises rawness, intensity and strong words, stage images that show acute pain or comfortless vulnerability, characterisation that prefers complicit victims to innocent ones, and a 90-minute running time that dispenses with the interval.[8]

A number of elements in Sierz's clarification are of interest in relation to *Normal, Penetrator* and *The Censor*. In particular, his notion of an experiential emphasis, a theatre that privileges felt experience in a theatrical context over other types of engagement, such as intellectual or aesthetic, offers a way of thinking about the intensity and affective power of Neilson's early plays. This is an element that the playwright has consistently privileged in his work: 'The hammer sequence in *Normal*, the whole end section of *Penetrator* and *that* moment in *The Censor*, all owed something to that element. Beyond that shock-effect it was a question of how to make it resonate, how to make it real and enervating in the moment. It was about being live.'[9]

By his own admission, then, Neilson is an experiential artist. None the less, while enabling in so far as it identified trends and shared preoccupations, an additional problem with the term in-yer-face theatre is that it has tended to over-emphasise similarities between writers and consequently to efface important differences. Thus Neilson becomes of interest because of his shared sensibility with, or influence on, writers such as Kane and Ravenhill. Reputations can be established by such emphases, by isolating certain characteristics in a playwright's work while inevitably sidelining others. In the case of Neilson this problem is exacerbated because, apart from the chapter in *In-Yer-Face Theatre,* the critical literature on his early plays is not extensive, and he tends to be mentioned in relation to the 1990s only in passing, as the comments by Daldry, De Monté, Saunders and Lane cited above demonstrate. Moreover, recent critical accounts of Neilson's work have focused almost exclusively on his work in the new millennium, when his theatre became marked by formal experimentation.[10]

I intend to argue in this chapter that Neilson has a particularly important and distinctive theatrical voice not so much because he utilises a particular set of theatrical techniques as outlined by Sierz, but rather because he articulates a consistent thematic preoccupation, one that is more personal than political, more concerned with subjective than social experience, and as such not straightforwardly relatable to the politics of its day. In common with a number of his contemporaries Neilson is temperamentally disinclined towards the moderate centre, where conflicts are usually resolved. He prefers instead to place his characters in situations of acute stress, examining their dilemmas through a juxtaposition of one extreme position and its opposite. *Normal* is a play about a naive young man who gets dangerously close to the mind of a serial killer, in *Penetrator* 'nasty violence with sexual overtones' erupts in the squalid living room of two ill-prepared layabouts and in *The Censor* a profoundly sexually repressed man comes into conflict with a sexually liberated young woman.[11] What distinguishes Neilson from his contemporaries in the moment of Cool Britannia is that in all three plays he stages a battle between inner and outer realities, one in which inner realities are privileged. His subject is not so much the spirit of the age, but subjectivity itself.

Throughout his career, Neilson has been concerned with characters who occupy margins and extremes, whose identity is under pressure and therefore relatively unstable. Alastair Galbraith, who played the Censor in the original production and also worked with Neilson on *The Year of the Family* (1994), believes that Neilson has 'always been writing pretty much about the same things since he started. He really likes people on the edge. He's particularly interested in madness.'[12] This focus on unstable identity in particular, and identity politics in general, might in retrospect be thought of as one indicator of Neilson's Scottishness. As Scotland's other major playwrights David Grieg and David Harrower have observed, the imperative to 'understand ourselves' acquired particular urgency for Scottish theatre artists in the run-up to and the aftermath of the referendum on devolution in 1997.[13] Such a preoccupation is especially apparent in Neilson's work in the new millennium, which consists substantially in a rejection of the conventions of realist narrative in favour of a formally innovative engagement with the problem of representing subjective reality in the theatre. For instance, this imperative entirely shapes the dramaturgy of *The Wonderful World of Dissocia* and its companion piece, *Realism*, which Neilson himself describes as an attempt 'to find a way of writing that somehow moves the way the mind moves'.[14] More recently, although *Relocated* (2008) represents a return to the darker subject matter explored in *Normal*, its most unsettling aspect is arguably the 'mood of tense unease' that Neilson creates 'with image and suggestion rather than lucid narrative': the play 'proceeds as a series of elliptical, enigmatic episodes'.[15]

In summary, a number of Neilson's major twenty-first-century plays consist in baffling concoctions of memory, fantasy and reality. Each in its own way complicates the inside/outside assumptions on which stable binary constructions of identity are usually based. A pattern of sorts emerges when we consider this consistent focus on subjectivity in Neilson's work. Moreover, looking back on his early work through the lens of his recent output can help us see this pattern more clearly. 'Something that deeply annoys, saddens and angers me about the human species,' Neilson remarks, 'is its capacity to adopt rigid positions, is its inability to step into the shoes of others.'[16] We might productively think of his work in the theatre as a sustained attempt to force the audience to 'step into the shoes of others'. In the event, a consistent, almost demented, preoccupation with subjectivity is what underwrites Neilson's distinctive theatrical voice and this is an obsession not necessarily shared by his London-based in-yer-face contemporaries, or indeed by other prominent Scottish playwrights of the 1990s, such as David Greig, Stephen Greenhorn, Chris Hannan and David Harrower.

Normal

Neilson's privileging of subjective experience over objective reality is apparent in *Normal*, his first London transfer (from Edinburgh), which bears the mark of this preoccupation in a number of ways.[17] It tells the story of Justus Wehner, a young defence lawyer tasked to defend Peter Kurten, a notorious serial killer who terrorised the German city of Düsseldorf in 1929, killing nine people before being arrested and later executed. The extent of Neilson's debt to the emotional intensity of German Expressionism is noticeable in the dreamlike quality of the play as well as in its choice of subject matter and distorted mise en scène. Kurten first appears '*at the foot of some twisted steps*', holding a pair of '*ludicrously over-sized scissors*' (p. 3). The shifts in tone and transformations that occur throughout the play quite obviously derive from earlier forms of theatre, and other movements influenced by these forms, most notably the films of Fritz Lang, especially *M* (1931) which also tells the story of a serial killer and is thought to have been based on the Kurten case. As in other classic Expressionist dramas such as Strindberg's *A Dream Play* (1901), the action in *Normal* is seen through the increasingly unsettled mind of the protagonist and consists of memories, experiences and even flights of fantasy. The play contains a number of disturbing sequences in which Kurten recounts in lurid detail both his appalling childhood, and his heinous crimes, and in making the link between the two explicit *Normal* privileges the notion that extreme criminality is a 'product of nurture, not nature'.[18] There is another sense, however, in which *Normal* is not really about Kurten but about the young lawyer and the impact on him of his intimate encounter with a cold-blooded killer.

In a pattern later repeated in *Penetrator* and *The Censor*, *Normal* charts a process of self-examination that proceeds from an inner struggle of conscience. Wehner begins the play as someone who by his own admission knows 'everything of the law, little of life, and less of love' (p. 5). Initially he is naively clear about the nature of the task ahead of him: 'It was a prestigious case, and in those still liberal times it seemed that it might easily be won. After all, I didn't have to prove him innocent, just insane, and he was surely that' (p. 6). The play is structured largely around a series of interviews between Wehner and Kurten. These meetings are ostensibly deigned to allow Wehner to construct a case for the defence, but as Joyce McMillan notes, the young lawyer's relationship with his client quickly becomes 'a kind of education sentimentale, in which he learns about the brutal undercurrents of his own sexuality, and about the brutality that is festering, and gradually coming to the surface in Germany itself'.[19] Wehner's developing self-awareness is a central concern of the play, while Kurten represents the archetypal criminal psychopath, unwilling to conform to agreed legal or moral dictates. Such an archetype presents particular challenges to the liberal mindset, as personified in the young lawyer. Like most liberal Westerners Wehner prefers to think of human actions as either self-directed and rational, or irrational and therefore insane. Ultimately, the question that disturbs Wehner – and by extension the audience – is whether Kurten's acting out of obscene subjective desires can be thought of as rational in any meaningful sense, or indeed meaningful in any rational sense.

In *The Censor* the acting out of a repressed sexual fantasy liberates the play's protagonist, and in so doing causes harm to no one. Obviously, in *Normal*, the acting out of subjective fantasies takes a rather more dangerous form, but it is important to note that Neilson's staging of Kurten's story is disturbing not only because of the killer's horrific crimes, but also because the playwright's attitude to him is marked by a certain ambivalence, not so much about the crimes themselves, but about the sense of personal fulfilment that Kurten is able to achieve by giving full vent to his subjective desires. It takes 'a strange kind of courage', according to Neilson, to follow one's 'own morality'.[20] It is this radically liberated aspect of Kurten that seduces Wehner. Not by accident, the moment of Kurten's self-realisation is of central importance structurally as well as thematically. In a play comprising thirty-one short scenes, the seventeenth, entitled 'Birth', tells of Kurten's return to Düsseldorf:

> And the sky was a bloody red just as it had been for Jack in London in 1888! Oh yes! I had read of him avidly (in prison no less) and I had thought; now there's a man after my own heart! And what with the clouds on fire, it was as if Jack himself was saying 'Peter, you are one of us now, one of the elite' [. . .] I felt like a king! No more denial, no more pretending [. . .] a thousand moments came together. I understood my true nature. The Düsseldorf Ripper is born. (pp. 33–4)

The significance of this moment, and of Kurten's subjective insurgency, is enforced by the fact that from this point Wehner's recollections, whether realistic or fantastic, are increasingly shaped by Kurten. For instance, while scenes nineteen and twenty-three, 'The reign of terror' and 'The reign of terror continues', function to provide explicit details of Kurten's crimes, they also, and more importantly, work to elucidate the inevitable trajectory of Wehner falling 'under the killer's spell'.[21] Neilson achieves this effect substantially through the organisation of speech patterns. Both scenes comprise extended stichomythic exchanges that have a kind of incantatory quality:

Wehner   Saturday August 23rd

Kurten   I went to a fair at the Flehe suburb

Wehner   Louise was fourteen, Gertrude was five

Kurten   I sent the older to buy some fags [. . .]

Wehner   While she was gone he took Gertrude's life [. . .]
When Louise returned he killed her too

Kurten But not before I got my

Kurten/Wehner Change (p. 39)

As the scene closes Wehner and Kurten speak the word 'change' in unison, a clear and explicit indication of Kurten's increasing influence on Wehner's psyche. In a more general sense, however, the use of stichomythia transposes the dialogue in this scene, and in scene twenty-three, into a kind of anti-realist chant whose hypnotic effects act as a prelude to Wehner's conversion. In particular, the spaceless-ness of the dialogue – it allows no room for reflection or response – calls to mind techniques of hypnosis.

The process of conversion does not stop there. In scene twenty-one Wehner succumbs, with Kurten's encouragement, to his baser sexual desires and has sex with Frau Kurten, who it transpires has been acting on her husband's instructions in seducing the lawyer. Subsequently, the stychomythic technique is reprised in scene twenty-three by which point Frau Kurten is also implicated:

Wehner August 29th, he killed Maria Hahn.

Kurten I stuffed her vagina with earth and leaves

Frau Kurten Attempted to crucify her on two nearby trees

Wehner But her body was too heavy

Kurten So I hid her in a shallow grave

Frau Kurten To which he sometimes would return

Kurten To discharge on the soil (p. 45)

As well as providing suitably gruesome detail, again the precise organ-isation of language in this sequence is the means by which Wehner is reoriented, wooed and promised insight into a new kind of freedom by Kurten.

The rhythm and tone of the dialogue in these scenes is in marked contrast to earlier exchanges between Wehner and Kurten, which are more realistic. It is useful to note, in fact, that in the play as a whole

Neilson merges two actions, two different levels of reality, and represents these in varying rhythms and contrasting styles. The outer action is the historical narrative that relates Wehner's failed attempt to save Kurten from execution by proving him insane. The inner action, which comes to the fore in the second half of the play, is concerned with the psychological effect of the encounter with Kurten on Wehner. The process of occupation I have been describing above belongs to the inner action of the play and finds its apotheosis in scene twenty-six, 'The art of murder', in which Kurten directs Wehner as he enacts the brutal fantasy of murdering Frau Kurten. While the murder sequence is clearly a fantasy – Wehner uses a deliberately over-sized hammer – it is uncomfortably long and Neilson is clear in indicating that it should be *'quite relentless'* (p. 52). After being struck by a hammer, Frau Kurten attempts an escape via the audience but is dragged *'kicking and screaming back to the stage'* by Wehner, who strikes her again and then, under direct instruction from Kurten, attempts to strangle her (p. 52). Subsequently Kurten *'directs him to break her legs, which he does'* (p. 52). By this time Wehner is in a state of exhaustion, but nevertheless:

> **Kurten** *sends him back to retrieve the hammer, and in his absence* **Frau Kurten** *comes round again. Wearily,* **Wehner** *walks to her and strikes her again, and again, and again.* **Wehner** *is like an animal beating her head. He screams a terrible triumphant scream.* **Frau Kurten** *dies.* **Wehner** *collapses over her body.*

> **Kurten** *straightens his tie, brushes down his suit as though nothing has happened and ascends the rostra.* (52)

This sequence lasted about six minutes in performance, and, as Sierz points out, it 'had a greater impact than all the others'.[22] A brief glance at the reviews confirms this assessment. Joyce McMillan, for instance, described the murder as 'horrifyingly convincing' and was particularly struck by the realism of Juliet Prew's performance as the victim.[23] For Ian Shuttleworth the murder scene was 'pornographically violent' and served only to undermine what he understood to be the play's central argument: that Kurten's dysfunctional childhood was the direct cause of his depravity.[24]

Shuttleworth's assessment is based on an understanding of *Normal* as a thesis play. It is worth unpacking because in failing to acknowledge the dynamic between the play's inner and outer realities it points to a recurring interpretative problem in relation to Neilson's work. The notion that *Normal* posits a hierarchy of nurture over nature in terms of the causes of criminality is sound enough and was picked up by a number of other reviewers.[25] The weakness in such a reading, however, is that it cannot explain the affective power of the murder scene described above, or indeed the play as a whole. It seems important at the very least to note that Neilson explores the impact of childhood experiences on adult behaviour not in a realist mode, but by means of subjectively distorted action, setting and character. It is choices such as these that compel us to think of the play in terms of discourses of subjectivity and Expressionism. As Sierz notes, the effect of the extended murder sequence was intensified 'because the lawyer moved in a dreamlike way' and because Kurten remained entirely impassive throughout.[26] In fact, the automatic quality in the staging of Wehner's subjectivity in this scene calls to mind Ernst Toller's assertion that Expressionist playwrights removed the individualising aspects of characters in a deliberate effort to get to the inner man: 'By skinning the human being one hoped to find his soul under the skin.'[27]

Neilson's focus on subjective experience, which dominates the second part of *Normal*, and his unwillingness to create hierarchies between the real and the imagined – the most powerful sequence in the play is a fantasy – also calls to mind aspects of psychoanalytic discourse. As Peggy Phelan has noted, one key characteristic of psychoanalysis is the refusal 'to believe that the empirical real is more impressive than the imagined or fantasized'.[28] It is a mistake, I would argue, to give too much weight to the empirical real, to the outer reality, in any reading of Neilson's work. His mode, especially in the latter half of the play, is much closer to Strindbergian dream consciousness than to traditional realism, hence the deliberate distortions of language and performance register. Like a dream, or more specifically a nightmare, many of the conclusions inferred by *Normal* remain contingent and mysterious. This is in no small part because

Neilson, by using a dramaturgy of illusion and suggestion, seems at once to both disapprove and yet also to approve of the notion that the subjective rebel, the individual who privileges inner over outer realities, should be true to his calling, whatever the cost. In his next major play, *Penetrator*, Neilson continues this meditation with similarly disconcerting and unsettling results.

Penetrator

Among Neilson's plays of the 1990s *Penetrator* is most often and most closely associated with the in-yer-face sensibility. There are a number of reasons for this. In the first place it has a contemporary setting, taking place 'in a grubby tenement flat in urban Scotland' during the first Gulf War.[29] Second, *Penetrator*'s language is extremely violent and peppered with expletives. Third, in its staging of violence and pornographic imagery it demonstrates the experiential emphasis Sierz identifies as a signature of in-yer-face theatre. Last, the play's focus on male relationships had the effect of positioning Neilson as a masculinist playwright, a forerunner of new laddism, and thus very much of his time.[30] New laddism, it might be remembered, was characterised by a 'rejection of the values of the feminist friendly new man' and the privileging of more 'rigid, conformist and conservative models of masculinity, including an adherence to misogyny and homophobia', and its effects were felt across culture.[31] Elaine Aston notes its impact on the London theatre scene with some disappointment, arguing that the considerable energies of 1980s feminist theatre dissipated in the 1990s to make way for a generation of disaffected masculinist playwrights. The Royal Court, Aston observes, 'remained heavily engaged with boys' drama throughout the decade', in particular, representing masculinity 'with a harsh and violent edge in the plays of Anthony Neilson'.[32]

In spite of the apparent simplicity of its narrative, *Penetrator* is a complex and sometimes mystifying play that contains a violent sequence of unusual power and intensity. Two young men, Max and Alan, share a flat. A third man, Tadge, who is a boyhood friend of

Max's, visits them unexpectedly. Tadge, who has gone AWOL from the army, cuts a strange and extremely menacing figure especially in relation to Alan whom he clearly does not like. Tension mounts. Eventually, Tadge produces a very large army knife with which he terrorises Alan. Finally, Alan leaves the flat at Max's request. Max and Tadge settle on the sofa and an odd kind of domestic harmony descends. Essentially, then, *Penetrator* consists of a comparison between two male relationships: the one Max has with Alan, and the one he has with Tadge, whose unexpected return is the catalyst for the play's action. In this sense it is straightforward enough. However, its ambiguities are apparent in the range of interpretations that emerged in response to the original production. For Sierz, the play's power to disturb is located in its experiential qualities: it 'stays in the mind', he argues, 'because of its intensity, not because it has a neat message'.[33] For Benedict Nightingale Neilson's message is clearer: 'Never be tempted to sentimentalise sex, for whatever the reason, or combination of reasons, it has the power to churn, twist, warp, brutalise and generally lay low the psyche.'[34] Other critics were less complimentary. For Caroline Donald, *Penetrator* is 'hooked on an annoyingly unresolved and non-cogent plot' that consists in a 'plumbing of the depths of the male sexual ego'.[35]

As with *Normal*, each of these interpretations has some value and is possible because the meaning of the play remains ambiguous. However, only an interpretation that attempts to tie the play's diverse elements together, to reconcile its inner and outer realities, can hope to explain not only the unusual trajectory of its plot but also its peculiar affective power. Sierz's account of the play is quite detailed and thorough in relation both to its experiential emphasis and its narrative, but it is possible to enhance this reading by focusing in more detail than he does on the play's language. Despite the centrality of verbal violence in *Penetrator*, the question of its significance, and the role which language itself plays in this parable of male friendship, has not yet been considered at any length. My aim is to make connections, in this the most Pinteresque of Neilson's plays, between the action of the play and its unusually vivid and sometimes aberrant language, in order to show how its themes, its exploration of subterranean as well as surface realities, are directly contained in the functioning of its language.

Penetrator echoes the central concerns of *Normal*, and *The Censor*, in that it consists of a meditation on, or even a battle for control of, the psyche of its central character. The play centres around Max, a slovenly and embittered twentysomething who shares a flat with his friend Alan. Max is the more assertive and self-assured of the two, but their relationship is one of easy familiarity. They talk about food and laundry, *Starsky and Hutch* and last night's excesses. They play cards and argue about who should make the tea. They sing 'The Trail of the Lonesome Pine', '*à la Laurel and Hardy*' (p. 72). In performance, the familiarity and credibility of the relationship is established primarily through distinctive dialogue, which slips seamlessly between idioms, and creates a private domestic world, sustained by imaginative word-play. As well as standard English they use demotic Scots, 'square goes' for fighting, and normative Scots, 'wain' for child (pp. 75, 69). Max's banter in particular mixes references to childhood games and television programmes with numerous expletives: 'Go *straight* to fuck. Do *not* pass go. Do *not* collect two hundred pounds' and '*Dr Who* was *shite*, for buck-toothed *fucks* in parkas' (pp. 64, 66). In these exchanges between Max and Alan, misplaced references and mis-associations do not simply exploit accidental intersections between alternative contexts of meaning: they are theatrically performed as a series of intentional misunderstandings – displaced meanings that act to create a private language game that binds the characters together in solidarity and friendship.

As well as employing references to popular culture both past and present, Neilson makes full use of a distinctively Scottish register of demotic swearing in the early exchanges between Max and Alan.[36] In scene three, for example, Max complains about his ex-girlfriend Laura, by whom he has been rejected, and who is the target for most of his misogynistic rhetoric: 'She knew *nothing* about sex when I met her. *Nothing*. She was Mary-fucking-Poppins when I met her and Mary-fucking-Millington when she *left* me' (p. 76). Here, the misplaced clause both replicates demotic Scottish speech patterns, and also recalls earlier Scottish drama, in which comic displacement is a key strategy in the production of meaning.[37] The early scenes also owe a debt to the traditions of the double-act, which have remained a potent mode in Scottish popular performance as evidenced, for example, by the success of Ford Kiernan and Greg Hemphill's *Still Game*.[38] So the playful language of the early scenes between Max and Alan establishes their relationship in a realist mode via a series of language games that bind them together in relatively cosy domesticity. However, Max's acute pain, caused by Laura's recent sexual betrayal, is also signalled by his refusal to take anything seriously and this cynicism is expressed primarily through language. His is a crisis of faith and as a consequence belief systems of all kinds become languages without meaningful referents in his world. In relation to the Gulf War, for instance, he quips, 'If they'd just start bombing again we could have some *decent* telly' (p. 67). Traditional languages of value are repeatedly rubbished when transposed into Max's rhetoric. In a hilarious sequence of pornographic puppetry he amuses himself by having Alan's teddy bears simulate copulation:

Max   You're too sentimental. The teddies like to fuck.

Alan   They *don't*.

Max   What do you think they do on their picnics? After the food's gone and they're tanked up on Bucky? They're beasts of the wild.

Alan   They're *not* beasts of the wild. They're part of the family.

Max   Families are built on fucking. Fucking and secrets.
(p. 74)

The sexualising of the teddies, as well as the inference that they drink cheap alcohol at their picnics, is transgressive because teddies are symbols of the innocence of childhood. Max extends this cynicism to the family as a whole: families are not built on love and trust, but on 'fucking and secrets'. His repeated verbal displacements are symptoms of a deeper confusion of signifying contexts, a confusion produced by the disintegration of his belief in the possibility of fidelity between men and women.

Tadge's arrival, which is prefigured in the play's opening scene, signals an attack not only on Alan's person but also on Max's cynicism because Tadge is fiercely and relentlessly intent on recapturing the intimacy of their boyhood. The spectre of Tadge first appears in the opening scene, hitchhiking towards an unsuspecting Max and blissfully ignorant Alan: '*A young man stands at the side of the road, thumb out. An army rucksack at his heel, like a patient dog.* [. . .] *His actions are slow and dreamlike. Over this, a voice, deep and subhuman*' (p. 61). The accompanying voiceover relates a pornographic fantasy, in which a surprisingly accommodating young woman picks up a male hitchhiker. 'She may have been barely old enough to drive', the voice tells us, but 'she had the dirtiest big tits I've ever seen' (p. 61). Before long the girl is begging him to 'fuck' her with his 'big tool' (p. 61). This is the language of mainstream pornography, widely available on the top shelves of newsagents and, as Sierz notes, it is not so much the language itself, as the transgression of conventions about where, when and by whom it should be consumed that causes acute embarrassment.[39] Fear and embarrassment are among the most affective of emotions and Neilson exploits these in *Penetrator* particularly in relation to the figure of Tadge, whose arrival is prefigured in a later sequence in which he is revealed looking up at a window that, in a similarly theatrical transformation, turns out to be the window of Max and Alan's flat. The threat of violence that accompanies Tadge is signalled in the soundscape both by '*a deep ominous bass rumble*' and also by the way the pornographic language of the voiceover in both scenes deteriorates into overt violence: 'I want you to shoot me' and 'We're going to shoot you' (pp. 62, 73). The conflation of a synonym for ejaculation with the discharge of a firearm is deliberate.

With Tadge's arrival an immediate switch in idiom is apparent. Most obviously he utterly eschews the comic banter characteristic of earlier exchanges between Max and Alan:

Max Sit down then. Take the weight off your cock.

Tadge (*pause*) Off ma what? (p. 78)

This exchange is in marked contrast to the one that introduces Max and Alan:

Max   Arsehole

Alan   Fuckface. How's life?

Max   Shite. What's in the bag? (p. 63)

Just as there are two levels of action in *Normal*, so there are two levels of speech in *Penetrator*: conversational or social speech, and private interior speech. Tadge experiences extreme difficulty with social speech. The simplest instruction causes him pain and confusion:

Tadge *gets up. They look at him.*

Tadge   Toilet.

Alan (*indicating*)   First on the left.

Tadge *hovers there, not moving.*

Tadge (*to* **Alan**)   Can you show me? (p. 80)

While the misunderstandings, disjunctions and displacements that pepper Max and Alan's exchanges are largely deliberate, Tadge's conversational, or outer, speech is marked by humourlessness and miscommunication. There is a noticeable discrepancy, however, between his stilted public language and the vivid language he uses to describe his disturbed inner reality. It seems important in this context to note that *Penetrator*, although it generates extraordinary tension in the expectation of violence, and involves an extended sequence in which Tadge menaces Alan with a knife, contains very little actual violence. One of Neilson's achievements in the play is to make the dismemberment of Alan's teddy by Tadge appear truly shocking. The play's most disturbing imagery is carried by Tadge's language. He recalls a bunkmate masturbating into a thermos flask filled with raw liver until his 'cock' dripped 'pus', for instance, and watching videos of girls 'sucking off pigs' (pp. 82, 116). But the central image of the play, the one that gives it its title, is drawn from Tadge's paranoid fantasy about being anally raped and subsequently pursued by a clandestine military organisation of Penetrators:

You don't know what it was like. In the dark. All shrivelled up.
Just my hatred keeping me alive. Their hands all over me. And
you never came for me. Their dirty cocks in my mouth, up my
arse. I know how to kill a man. I'm not afraid. I've seen guys
get their ears cut off. I've seen lassies with their cunts shot out.
(p. 109)

This speech occurs towards the end of the play and is the last in a
number Tadge makes about his ordeal. His hostility towards Alan is
fuelled, or at least appears to be fuelled, by the conviction that Alan is
a member of this hated organisation. The speech above is also notable
for the plaintive accusation, 'you never came for me', that punctuates
the otherwise relentlessly violent imagery. As Dan Rebellato has noted
in relation to the 'proliferation of images involving bodily mutilation
and dismemberment' in 1990s drama, 'the ghost of a better world, a
better way of being with others' often accompanies such images.[40] In
Tadge's case the better world is the world of childhood intimacy he
shared with Max and he is prepared to go to extreme lengths to recap-
ture it. At the play's climax he terrorises Alan at knifepoint in order
extract a confession from Max about a proto-sexual homoerotic
moment they shared as boys in the woods. Only after Max confirms
that he remembers 'the smell' of Tadge, does the latter release Alan.

The dynamic between subterranean and surface realities that
animates *Penetrator* is directly contained, then, in the functioning of
its language. Following Tadge's arrival, Max tries initially to placate
Alan, who is uncomfortable with Tadge's presence, but ultimately the
play charts Max's transition away from Alan towards Tadge. Max's
playful linguistic strategies in the early part of the play represent an
attempt to ward off pain and thus avoid reality, while Tadge's rhetoric
returns repeatedly and mercilessly to images of suffering and mutilation, but also, and importantly, to genuine intimacy. On a surface
level Max's final rejection of Alan hinges on a rather mechanical plot
twist – the discovery that Alan has had sex with Laura; however, on a
deeper level the shift represents a rejection of surface realities and the
sophisticated linguistic strategies that support them in favour of a
much deeper, if altogether cruder, reality personified in the figure of

Tadge. It is noticeable that as the play draws to a close language begins to break down completely. After Alan's departure, Tadge begins a speech about the video nasties he watched while stationed in Germany but quickly becomes confused, '. . . no, he had a cock up his arse and *that* guy, he had a *cock* up *his*' (p. 116). Soon, Tadge's '*voice fades until all we can hear is a steam of murmur, punctuated by obscenities* [. . .] cunts, cocks, cock, cock, cunt' (p. 116). Max's response to this final outpouring is to tell Tadge to shut up, which he does. After a long pause, the play ends with the two humming to themselves and sharing a packet of Rolos on the sofa, '*lost in their own worlds*' (p. 116). This image of domestic harmony, in combination with Tadge's final line, 'I used to like coming to your house', signals the completion of the reversal that structures the play (p. 117). Neilson's privileging of interior realities, here as elsewhere, makes Tadge's victory inevitable. Madness is after all the ultimate triumph of subjective over external reality. The importance of acknowledging, coming to terms with and celebrating inner realities continued to be a focus in Neilson's work as the decade progressed.

The Censor

Neilson's next major play, *The Censor*, was to become his most critically acclaimed of the 1990s. Structured around a series of encounters between a young female pornographic filmmaker, Miss Fontaine, and the low-level official who holds the licensing scissors, it won the Writers Guild Award for Best Fringe Play of 1997 and the *Time Out* Live Award. Like its predecessors, *The Censor* is an ambiguous work that has been interpreted with different emphasis both by critics and in performance. Broadly, readings fall into two camps, although there is typically an overlap. First, the play has been interpreted as a treatise on censorship and its role in society, particularly in relation to pornography. Second – and this is the reading Neilson himself privileges – it has been read as a love story. According to Alastair Galbraith, in rehearsal the playwright 'consistently talked about it being a love story' and focused on little else.[41] This interpretation continues to have efficacy and is picked up in the publicity for a recent production in Chicago, directed by Mike Rice at Ebb and Flow Theatre (2010). The play is advertised as a 'gripping encounter between a movie rating board official and a pornographic film maker, which spins into a moving yet tragic love story'.[42] Chris Durnall's 2009 production for Faction Collective in Cardiff, by contrast, was staged in direct response to the cancellation of a controversial book launch in the city, and was thus explicitly implicated in a wider debate around censorship.[43] According to Durnall, *The Censor*, as well as being a love story, is an example of 'provocative, socially exciting drama'.[44] Durnall's decision to screen extracts from a pornographic film at pertinent moments throughout his production gave particular weight to the intellectual and philosophical arguments about pornography contained in the play, thus emphasising its political dimension.

The relative success of both revivals evidences the tension between the personal and the political that usually animates Neilson's work. However, I want to suggest that *The Censor* is not fundamentally concerned with changes in the social structure, with challenging censorship legislation or attitudes to pornography, nor is it a love story. The arguments Miss Fontaine offers the Censor when advocating absolute freedom of expression do not stand up to robust analysis, and in any case her character is so partially drawn as to deliberately allow for the possibility that she could be 'a figment of his imagination'.[45] Instead, the play is best understood as a narrative of repression and liberation. Its subject is the complete transformation in the psychological condition of one man. The most revealing way of looking at Neilson's work is to see it as a sustained examination of subjectivity, and of the various implications of selfhood in a contemporary context. What does it mean, his plays ask, to realise oneself in the world? Which version of the self should take precedence? In *The Censor* he addresses these questions more explicitly than in any of his other 1990s plays. The Censor's internal struggle is staged as a battle between two aspects of the same man and these two aspects are so deeply in conflict that victory for one inevitably means defeat for the other. It is, I would argue, the absolute seriousness of this subject matter that gives the play not only its unusual intensity and power, but also the quality of a parable. Behind Neilson's demand for a new beginning for his protagonist, we sense the desire to fashion a new world in which personal liberation becomes the ultimate value.

This symbolic dimension of the play is realised in a number of ways. The fact that neither the Censor nor his wife has a name, at least until the final scene, is, for instance, a contributing factor. Also, in Julian McGowan's design for the original production, the Censor's office was clearly set deep in the bowels of a large, faceless government building, and this worked to inform the protagonist's character. Large industrial fans hummed overhead; there were no windows and hence no natural light. McGowan's design had the effect of concretising the Censor's difficulty – he is buried, trapped in 'some dark limbo of his imagination' – but also gave the proceedings an abstract quality.[46] As Galbraith observes, 'There isn't a very strong sense of time or place. It could be anywhere.'[47] A naturalist setting typically proposes that in one way or another the environment determines character, but in this case the setting is more expressionistic in that the Censor's office 'ceases to be a physical representation of the world and becomes a projection' of his 'inner self'.[48] The play's most significant events take place in this isolated space. References to the outside world, to current events, popular culture or even the weather are almost completely absent.

Neilson objectifies the Censor's internal conflict by providing him with two antagonists, his wife and the pornographer Miss Fontaine, both of whom are only partially realised as characters. The wife is only ever staged in conversation with the Censor in their kitchen. According to Neilson these importance of these scenes is often ignored:

> The fundamental thing that happens when *The Censor* is revived is that people skip over the silences. The scenes between him and his wife, in particular, are long. They're a lot longer than they read. The silences should be so big you could drive a massive bus through them. Those scenes are important. In a lot of productions, I've seen them used rather functionally as a

kind of cut-away, cut-back device. But in the original production those scenes had almost as much weight as the others.[49]

These extended silences underline the breakdown in communication
that characterises the Censor's marriage. He and his wife have reached
an impasse, a situation that is emphasised through a series of revisions
and extensions, in which it becomes clear that their domestic
exchanges are fragments of the same scene, replayed, extended and
revised. We discover that the wife has been out late the night before:
that she has slept in the spare room, that she has a lover, that her lover
wants to meet the Censor, that the Censor is ambivalent about such a
meeting and that his ambivalence infuriates his wife. While the scenes
between the Censor and Miss Fontaine are played out in chronolog-
ical order, it is significant that the Censor's domestic reality is
produced through a process of forgetting and remembering. The
Censor is unable to be his authentic self at home, trapped as he is in a
sexless and loveless marriage with an adulterous wife. This absence of
authenticity is communicated at the level of structure. Partly because
it is being constantly revised, his home life seems less real, and as a
consequence the precise version of it that emerges is opaque in
comparison with the intensity of the scenes between the Censor and
Miss Fontaine which form the core of the central liberation narrative.
As in *Normal*, Neilson utilises voiceover for exposition:

> It started with a pornographic film [. . .] The film was hard-core
> and unpassable as it stood but she requested a meeting with me
> to challenge the ruling. I could've refused. To this day I still
> don't know if things would've turned out better if I had. But I
> didn't, and she came to try to change my mind, the only way
> she knew how. (p. 245)

This is a kind of memory play, then, its narrative unfolding in the
past, and its opening section privileging the discourse of its central
character, whose story it tells. The play is structured around a series of
meetings between the Censor and Miss Fontaine during which she
attempts to persuade him that her film has artistic and social value,

and that he should support its distribution. She repeatedly asks him to look beneath the surface of the images. Their encounters involve some detailed discussion of the explicit content of the film, which we never see (at least not in Neilson's own production), but from the outset Miss Fontaine's tactics also include sexual provocation. In the first scene between them she removes her shirt and threatens to unclip her bra, and in the second she attempts to masturbate the Censor, 'to no avail' (p. 253). It quickly becomes clear that the Censor's impotence, which is revealed in this scene, is caused by a repressed sexual fantasy. It is the expected revelation of this fantasy which generates suspense, direction and intention in the plot. From this point on there is a growing sense that he will have to deal at some point with this repressed desire and that Miss Fontaine will be the catalyst for this release. The narrative thus builds towards the play's most infamous moment:

> **Miss Fontaine** *lays newspaper down on the floor. The* **Censor** *watches.* **Fontaine** *encourages him to touch himself. She raises her skirt and squats. The* **Censor** *watches, touching himself more vigorously. It takes her a while but eventually she defecates. She cleans herself then moves away. The* **Censor** *is in a state of extreme arousal. She beckons him to come forward and make love to her. He does.* (pp. 276–7)

For some critics this sequence is mere gratuitous affect.[50] Affect, it should be remembered, is the term critics use to describe a kind of basic physiological emotional response that bypasses the intellect, is 'immediate, uncontrollable', involuntary and 'skin-level', and thus literally sensational.[51] The most affective of emotions – embarrassment, fear and disgust – are experienced as involuntary and the use of such provocations became synonymous with Neilson's early work and with the shock tactics of in-yer-face theatre in general. Interestingly, Galbraith does not recall disgust being a primary response to the scene:

> The big moment ten minutes before the end would normally get quite a riveted silence, or the odd nervous giggle, but it

never got a yuck or any kind of expression of disgust. Audiences found themselves neither embarrassed nor disgusted – they seemed to feel it was all right although I don't think they were expecting it.[52]

The Censor is a man for whom the repression of authentic desire has become physically and emotionally disabling, but he is also, and importantly, a good man. The unveiling of his fantasy is a moment of crucial importance to the dramatic effectiveness of the play because so much suspense has been generated around it and because it needs to effect the physical transformation that signals his liberation. The hidden desire therefore needs to be surprising and unexpected, shameful even, but also essentially harmless. Thought of in these terms the climactic scene is perfectly judged and neither shocking nor gratuitous. As Dominic Dromgoole has observed, Neilson's vision is essentially one of 'a better world' and the playwright often seems 'almost reluctant to describe the acts he does'.[53] In *The Censor* the importance of the central revelation, and the recovery it initiates, is further evidenced by its being positioned late in the drama. Shortly after the big event Miss Fontaine departs for New York, and in scene thirteen – which is the longest of the domestic scenes and consists in an amalgamation and extension of all previous exchanges – the Censor seems on the point of divulging something genuinely important to his wife when she reads a newspaper report of Miss Fontaine's murder in a New York hotel room. This shocking revelation precipitates a breakdown in the Censor, which his wife welcomes, mistakenly believing it to be evidence of emotional engagement in their marriage. It is this plot twist that led to the play being labelled a 'tragic love story'.[54]

As I have been arguing throughout this chapter, Neilson is always preoccupied with the expression of personal rebellion, with the privileging of inner over outer realities. This element, however muted or disguised, is never completely absent from his work and other themes, while certainly present, are generally subservient to it. The resolution of *The Censor* provides a good example. The romance between the Censor and Miss Fontaine has little efficacy in terms of this theme after she has performed her function in bringing the Censor's repressed desire into the open. In the play's final scene, the Censor is alone. He *'sits in his office, watching the film. And, after a while, he smiles'* (p. 285). This closing image suggests that the Censor's rehabilitation has not been derailed by the murder of his lover. He has come to a greater understanding, not of the film but of himself, and this knowledge is authorised, not by any external order but, by 'the certainty that clear and distinct perception is unconditional and self-generated'.[55] This focus on the liberation of the individual partly explains the play's success with the right-wing press who, as Ruth Little and Emily McLaughlin have noted, 'might have been predicted to vilify it'.[56] In addition, failure to appreciate the importance of Neilson's central theme led to the ending of the play being misread as 'a little limp' just as *Penetrator* was judged 'annoyingly unresolved'.[57]

Conclusion

A significant number of plays written in the aftermath of Thatcherism focused on questions of individualism and individuality because, at least partly, Thatcher's policies and rhetoric – her most quoted remark was 'There is no such thing as society' – polarised views on these subjects.[58] In *Shopping and Fucking* (1996) and *Some Explicit Polaroids* (1999), for instance, Mark Ravenhill emphasises the debasement of human beings by the rampant consumerism of late capitalism, while Sarah Kane explores the political landscape of Europe in the 1990s through 'boldly experimental theatrics, neo-mythical form, and unrelenting focus on physical and psychic pain'.[59] The question of Neilson's relation to his historical moment, to the zeitgeist, which it should be remembered is a key characteristic of Sierz's definition of in-yer-face theatre, is rather more complex. This is largely because his subject matter seems more focused on the personal than the political, and more concerned with subjective than objective realities. In the event a presumed lack of expressly political engagement has led to Neilson's work being condemned or dismissed by some critics. For Vera Gottlieb, for example, he was one of a 'younger generation, who seem virtually to have abandoned perspectives on the past'.[60] My writing in this chapter is obviously intended to challenge this position.

In a recent chapter on Scottish political drama of the 1990s, David Pattie, while making no mention of Neilson, identifies a preoccupation with identity and its representations as a signature of contemporary Scottish drama.[61] As Adrienne Scullion has argued elsewhere, the 'dynamics of identity and representation' were to become 'key themes across the whole of Scottish culture' in the years immediately before and after devolution in 1999.[62] Of Neilson's three major 1990s plays, two were created and originally produced in Scotland, and all three are without exception deeply, even obsessively, preoccupied with identity and its representations. In this sense, Neilson's Scottishness can be considered a significant factor in shaping his theatrical output. According to the playwright, he learned in childhood 'to think of the personal, political, emotional and theatrical as intricately entwined', substantially through the experience of watching his parents rehearse Donald Campbell's two powerful plays, *The Jesuit* and *The Widows of Clyth*.[63] It is certainly the case that the palpable quality of lived experience, whether highly pleasurable or intensely painful, is determinedly and consistently placed at the centre of his work.

In each of these three plays Neilson engages creatively and boldly with a problem that has preoccupied dramatists for centuries, that is, how to express or represent interiority on stage, how to allow the audience to get inside the heads of the characters. The fact that he employs sensationalist tactics in the exploration of this problem suggests that for Neilson, and perhaps for his generation of playwrights, understanding what is meant by interiority, and staging it effectively, is not straightforward. He returns to this problem again and again, not only in his plays of the 1990s but also in his more recent work – especially *The Wonderful World of Dissocia*, *Realism* and *Relocated* – and most recently in his children's show *Get Santa!* (2010) in which a teddy bear is afforded an amusingly vocal subjectivity by a misplaced magic spell. Having received the ultimate prize, the bear, in a plot line reminiscent of *Blade Runner*, goes to extreme and quite sinister lengths to preserve it. Here, as elsewhere, Neilson privileges an identity politics that transcends narrow or fixed definitions, or at least insists that lived experience must and should take precedence over externally imposed constructions of identity. So, in each of his plays, and in a variety of ways, Neilson privileges subjective experience, assigning particular value to authenticity and honesty as pathways to self-knowledge and self-realisation. The claustrophobic and obsessional qualities in *Normal*, *Penetrator* and *The Censor* draw much of their subversive power from their privileging of subjectivity over rationality. They hint at the necessity of a full-scale subjective insurgency, and in this sense they can be understood as genuinely antisocial. Their exact meanings, however, remain contingent. Carefully constructed ambiguities in combination with subtle shifts in point of view, and an irritating sense of always being on the verge of some kind of interpretative synthesis without ever actually achieving it, give these plays their lasting appeal.

MARK RAVENHILL
By Graham Saunders

> **Gary** I'm not after love. I want to be owned. I want someone to look after me. And I want him to fuck me. Really fuck me. Not like that, not like him. And, yeah, it'll hurt. But a good hurt.
>
> – Mark Ravenhill, *Shopping and Fucking*, 1996

Introduction

If the work of any dramatist exemplifies the much-overused term zeitgeist it would be the 1990s plays of Mark Ravenhill. While his contemporary Sarah Kane has been widely lauded as the most significant playwright of that decade, it was Ravenhill who best caught its mood. But that does not mean that he is merely a 1990s playwright. When interviewed in 1997, director Stephen Daldry correctly predicted that Ravenhill would be a 'long-distance runner among new writers'.[1] Since then he has moved on from being a youthful *agent provocateur* to becoming an established figure in British theatre, an associate of the National Theatre and a mentor to younger play-wrights. The other distinguishing feature of Ravenhill's early work has been the number of different responses it has attracted from critics in terms of claiming both the writer and the work as representative of a particular ideological position or theatrical style. Allied to this has been the polarisation of attitudes towards Ravenhill's work: for some, he inherits the mantle of Brecht, developing political playwriting in new directions in response to the breakdown of clear ideological posi-tions after the fall of the Berlin Wall; to others, his work is symptomatic of the vacuum left in the wake of the end of the Cold War.

The first and perhaps still most influential response to Ravenhill's work has been that of Aleks Sierz, whose study of the new playwriting culture of the 1990s, *In-Yer-Face Theatre*, continues to some extent to define – and some might say misrepresent – the playwright's oeuvre. Sierz saw him as an arch provocateur, who articulated the mood of the late 1990s with a mixture of criticism and celebration.[2] But while there is much in Sierz's assessment that still holds true, his interpreta-tion does downplay one central part of the playwright's work – his treatment of gay sexuality. And it is this that has made the most lasting impact. In the short period of time between *Shopping and Fucking* (1996) and *Some Explicit Polaroids* (1999), Ravenhill has quietly brought about a transition from what had formerly been understood as gay drama to one which can more properly be termed queer theatre. In fact, it now seems clear that *Shopping and Fucking* and *Some Explicit Polaroids*, together with *Mother Clap's Molly House* (2000), constitute a loose, yet none the less cohesive trilogy of plays on the subject of AIDS.

In 2001, the same year as Sierz's book was published, Dan Rebellato's 'Introduction' to Ravenhill's first collection of plays provided an important alternative assessment: here the voguish writer with a scandalous reputation was interpreted as a serious dramatist, one who wrote about the issue of globalisation and its perfidious effects on culture and social behaviour.[3] Allied to this, Rebellato also cites Ravenhill as the key example of a new style and sensibility in playwriting that marked the end of a particular era: namely, the state-of-the-nation model that had dominated the stages of major British subsidised theatres since the 1970s and 1980s. In its place, in 1990s theatre, a focus on the contemporary superseded the epic sweep of history; characters discoursed tersely about ready meals and their addictions to drugs and sexual encounters rather than giving fifteen-minute set speeches on the state of the nation or the progress of socialism. In short, plays became postmodern and fractured, and their half-glimpsed truths replaced the dramatic thesis that under-pinned the typical state-of-the-nation play, where the workings of history and opposing political ideologies were clearly defined and set against each other, often in the form of dialectical argument. By contrast, Ravenhill attempted to find ways of dramatising less defin-able but none the less powerful forces, such as the rapid movement of global capital, or the collapse of what the philosopher Jean François Lyotard has called 'the grand narratives' of political and religious belief systems – changes that collectively were shaping even the tiniest and most mundane aspects of everyday life.[4]

Ravenhill's importance, like that of the 1968 generation of drama-tists who came before him, was that he rose to the challenge of creating a new type of political theatre whose project was to make sense of the rapid changes taking place within the systems of economics, politics and technology during the 1990s. Considered in this light, the generational divide between Ravenhill and dramatists such as David Hare, Howard Benton and David Edgar begins to narrow. A case in point is Edgar, whose career since 1970 has been memorably described by Michael Billington as resembling that of a latter-day Balzac, fulfilling the role of a secretary for his times: in *Destiny* (1976) he charted the rise of the British far right; in *The Shape of the Table* (1990), the collapse of Eastern European communism, and in *Playing with Fire* (2005), the Bradford race riots.[5] Yet Ravenhill can also lay claim to fulfilling these very same secretarial functions, although with one crucial difference: rather than simply reporting events such as the collapse of socialism as a belief system, plays such as *Shopping and Fucking* and *Some Explicit Polaroids* not only set out to dramatise its replacement by the ethics of consumer capitalism, but demonstrate its effects by using Brechtian-inspired *gestus*. As the 1990s gave way to the new millennium, plays such as *Mother Clap's Molly House*, with their historical settings, linear narratives and more clearly defined political subjects, have even begun to display remnants of exactly those features that Dan Rebellato claimed Ravenhill's drama replaced, namely the state-of-the-nation play.

Sometimes these references to past forms are made explicit. In *Shopping and Fucking* one of the most frequently cited moments is the speech that Robbie makes about the erosion of 'big stories' such as 'The Journey to Enlightenment' and 'The March to Socialism' (p. 66). In political plays of the 1970s and 1980s, such speeches were a familiar and expected feature, but in the world of *Shopping and Fucking*, when placed among the ephemera of Ecstasy tablets and ready meals, Robbie's speech appears to come from nowhere. Moreover, there are several other comparable speeches in the play, such as Brian's discourse on the loss of an earthly paradise (p. 46), or Robbie's Ecstasy-induced meditation on observing the world from above, seeing 'this kid in Rwanda crying' and 'this granny in Kiev selling everything she's ever owned' (p. 39). In *The Full Room*, Dominic Dromgoole detects the shaping hand of fellow director Max Stafford-Clark – whose reputation comes from working with socially committed writers – in Ravenhill's finished work.[6] Yet a closer look at the occurrence of these declamatory speeches shows that they have not just emerged arbitrarily, or because of a directorial whim. For instance, Robbie's speech about stories comes out of Gary's own self-constructed fantasy narrative of wanting to find a lover who is also a stern father (pp. 65–6); in addition, Brian's lament comes after hearing his son play the violin, and Mark's speech about a world in crisis seems prompted by Lulu's outburst, 'Why is everything such a mess?' (p. 65). Taken together, all of these speeches are a direct response to Lulu's question, and stand as attempts by the characters to create meaning for themselves in a society that appears to be brutal and alienating.

One of the principal functions of the state-of-the-nation play was to analyse the workings of history. In his recent cycle of short plays

about the occupation of Iraq and the War on Terror, collectively entitled *Shoot/Get Treasure/Repeat* (2008), Ravenhill names one of the
pieces *Paradise Lost*. Like the 1970s political dramatists before him,
who tried to understand through their drama why revolutionary
socialism had failed to materialise, lost pasts are a recurring obsession
in Ravenhill's work. When invited to give the Shakespeare Lecture at
the Cheltenham Festival of Literature in 2004, Ravenhill chose as his
title 'Paradise Forgotten' and spoke about Edenic visions in
Shakespeare's *As You Like It* and *A Winter's Tale*, and throughout his
1990s plays Ravenhill's characters also desperately search for these
same briefly glimpsed visions of Eden: Brian in *Shopping and Fucking*
mourns its fleeting memory, summoned by a piece of music or a poem
(p. 46); and all of the other characters collectively mourn a barely
remembered world based on moral certainties. Similarly, Nick in
Some Explicit Polaroids tries to regain it through the spirit of political
idealism remembered from the 1970s. Concerns for a lost
pre-lapsarian past still cling to the hedonistic and brutal worlds that
Ravenhill depicts, and provide an alternative perspective on a writer
who has frequently been seen as a detached and ironic observer of
events.

Yet, this view of him as a morally and politically motivated dramatist is one that continues to be fiercely contested. For instance, in
Suspect Cultures, Clare Wallace argues that the main reasons why
advocates such as Sierz and Rebellato were so keen to see Ravenhill as
a morally committed playwright firmly rooted in the traditions of the
left was in order to stave off earlier criticisms from theatre scholars
such as Vera Gottlieb, who saw Ravenhill and his contemporaries as
essentially apolitical.[7] Others have also accused the plays of being
ironic and detached, prurient exercises in cultural tourism or revelling
in the very consumerist culture they purport to critique.[8] In the same
vein, playwright Christopher Shinn claims that he was driven to write
his Royal Court debut, *Other People* (2000), in response to *Shopping
and Fucking*, which he saw as a cynical exercise in offering its characters' emotional pain for the edification of audiences who could
subsequently enjoy their guilt after it had been sublimated, 'sexual-
ized, [and] aestheticized into something cool'.[9] This polarisation of

attitudes provides difficulties when attempting to come to an understanding of Ravenhill's work. It is time to offer some new perspectives.

Shopping and Fucking

Alongside Kane's *Blasted* (1995) and Patrick Marber's *Closer* (1997), *Shopping and Fucking* ranks as one of the most significant new plays of the 1990s, having enjoyed two successful runs in the West End, a national and international tour and numerous productions around the world. Set in a shared flat, and various other urban locations, the play's thirteen scenes show the attempts of four young people – Robbie, Mark, Lulu and Gary – to survive, whether in poorly paid jobs, or by selling sex. In the process, they come under the influence of Brian, a powerful yet sentimental criminal boss. Although one strand of the play shows Mark's attempts to kick his addiction to drugs, another tells the grim story of Gary, a young teenager working as a rent boy, who associates sex intimately with violence. Perhaps the most concise yet accurate description of what the play is actually about is Rebellato's observation that it shows us what happened when Britain 'turned from a nation of shopkeepers into a nation of shoppers'.[10] Yet, since its first production in 1996, the intervening years have brought many different interpretations. Rebellato's view that it is chiefly about the effects of globalisation makes it a far more directly political play, and one which challenges Sierz's experiential interpretation – namely that it set out to deliberately shock and discomfort audiences for its own sake. While this holds true at certain moments – such as the penultimate scene where Gary is sodomised in turn by Mark and Robbie, with Lulu as a goading onlooker (pp. 81–5) – there is another significant incident in the play's history that not only challenges Sierz's reading, but exposes a surprising degree of coyness from a playwright who supposedly set out to break taboos.

While Sierz has convincingly argued that much of the play's initial notoriety arose from its title as much as its content, its original name, *Fucking Diana*, would arguably have been even more controversial.[11]

In the published text that accompanied the first production strong traces of the original title can be found in an incident where Mark recounts a supposed encounter with Princess Diana in a nightclub toilet: 'I'm fucking Diana, it's pumpity-pump against the cistern', before they are joined in the cubicle by Sarah Ferguson (the Duchess of York), who enthusiastically fellates him ('Oh yah. Chock's away').[12] Both women are dressed as police officers, and while Mark's story is fanciful, the incident itself is loosely based on a widely reported 1986 tabloid newspaper story that on the eve of Prince Andrew's wedding in July of the same year, the two women dressed as police officers in an attempt to gatecrash his stag-night celebrations. Ravenhill's scurrilous and highly amusing retelling of the incident did much to establish *Shopping and Fucking* as a play that set out to be daring and provocative.

However, the death of the Princess of Wales on 31 August 1997 marks the point when the play's claim to be the epitome of in-yer-face theatre looks far less convincing. The reason for this is that, with the play still touring in the UK, Ravenhill hastily rewrote the scene, excising Mark's account of having sex with Diana, but retaining the incident with Sarah Ferguson. Dominic Shellard's *British Theatre Since the War* gives an interesting account of seeing the touring production of *Shopping and Fucking* in Leeds two days after Diana's death. During this time a mood of mawkish hysteria was sweeping the nation, and in his account of the audience's mounting panic as the scene unfolded (prompted by their familiarity with the tabloid story of the two royals disguising themselves as policewomen), Shellard suspected that, given the play's scandalous reputation, the scene with Diana would be left intact, but feared 'a verbal or literal invasion of the stage'.[13] However, while the rewritten scene continues with Mark's story: 'door opens and there's another woman. Another policewoman . . . with blonde hair', Robbie abruptly silences Mark before he can go any further: 'SHUT UP. SHUT THE FUCK UP' (p. 77). In Robbie's hysterical interruption a definitive boundary line in the detached aesthetic of Cool Britannia had been reached. The incident not only marked a crucial moment for Ravenhill's place within the narrative of 1990s in-yer-face theatre, but for in-yer-face theatre itself.

The decision to rewrite the scene can be interpreted in one of two ways. As theatre's poster boy for outrage, Ravenhill's decision could be seen as one of craven cowardice, betraying the very sensibility that *Shopping and Fucking* appeared to celebrate, giving ammunition to those detractors who saw the play as little more than a cynical attempt to *épater le bourgeois* with its timid excursions into the world of rent boys, and rimming. The other interpretation one can give to the rewrite and its subsequent retention in published editions of the play is that by keeping the Diana story after her death Ravenhill knew that it would fatally mire the play for ever with associations of prurience, and compromise what Rebellato has called its 'profoundly moral' centre.[14] Yet Ravenhill's motives for writing the play have always raised suspicions, and even its director believed that the title, while generating immediate publicity, obscured the play's true intentions.[15] In fact, it could be argued that the accusations levelled at the play's amorality and self-conscious modernity were exacerbated in the first production by Stafford-Clark himself through decisions taken about its design and lighting. These included the memorable neon signs that formed words to suggest specific locations, themes or moods, such as 'Bedsit', 'Money', 'Fuck', 'Sweet' or 'E', and the loud club music that played between scenes. These decisions were taken quite deliberately at the time, with designer Julian McGowan describing the overall intention as being 'quite hip; hip, grungy, neo-commercial and brash'.[16] Yet this stage style has also risked for ever associating *Shopping and Fucking* with the 1990s. Johanna Town, who designed lighting for the original production, in 2007 spoke about still receiving requests to explain how the neon light effects were achieved, the assumption behind the enquiries being, 'Well that's how the play has to be done.'[17] Such responses not only risk making the play into a museum piece, but also add fuel to its detractors, who criticise *Shopping and Fucking* for being little more than an exercise in style over substance.

The dichotomy in critical response that the play has attracted has been one of its principal features. Playwright Rebecca Prichard believes that the very different critical responses come from a Janus-faced quality in Ravenhill's writing, where 'sometimes he winks ironically [while] at other times he surprises [. . .] with raw feeling and shock'.[18] Rebellato's summary of the contradictory responses to the play shows that if anything, the multiplicity of reactions is even more various and complicated:

> Some critics found the explicitness of the play part of its virtue; others thought it a distraction. Some found the play's structure solid and traditional; others found it trendily fragmented. Some saw an urgent and important moral message in the play; others described it as morally slight; still others thought it heavy-handed in the delivery of its message.[19]

Yet these diverse and contradictory qualities are the very ones that illustrate the essential fabric of the play. These same incongruities can also be discerned in its simultaneous displays of both conservative and experimental impulses. Subsequently, this can allow Prichard to note both 'its traditional three act structure' and 'ironically "domestic" setting', while David Edgar can also wryly note that 'forty years after drama was dragged kicking and screaming from the drawing room into the kitchen', Ravenhill and his contemporaries appeared to be 'dragging it right on back again'.[20] This has been used against the play-wright by critics who see his self-conscious displays of postmodernism as masking an inherent conservatism – playwright Edward Bond, for instance, sees the Royal Court's embrace of in-yer face writers as no more than a bid to 'supply the market with Terence Rattigan spiked with bad language and imitated sex'.[21] Yet despite Ravenhill's own admission that *Shopping and Fucking* shares a number of qualities found in traditional forms of playwriting, it also demonstrates some radical departures: these include the 'rape' of Gary in scene thirteen where formal narrative is abandoned and the experiential dominates over the analytical.[22]

However, it is one particular aspect of *Shopping and Fucking* – and one that went largely unnoticed at the time – that has been its most innovative quality: namely, the transition it made from what had been generically termed gay to queer drama. Looking back, it is remarkable that in a play involving two bisexual men and a fourteen-year-old rent boy this aspect of the work had passed almost unnoticed by critics. In some respects, this came about because of the furore over Kane's *Blasted* that had preceded it, which meant that *Shopping and Fucking* became identified as the next representative example of a play that captured the bravado and energy of Cool Britannia. Consequently, Ravenhill became closely associated with a group of writers with almost exclusively heterosexual concerns, exemplified in plays such as Nick Grosso's *Peaches* (1996) and Marber's *Closer*. The only plays in Sierz's study which at times directly address gay sexuality were Phyllis Nagy's *Weldon Rising* (1992) and *Butterfly Kiss* (1994), Philip Ridley's *The Pitchfork Disney* (1991) and *The Fastest Clock in the Universe* (1992), and Sarah Kane's *Cleansed* (1998). Yet, its assessment in such terms meant that it became difficult to appreciate how queer *Shopping and Fucking* really was.

While Sierz's *In-Yer-Face Theatre* briefly questions the extent to which Ravenhill could be seen as a gay writer, its main intention was to associate him with the group of playwrights identified as reflecting the prevailing mood of the times.[23] Therefore, even while he might have winced at being labelled an in-yer-face playwright, Ravenhill had nevertheless successfully managed to escape the arguably more restrictive label of being a gay playwright. Perhaps most importantly of all *Shopping and Fucking* simply does not feel like a gay play. But it does have a queer sensibility. Although the term queer is a complex and contested term, with its uses ranging from the political activism that came out of the gay community during the AIDS crisis of the 1980s to the coded representations of homosexuality in Anglo-American film and theatre before the relaxation of censorship in the late 1960s, Ravenhill's 1990s work can be understood as displaying the following: a polyvalent view of sexuality where characters such as Mark and Robbie in *Shopping and Fucking* move unconsciously and without censure between heterosexual and homosexual modes, and a willingness for gay lifestyles and politics to be held up for scrutiny and criticism. Ravenhill's early work also rejected the portrayal of gay men as doomed victims that had characterised earlier British plays such as Julian Mitchell's *Another Country* (1981) or Hugh Whitemore's *Breaking the Code* (1986), a time when, in Nicholas de Jongh's words,

'The homosexual as he emerged in theatrical form was therefore pathetic, introjecting society's view of him and succumbing to guilt and self-pity.'[24] By contrast, homosexuality in *Shopping and Fucking* is predatory, promiscuous and dangerous. His theatrical predecessors can be found in Joe Orton's *Entertaining Mr Sloane* (1964). Like Orton's, Ravenhill's gay figures are highly problematic but also highly exhilarating stage figures.

Yet Ravenhill is also often critical of them. At one point in *Shopping and Fucking*, Lulu turns on Robbie after discovering that he has given away three hundred of Brian's Ecstasy pills, partly because he had been attracted to his male customers at the nightclub where he was supposed to be dealing. At the same time as attacking Robbie physically, Lulu lets forth a stream of homophobic invective: 'Pillowbiter (*hit*). Shitstabber (*hit*)' (p. 39). This is followed by a condemnatory speech: 'Boys grow up you know and stop playing with each other's willies. Men and women make the future. There are people out there who need me. Normal people who have kind tidy sex [. . .] And boys? Boys just fuck each other' (p. 39). Such critiques of gay men were to become a notable feature of Ravenhill's plays and a radical departure from how homosexuality had previously been represented onstage. Not only was this aspect of his work missed at the time, but, as Rebellato observes, the generally positive reviews for the original production of *Shopping and Fucking* belied a real misunderstanding over what he calls 'its *attitude*'.[25] Ravenhill's next major play, seen by many at the time as the follow-up to *Shopping and Fucking* (despite the fact that he had written several other plays in the meantime), set out to make his intentions even clearer.

Some Explicit Polaroids

At first glance, connections with a previous tradition of political drama are the most apparent feature of *Some Explicit Polaroids*. Nick, just released from prison after serving fifteen years for torturing the financier Jonathan in an act motivated by class warfare, is contrasted with young Victor, a one-time Russian citizen from the communist regime, who has been acquired via the internet by Tim as his sex slave. While in a previous play, *Handbag* (1998), Ravenhill had used parallel timescales to compare family and parenting in the 1990s with that of the Victorian period, Nick and Victor introduced a historical frame-work that had been notably absent in previous work: here the socialist values of Nick and his ex-partner Helen are explicitly set against the 'happy world' of 1999 (p. 302), where engaged political ideology has been replaced by hedonism and pop psychology. In the action of the ten-scene play, which is set in London, there are a series of dialectical encounters between Nick and his past lover, some new acquaintances (Tim, Victor and Nadia), and finally with Jonathan himself. Completed in the autumn of 1999, *Some Explicit Polaroids* was Ravenhill's last *fin-de-siècle* play. This can be seen in its countervailing moods – of simultaneously looking out to the future and back over the past. The playwright has also acknowledged that the adult children, Tim, Victor and Nadia, are revisitations of Mark, Robbie and Lulu from his debut.[26] Clare Wallace also sees *Some Explicit Polaroids* as a 'reconsider[ation of] the terrain of *Shopping and Fucking*'.[27] Yet Ravenhill has also spoken of *Some Explicit Polaroids* as being the play that made him realise that 'my writing had broken free of a pattern', and it certainly feels like a coda of sorts: it is notable that his subse-quent plays in the following decade bore few traces of the concerns or indeed style of the 1990s.[28]

Both plays take very different approaches to British political history. While *Shopping and Fucking* marks the final years of John Major's administration, and a Conservative Party which had been in power since 1979, *Some Explicit Polaroids* is associated with Tony Blair's New Labour after its decisive election victory in 1997. However, it is also among the first to voice its disenchantment with the new administration after just over two years in power, where Helen's ambitions as a New Labour councillor extend no further than to trying to improve the local bus service for her constituents. The wider historical and political framework in *Some Explicit Polaroids* is also made clear through the comparisons made between its characters. Nick, bewildered at leaving prison and finding himself suddenly having to integrate within 1990s British society, is contrasted with

Victor, who hedonistically embraces the lifestyle afforded by consumer capitalism. Both characters' experiences of the past – Nick as a revolutionary socialist in the West during the 1980s; Victor growing up under drab Soviet communism – set up a Brechtian dialectic. Whereas Victor embraces the 'happy world' of the 1990s, Nick is appalled by a culture where 'Nothing's connected [. . .] and you're not fighting anymore' (p. 269). With such a clear sociopolitical framework derived from Brechtian theatre and English state-of-the-nation plays it is unsurprising that a critical consensus argues for *Some Explicit Polaroids* being Ravenhill's best play of the 1990s.[29] Stafford-Clark, who directed it, observed that its greater political engagement had also led to the characters being far more emotionally engaged than their coolly detached counterparts in *Shopping and Fucking*.[30] It is always difficult to attribute the exact causes of theatrical success, but it is possible to speculate that the extended period of rehearsals and workshops for *Some Explicit Polaroids*, lasting from March until September 1999, allowed for greater direct input from Stafford-Clark, whose own responses to the material are likely to have been shaped by previous work on plays – such as David Hare's *Fanshen* (1975) and Caryl Churchill's *Top Girls* (1982) – that had a clearly defined sociopolitical framework.[31]

The success of *Some Explicit Polaroids* also provides an opportunity to reassess interpretations of earlier work. For instance, Rebellato's claim that the plays rejected the state-of-the-nation model now looks more uncertain.[32] Steve Blandford in *Film, Drama and the Break Up of Britain* argues that beneath the depthless postmodernity of *Shopping and Fucking* lurks a deracinated state-of-England play prior to what he calls the 'internal de-colonization' of Scotland and Wales after 1997.[33] This is not to say that Rebellato's interpretation, or indeed Ravenhill's own explanation, that globalisation is the play's principal theme, is wrong.[34] For instance, it abounds with references to the porosity of national borders against the flow of capital; Victor is 'downloaded' (p. 283) by Tim, and Jonathan points out that national governments can do little against the combined might of 'the multinationals, the World Bank, NATO, Europe' (p. 259). So Blandford for instance recognises that the 'directionless, rootless world' of

Shopping and Fucking (and here *Some Explicit Polaroids* can also be included) is entirely symptomatic of this position.[35] However, he also observes that audiences in Europe have interpreted *Shopping and Fucking* (and again this can be applied to *Some Explicit Polaroids*), not as a play about globalisation but as 'one of the key theatrical representations of England'.[36]

Shopping and Fucking and *Some Explicit Polaroids* also have other shared themes, the most important of which are the responses they give to AIDS. In British theatre of the mid-1990s, despite a number of so-called gay plays, one could be forgiven for believing that AIDS had never touched British shores. Kevin Elyot's *My Night with Reg* (1994), a traditional well-made West End-orientated play, became one of the few instances where the effects of AIDS upon the gay male community was openly addressed. *Shopping and Fucking*, contrary to Rebellato's description of it being 'a defiantly young, queer strutting play', is actually highly reticent, to the point of silence, on the subject of AIDS.[37] Yet the disease nevertheless inscribes itself insidiously throughout the play as a spectral presence. David Ian Rabey notes 'the surprising persistence of blood [as] a running motif [. . .] as a source of danger and infection', and arguably the one genuine moment of in-yer-face shock comes when, after rimming Gary, Mark emerges with '*blood around his mouth*' (p. 26).[38] The audience's unspoken fear is articulated by Gary: 'Didn't think that happened anymore. Thought I'd healed, OK [. . .] I'm not infected OK?' (p. 26). What the scene manages to avoid is overt didacticism or what Rebellato calls the 'elaborate earnestness' of Elyot's *My Night with Reg*.[39] Instead, the scene succeeds in conveying not only the fear and threat of infection, but the idea that homosexuality itself is a dangerous yet thrilling condition – which is an idea far removed from the fey virtuous gay men portrayed in Anglo-American film theatre and television during the 1980s and early 1990s.

While allusions to AIDS in *Shopping and Fucking* largely function as metaphor, *Some Explicit Polaroids* gives room to a more direct engagement, yet Ravenhill – who is openly HIV positive – found the issue difficult to write about. This was not due to shyness about his own personal situation, but because American AIDS plays of the

1980s – such as Larry Kramer's *The Normal Heart* (1985) – had so colonised British theatre that, despite his best efforts, Ravenhill kept 'hear[ing] American voices and see[ing] American pictures' when he attempted to write about the subject.[40] This should not seem so surprising when one considers the dominance that not only American gay and lesbians command in cultural life, but the queer activists whom Jarrod Hayes takes to task for 'assuming the history of US lesbian, gay, bisexual, transgender, and or queer resistance holds a monopoly on inspiration for a global queer politics'.[41] However, *Some Explicit Polaroids* does manage to break free of the clichés of the 1980s AIDS play. Although it contains a deathbed scene, this is not a touching or sentimental farewell: Tim rejects the antiviral drugs (which had only become available since 1996, the year that *Shopping and Fucking* was produced) that manage his illness, choosing instead to die from the certainty of an AIDS-related illness rather than living the precarious existence that the new antiviral drugs bring with them (pp. 288–9). Not only that, but the second hospital scene is infused with sexuality as the grief-stricken Victor talks with Tim's ghost, who wants him to relieve his erection (p. 298). In this fantasy scene, as he masturbates his dead lover, Victor realises that 'Revolution never saved us. Money never saved us' (p. 299). Not only is this a troubling AIDS play, but it also simultaneously becomes a commentary on the state of the nation and the globalised world.

Despite the critical orthodoxy that maintains that *Some Explicit Polaroids* is Ravenhill's best 1990s play, Stafford-Clark points out that in terms of dissemination – playing to an estimated seven thousand people during its London run in comparison to the seventy thousand or so who eventually saw *Shopping and Fucking* – it is at odds with its critical reputation. Stafford-Clark then goes on to compare the reception of the two plays in Germany, where in terms of the number of productions both are held in equally high regard, yet each playing in a different size of theatre, 'often with *Some Explicit Polaroids* in the main theatre and *Shopping and Fucking* in the studio'.[42] Regarding both plays as so integrally connected allows audiences to give them a more mature consideration, especially as regards the often clouded debates that still hover over Ravenhill's work, and especially those that question his seriousness as a political dramatist or the extent of his commitment to a moral position.

Mother Clap's Molly House

While its debut on the National Theatre's Lyttelton stage in 2001 comes a couple of years after Ravenhill's 1990s work, *Mother Clap's Molly House* functions like a jigsaw piece that retrospectively allows his previous work to be assessed more cohesively. At the same time, this play with songs also marks a new departure and provides clear indications of the shape that Ravenhill's work would take in the first decade of the new millennium. The play combines two stories set in two separate eras. Act One is set in the 1720s and shows Mrs Tull, after the death of her husband, taking on the management of his dress-hire shop and after his death turning it into a molly house, a kind of same-sex club where men can gather to drink, talk, sing and have sex. In this Hogarthian London, whores and backstreet abortions provide an ironic contrast to the hedonism that takes place within the molly house. Act Two introduces three scenes set in today's London where a group of homosexual men give themselves over to licentious sex and drug taking.

The play is certainly Ravenhill's most ambitious to date, with a cast of fourteen and a score for a small orchestra. The move from having work staged at the Royal Court's Theatre Upstairs to one of the National's main stages in just over five years also marked a transition from the playwright's role as the *enfant terrible* of the 1990s to a place in the higher reaches of the theatrical establishment. If further confirmation was required, this came the following year when Ravenhill was appointed an artistic associate of this flagship. But with its device of parallel historical narratives, in some ways *Mother Clap's Molly House* is a throwback to the epic history plays of a previous era, such as Howard Brenton's *The Romans in Britain* (1980) and Edgar's *Maydays* (1983). However, the play it comes closest to resembling is Edward Bond's *Restoration* (1981). This is apt because Bond was in many ways a godfather figure to writers such as Ravenhill and Kane, and his iconoclastic plays – such as *Saved* (1965), *Early Morning* (1968) and *Lear* (1971) – were a source of inspiration. Kane acknowledged her indebtedness to Bond's work while Ravenhill has recalled his student days, when he attempted to steal all of Bond's published plays from a bookshop.[43] *Restoration*, as its title implies, is also set in the early eighteenth century, and Ravenhill incorporates many of its formal qualities into *Mother Clap's Molly House*: these include Bond's inventive use of quasi-Restoration language, musical numbers and perhaps most importantly (and in turn appropriated from Brechtian theatre), a series of clear dialectical arguments set up throughout the narrative.

With its three scenes located in 2001 and the remainder in the London of 1726, one of the most obvious breaks that *Mother Clap's Molly House* makes with Ravenhill's previous work is through its historical setting. However, this was not the first time that the playwright had set a play in the past: *Handbag* (1998) appropriated characters from Wilde's *The Importance of being Earnest* (1895) and moves between the Victorian period and the present. *Mother Clap's Molly House* also incorporates parallel time frames but does so in order to return to what has already been identified as an important subject to Ravenhill – namely lost Edens. The play dramatises a brief pre-lapsarian moment of sexual history in the early eighteenth century where male homosexuality, while still illegal and therefore hidden, was still largely free from codes of prescribed behaviour. During this time, meeting places for homosexual men, known as molly houses, were established. But, in their original form, these should be distinguished from the commercially run male brothels of Victorian London: in the molly house, no one paid for sex. Ravenhill's chief argument in the play is that during this historical moment there existed many opportunities for innocent sexual celebration before the forces of capitalist enterprise transformed sex into a commodity. As he observes, 'It's quite a quick transition from discovering pleasure to paying for it.'[44]

Through the incorporation of some features from the genre of Restoration city comedy, Ravenhill also discovers the ideal historical-theatrical form by which to continue his major preoccupation from the 1990s: namely, the effects of commerce on human behaviour. Brian's credo from *Shopping and Fucking*, that 'money is civilisation' (p. 87), is revisited in the opening scene of *Mother Clap's Molly House*, where the Chorus and figure of God join in extolling the spirit of enterprise. God reveals that 'Enterprise shall make you human [. . .] This my gift to you poor human', while the Chorus pleads for 'enterprise, come light our darkness/Business, shape our heart and hand'. The play also contains one of the funniest, yet at the same time chilling moments in Ravenhill's work to date. In a scene borrowed from one of the tropes of Restoration comedy we see the arrival of Amy, a girl fresh from the country, who has come to London to make her fortune as a prostitute. Amy's perception of herself, expressed in a Brechtian demonstration, is the clearest example in Ravenhill's work of a character whose selfhood is defined wholly in terms of being a marketable commodity. For example, on learning of the price (twenty guineas) that men would be prepared to pay for her maidenhood Amy exclaims, 'In't it a marvel what a body's worth?' (p. 13), and praises the day 'when a girl finds her body in't just eating and shitting, in't' it? Day when a girl discovers she's a commodity' (p. 14). Eventually it is this very self-knowledge, of the body as commodity, which slowly corrodes the mood of innocent licentiousness within the molly house, as the new code of paying for pleasure slowly encroaches. These glimpses of a fading pre-lapsarian past are contrasted with the two scenes set in 2001 at the flat of a wealthy pair of homosexuals, Josh and Will, who are organising a sex orgy. The switch from the eighteenth century to the twenty-first presents a continuum of gay history where the innocent beginnings of Mrs Tull's molly house in the eighteenth century end up with contemporary debauchery, thus presenting a situation that Ravenhill describes as being one of 'absolute sexual liberty but no sense of pleasure or of relationships whatsoever'.[45] This in turn also functions as a wider metaphor that reaches beyond a gay enclave to address a hedonistic, selfish and consumer-obsessed society.

With its analysis of homosexual relations from the eighteenth century to the present, *Mother Clap's Molly House* has been Ravenhill's only play to date that concerns itself exclusively with queer culture – for while *Shopping and Fucking* and *Some Explicit Polaroids* featured gay characters, critics never identified them as being specifically gay plays. Dodging this particular categorisation has been a longstanding mission on the playwright's part, and it is notable that most of his output in the 2000s has avoided any direct engagement with gay/queer issues.[46] Yet following on from an identification of Ravenhill as a queer writer, de Jongh also talks of a 'queer sensibility permeating the action' rather than the gay one in *Mother Clap's Molly House*.[47] This is an important distinction to make, for while heterosexual audiences can potentially identify with a play featuring gay characters or discussing related issues, de Jongh argues that any sense of didactic impulse in *Mother Clap's Molly House* is notably absent. This is because the play was intended neither for them, nor for an exclusively gay audience wanting to see their own interests addressed. Rather, it was directed at an audience – whatever their sexual orientation – that de Jongh believes 'feel a total outsider within a heterosexual context'.[48] Without such a sensibility, he argues that audiences would struggle to understand the scenes in the first act set inside the molly house, where codes of behaviour have not yet been fully established by societal forces. While this argument has much to recommend it, the beginning of the play is actually at pains to establish a strictly normative heterosexual world in order to make the later split with the sodomitical one all the more extreme. In the early scenes, much of Mrs Tull's education and gradual transformation into Mother Clap comes from her struggle to accept a queer world. For instance on first meeting Princess Seraphina, '*a large man in a dress*' (p. 7), she relies on biblical and patriarchal ideology to dismiss the existence of such inverts: 'See – good Lord made two natures [. . .] Thass man. And then – bit of his rib – woman [. . .] There in't no room for third sex' (p. 9).

Yet the play itself goes beyond notions of a 'third sex' to show a whole spectrum of queer sexualities including Seraphina, a heterosexual male who inhabits drag, to Lawrence, whose visits to the molly house are not governed purely by expediency: 'cos woman's needy and whores want paying' (p. 89). Alan Sinfield believes that men like Lawrence may be the true sexual dissidents, who by escaping strictures, both societal and self-imposed by the homosexual community allow such individuals to 'effectively blur and resist conventional

181

categories'.[49] Judith Butler also recognises that with men such as Princess Seraphina 'it would be a mistake to think that homosexuality is best explained through the performativity that is drag'.[50] Rather, in these cases Butler sees the act of cross-dressing 'to be the allegorization of heterosexuality and its constitutive melancholia',[51] a state which Seraphina intuitively recognises: 'See, when I'm dressed in trousers I get awful vicious. I think the world's against me and I strike out with my fists. But in a dress –' (p. 9).

However, by Act Two any residues of heterosexual conduct have been supplanted entirely by a queer world. In the song 'The Whore's Prayer', Amelia, Cranton and Bolton lament the transformed state where 'ev'ry man's turned molly' and 'ev'ry maid's alone' (p. 86). On the one hand, this dramatises a utopian vision upheld by some queer theorists, such as Michael Warner, from the early 1990s, who spoke about the queering of America.[52] On the other hand, the song can be interpreted as a wry commentary on this position, or even serve to draw attention to criticisms of the exclusiveness and exclusivity of the sodomitical world presented in the scenes from 2001. Here one is not only reminded of Mrs Tull's earlier revulsion at male effeminacy, while Tina's discomfort and in the contemporary all-male-sex party scenes could also be interpreted as a bid to protect her own marginalised position as a displaced heterosexual woman in a queer world.

While *Mother Clap's Molly House* is a triumphant 'coming out' play, it is also illustrative of Eve Kosofsky Sedgwick's ideas about queer identity and its defiance of the heteronormative residing in gay shame. For example, Martin's surreptitious visits to 'Sodomites Walk' (p. 30) in London's Moorfields district mark the beginnings of this process but Martin's identity is finally realised in his simultaneous attraction and repulsion to Orme's openly queer sexuality. Orme in turn realises both Martin's shame and its latency in determining his queerness:

Orme   You ever have your prick touched?

Martin   No.

Orme   Well, you feel such shame and then you feel lost and you don't know which way to turn. (30)

It is these very feelings of shame that constitute for Sedgwick what she calls 'powerfully productive and powerfully social metamorphic possibilities' in forging a new identity.[53] These same forces erupt during the song 'End of Act One'. In this defiant and celebratory affirmation of a queer identity the mollies proclaim, 'We are the future / We are the light' and 'Shit on those who call this sodomy / We call it fabulous' (p. 56). The song is also reminiscent of an expression of the utopian ideals held by earlier generations of gay liberationists pre-Stonewall, but in the play becomes the moment when the forces of God (who promotes enterprise) and Eros (who desires pleasure) are momentarily reconciled; now the pursuit of pleasure and profit exist harmoniously as the mollies join in chorus to proclaim, 'Pleasure in profit / Profit in pleasure' (p. 56). It is also here that *Mother Clap's Molly House* severs another association with in-yer-face theatre in the strong, but unquestioned, correlation in much of the drama from this period between stagings of anal intercourse and its use as a metaphor for abuse. In this respect, Ravenhill was as guilty as anyone else, where in *Shopping and Fucking* the trauma of Gary's past abuse at the hands of his stepfather manifests itself through his obsession with being sodomised by a knife. By contrast, *Mother Clap's Molly House* and its defiant celebration of sodomy succeeds in tearing down what Ravenhill calls 'this theatrical Berlin Wall [. . .] that separates horrific male rapes [. . .] [and shows] men on the British stage having anal sex as they do in life – frequently and for fun'.[54]

Mother Clap's Molly House, like Ravenhill's *Handbag*, also continues a theme of some of the playwright's 1990s drama: the exploration of alternative forms of parenting. Orme's observation that the 'Lord intended each of us to have a father and a mother and if Nature don't provide 'em, we must do what we can' (p. 34), is a neat summation of the family structures that occur in the playwright's previous work. *Mother Clap's Molly House* offers a more optimistic outcome, with the eponymous central figure retiring to the country with her 'family' of mollies. Compare this Arcadian ending with the lost boys in *Handbag* who either are given over to the repressed pederast Cardew or endure the fate of the baby left in the care of the drug addict Phil, whose attempts at resuscitation are to stub a cigarette out on the infant's body and afterwards dispose of it in a bin bag (pp. 222–6). While preferable to either of these fates, the alternative family structures in *Mother Clap's Molly House* never seriously challenge the innate legitimacy of the traditional family. In a significant moment, Orme tells the molly community, 'We must *play* at families' (33, my italics), where the acts of birth and mothering are self-consciously performed by men in drag rather than directly experienced. In Leo Bersani's discussion of Jennie Livingstone's *Paris is Burning* (1990) (a film that in its exploration of the various 'houses' and affiliated families of drag queens in 1980s New York, bears some notable resemblances to the eighteenth-century molly-house community), he questions Judith Butler's argument in her influential book *Gender Trouble* of drag being subversive parody, and argues instead that 'the heterosexual matrix [being] reduced to more or less naughty imitations of the matrix', far from disrupting gender relationships, exposes 'elements of longing and veneration in parodistic displays'.[55] The 'birthing' scene in *Mother Clap's Molly House* is an illustrative example of this process, where the enactment of Martin's mock pregnancy and the 'birth' of the wooden doll is less a display of subversive high camp than an instance of Martin pleading to his reluctant lover Orme to commit to heterosexual norms of family and marriage (p. 76). Orme's rejection of the doll is also a rejection of monogamy and the traditional family associated with the heterosexual world.

In some ways Orme's behaviour should not surprise us. Ravenhill's previous work has also found the traditional family either absent, such as Lulu's vague statement in *Shopping and Fucking* that her family 'spend Christmas together. On the whole' (p. 10), or sinister, such as Nadia's disturbingly insouciant response in *Some Explicit Polaroids* that she has never met a paedophile before except her father, 'but I don't count him' (p. 257). But then this is to be expected: a queer sensibility is antagonistic to the traditional family through its outlaw status in comparison to the ideal of stability achieved through heterosexual normative relations. In this context, families are places that one abandons, or structures that need reinventing.

Conclusion

All three of Ravenhill's plays discussed here can be read as an AIDS trilogy. *Shopping and Fucking*, with its associations between blood and anal intercourse (pp. 26–7, 32, 83–4), captures something of the culture of fear and silence that the disease spawned during the 1980s and early 1990s; *Some Explicit Polaroids* was among the first British plays to look at the introduction of retroviral drugs and combination therapy in treating the disease and the challenges suddenly presented to homosexual men such as Tim who could now opt to 'spin it out for years and years' (p. 268); and *Mother Clap's Molly House* in the two scenes set in 2001 also returns to the same idea where we see how men such as Edward have, through treatment, been bought back from the brink of death (pp. 82–3). Here, as in so many other respects, what becomes most apparent is Ravenhill's role as a perspicacious and saga-cious chronicler of the rapid changes that marked the *fin de siècle* and the first decade of the new millennium. From early debates about the impact of the internet and virtual reality, to celebrity culture and the 'me generation', taken together the plays become an *assiette* of contemporary preoccupations. Yet Ravenhill's analysis of current obsessions is not governed by a journalistic impulse. De Jongh has called him 'perhaps the first true English queer playwright', with *Shopping and Fucking* allowing for a new representation of homosexu-ality that can be seen in subsequent plays such as Samuel Adamson's *Southwark Fair* (2006).[56] Yet, while such changes in representation largely passed unnoticed at the time, it is sobering to remember that in 1994, just two years before the arrival of *Shopping and Fucking*, the central revelation in Terry Johnson's popular West End hit *Dead Funny* was that one of its characters was a homosexual.

Other critics agree that Ravenhill has altered our perceptions of both homosexuality and queer theatre. For Dominic Shellard, his willingness to critique the proclivities of gay men brought about a 'new resilience [to] gay drama', and Sarah Jane Dickinson has argued that Ravenhill 'restores a sense of danger invoked by homosexuality' together with an 'ability to tap into the persistent anxiety connected to homosexuality: the fear of the queer'.[57] Young teenagers such as

Gary in *Shopping and Fucking* and Victor in *Some Explicit Polaroids* not only attract the pederastic attentions of older men but also seem to revel in their power to do so: for example, Victor proudly tells Nadia that at fourteen both his brother and father went 'crazy for my body' (p. 239), while Gary craves an enactment of abuse from a succession of father figures. Like Joe Orton's unscrupulous (and murderous) Mr Sloane, these characters either attempt to disrupt the normative heterosexual world with an amoral and hedonistic alternative, or else set out to tempt characters such as Martin (in *Mother Clap's Molly House*) who waver precariously on the brink of homosexuality. Such figures are contentious, not only because of their age (how different would have been the reception of *Shopping and Fucking* if Gary had been a fourteen-year-old girl?), but also because of their precocious knowingness about the world of gay sex. Certainly, these stage characters are more thrilling, and often more disturbing, than the rather bloodless and domestic gay characters that people the plays of a previous generation of playwrights. A good example is Guy's hobby of knitting in Elyot's *My Night with Reg*; the character says that his current project, 'a cover for my door sausage', is 'a sort of lust-depression'.[58] Guy is a representative of a type of homosexuality that is cosy, non-threatening and assimilationist. Ravenhill's characters are the very opposite.

Yet, in any assessment of Ravenhill as a queer dramatist, it should also be remembered that prior to *Shopping and Fucking*, the 1993 London New Play Festival staged an earlier work by him entitled *Close to You*. Here its subject matter, concerning the exposure of an MP as a homosexual, followed the more familiar discourses to be found in gay playwriting at the time.[59] The writer, director and former artistic director of the Lyric Hammersmith, Neil Bartlett, whose own work in the 1980s such as *A Vision of Love Revealed in Sleep* (1986) did much to promote a new gay aesthetic in theatre, has also commented that while *Mother Clap's Molly House* appears to have been spawned from 'the "queer" 1990s', its reclamation of gay history in fact mines the very same territory as theatre groups such as Gay Sweatshop did in the 1970s.[60] Ravenhill's interest in history also goes against what Donald Morton calls the 'non-ordered atopia (a no place outside history)' that pervades much queer theory where the future becomes merely 'an ever expanding region of sensuous pleasure' – and in turn a reflection of the workings of late capitalism.[61] Morton's analysis uncannily reflects the outlook of the 2001 partygoers from *Mother Clap's Molly House*, where Tom divides his coming out as a separation between past and present: 'Old Me was living in the Olden Days. History and that. Really, really old fashioned . . . And now there's new me – and I'm like totally today' (p. 64). Tom's sense of his new queer identity produces a shrinking of history: 'Two months and I've travelled hundreds of years into the future. Only the future's like now' (p. 64), but it is one governed only by the ethics of consumption and hedonism that is symptomatic of late capitalism: 'Clubs. E. Shagging all sorts of blokes' (p. 64).

One other feature of Ravenhill's work already alluded to has been the critical dichotomy between robust praise and vociferous denigration. This dissension is just as much part of the fabric of the plays as their content. One such area where the critical fault lines have opened is over the playwright's eclecticism. Clare Wallace, for instance, sees him as 'neither a formal innovator nor a particularly cogent observer of postmodernism', where his representation of the ideas of philosophers and theorists such as Baudrillard, Foucault and Lyotard is 'fragmented, superficial and exaggerated' and operate as little more than 'beginner's guide' digests.[62] In a similar vein, Ravenhill's plays could also be accused of being too knowing, alluding to and then shying away from confronting serious subjects. Yet such criticisms fail to take into account the response of actors, who at times seem to have been all too readily beguiled by a camp sensibility that, in the right hands, disappears after a first reading of the work. For instance, the actor William Osborne – who played the roles of Philips and Will in *Mother Clap's Molly House* – commented that while he enjoyed 'the frock side of things', he could also see the dangers of 'a lot of potential campery'.[63] The play's director Nicholas Hytner also observed during rehearsals that 'the actors are having such a good time I'll have to keep an eye on them', otherwise they potentially risked 'ingratiat[ing] themselves with the audience'.[64] The audience itself has also been a highly problematic element in the reception of Ravenhill's work. For example, the youthful contingent who originally went to see *Shopping and Fucking* often seemed to view the play as a celebration of what it sought to condemn, while Ravenhill has observed that audiences of his more recent plays appear to be cut adrift from any real sense of moral or political conviction, whereby their 'sense of values just gets woollier and woollier, and is simply a mixture of liberalism and postmodernism'.[65]

Perhaps misinterpretation is destined to follow Ravenhill around, particularly so with the early group of plays that made his name; similarly, attempting to place him within any formal category is still difficult. Even a cursory glance at the already considerable (and growing) body of critical writing on this playwright soon reveals the difficulties critics have found in coming to any sort of consensus about a writer who manages to shape-shift one moment from being an arch commentator on postmodernism to the writer of a popular pantomime, *Dick Whittington and His Cat* (2006), in the next. However, the theatre scholar Patrice Pavis in a comment made about *Shopping and Fucking*, but one that applies to all of the playwright's work, categorises it as a problem play rather than a thesis play.[66] Problem plays by their very nature elude classification or explanation, and while *Shopping and Fucking* and *Some Explicit Polaroids* are in some respects examples of plays that clearly represent a specific period, their troublesome qualities that refuse easy interpretation will continue to make them of lasting relevance for some considerable time to come.

CHAPTER 3
DOCUMENTS

Philip Ridley: *Vesper* – a Monologue

An earlier version of Vesper, *a monologue by Philip Ridley, was first performed as a live art piece by him at St Martin's School of Art as part of the* Ten Painters Exhibition *in 1986.*

What's that? Shhh!

Slight pause.

Outside the front door. I thought I heard a – Listen!

Slight pause.

Hear that? Someone's there. What can they want? It's the middle of the bloody night, for chrissakes – They're rattling it! They won't get in. Oh, no. It's securely locked. Two locks. And there's seven bolts. I've sealed up the letterbox too. You can't be too careful – What's that? Shhh!

Slight pause.

They're outside the window now. Don't worry, I've sealed it shut. Cement and nails. Fresh air? Who needs it? When was the last time anyone breathed fresh air anyway? Not since Tyrannosaurus Rex bit the head off a . . . whatever. Pterodactyl! – What's that? Shhh!

Slight pause.

Footsteps. They're prowling round the house. Oh, this is not friendly behaviour, is it. Well, *is* it? Do not try telling me whoever's out there means me no harm. Why me? That's what I'd like to know. I try my very best not to be a nuisance to anyone. You know what my motto is? Don't get involved. All I want to do is float through life without causing so much as a ripple. If nobody knows I exist, that suits me just fine. Invisible. That's my preferred state –What's that? Shhh!

Slight pause.

Hear that? . . . Oh, come on, you *must* have heard that. It was a bottle, for fuck's sake. A bottle being smashed. Smashed in anger. By a man. Oh, yes. It's a nasty man out there I reckon. A drunk man. Muscles. Tattoos. Tiny vein on his forehead going throb, throb, throb. You know the sort. We all do. He's picking up another bottle now and he's . . . Oh, no! He's throwing it at the house. Perhaps it'll smash through a window. Perhaps it's full of petrol. A Molotov cocktail! Perhaps he's got lots of Molotov cocktails. Hundreds. My skin will shrivel and melt like wax. I'll scream but no one will hear me. No one will care – No, no, no! I have to stop thinking like that. Why didn't you stop me thinking like that? Eh? Haven't you got feelings, for fuck's sake? Haven't you got a conscience? – What's that? Shhh!

Slight pause.

I'm sure I heard . . . another bottle – Did you hear it? Another beer bottle being smashed – Oh, no! The man's shoving the broken bottle in the face of another man. A younger man. He's no more than a boy. It *is* a boy. A child. Can you hear the child screaming? Oh, don't tell me you can't hear that? There's blood! Blood all over the place. I know there is. You know it too. I know you know – Bone! Oh, my God, I can see boy's skull! There's a child out there having his head peeled like a tangerine and all you can do is sit there like . . . like staring things – Zombies! Haven't you got feelings? Haven't you got a conscience? The boy's on the ground now. The man is stomping on his head. Skull breaks. Stomp! Crack! Stomp! The man's flattening the boy's head to a . . . a . . . – Police! I'll phone the police. No! Don't get involved. I'll be asked to give evidence at the trial. I'll have to stand in the witness box and say, 'I saw a man peel a child's skull like a tangerine and stomp on it till it was flat as a pancake.' A lawyer will tell me to point at the man who committed the crime. I'll have to point at the man who did it. He'll stare back at me. Oh, that look! Goosebumps – See? The jury will retire to consider their verdict. I'll be shaking. I'll rush to the public toilets and throw up. A policeman will be standing at the urinal. He'll say, 'You did the right thing, sir. We can't have nasty men like that walking our streets.' I'm about to thank him when I hear an announcement over loud speakers: the jury are returning with their verdict. I rush back to the courtroom. The head of the jury stands up. The judge asks, 'Do you find the nasty man guilty or not guilty?' The head of the jury says, 'Not guilty.' The nasty man lets out a shriek of joy. It sounds like a Tyrannosaurus Rex having its head bit off by a . . . whatever. Pterodactyl! And then . . . then the nasty man looks at me. He grins and slides his finger across his throat. He wants to kill me. I run out of the courtroom. I run to the nearest police station. I ask the police for protection. They give me a new name and set me up on a farm somewhere in the Cotswolds. I look after livestock. Cattle – No! Ostrich! I'm an ostrich farmer. I wear tweeds and grow a beard. I learn to walk down country paths as if I've been doing it all my life. I'm happy here. *Ostrich Paradise – Lean and Healthy Meat for the Whole Family.* I'm a one-man business. It's hard work but I don't mind. The satisfaction I get when I stand here – on this typically green and pleasant hillside – and look down at my farm . . . oh, it's worth every hour of sweat and toil. You see my little cottage over there? That monkey tree in the garden was a gift from a neighbour, an Ex-World Champion Surfer, who lost his leg to a capricious manta ray somewhere off the coast of Malaga. And over there – oh, my pride and joy. My ostriches. In their pen. See them? I've got fifty-seven in all. My free-range ostrich meat is well known across the whole county. Oh, yes. And it's one hundred per cent organic too. I feed the birds a mixture of seaweed, saffron and par-boiled terrapin. They love it. Can't get enough. And I must say it gives their meat a distinctly gamey twang. I sell the meat here too, you know. Oh, yes. This is a farm, abattoir and butcher all in one. Now, I know what you're thinking. How do those happy, fluffy feathered, long necked 'n' legged fuckers become ostrich steak and two veg please. It's a gory story but if you want to know. I'll tell you . . . *Do* you want to know? Course you do. Time for slaughter – What's that? Shhh!

Slight pause.

I'm in the ostrich pen. I'm twirling a lasso. The ostriches start running away. I chase after them. I need a horse really. Rodeo style. You know? 'Yee-haa!' I can't afford a horse. And I haven't got a cow. But I can still go, 'Yee-haa!' The ostriches are scattering all over the place. Look at their legs go. The trick is not to get distracted by all the whole flock running around like that. You have to pick just one bird – that one, say! – and stick to it. 'Yeee-haa!' It's flapping its useless wings in panic. Feathers fly everywhere. 'Yee-haa! . . . Yee-haa!' I've trapped it in a corner. Throw lasso. Ostrich runs. I miss. Gather up rope. Chase. Flapping feathers. Twirling lasso. Throw – Got it! Fuck, it's strong. Hold the rope tight. Pull hard. The ostrich is on the ground. I've got to move quick. Tie rope round its legs. They're kicking – Careful! Careful! Tie! Quick! Tie! Not kicking and flapping now, are you, ostrich, eh? Look at it. Just a long neck sticking out of a ball of trussed-up body. A vein on its neck is going throb, throb, throb. The other ostriches are gathering round now. There's vengeance in their gleaming black eyes. Fifty-six angry ostriches can be a lethal thing. Oh, yes. One ostrich farmer I heard about in Australia – an Aboriginal who could floor any kangaroo out with a single punch – was stomped to death by his birds purely for being a few minutes late with their feeding time. I grab the rope round the ostrich's neck. I tie the other end to a conveniently nearby tractor – 'Stay back, you feathered fuckers! Back! It's a man eat bird world. Read your Darwin.' I'm in the tractor now. Start engine. Accelerator. Move forward. I'm heading for that shed up ahead. See it? I've painted it black. It looks like hole in the landscape. But it's not a hole. It's the abattoir – What's that? Shhh!

Slight pause.

Meat hook! That's what the ostrich is hanging from. See it? Oh, it's dead now. Dodo dead. All that tractor dragging strangled it. Okay, okay, not the most humane death, I grant you, but have you ever tried chopping the head off an ostrich with a fifteen-year-old and somewhat blunt electric meat carver? Well, have you? Let me tell you it is a messy and time-consuming business. So do not judge me if a handy motorised farming vehicle incidentally – and, yes, yes, I admit it, conveniently – strangles an animal in transit. I have more than enough work to do on the farm without spending all day beheading a fully grown ostrich the size of a . . . a fully grown ostrich. Now . . . I've cut the ropes off the bird, as you can see, and the meat hook is stuck in here, through the ribcage, as per official government guidelines. The bird is plucked clean. I've swept all the feathers up. They're in that bag over there. I sell them to a seventy-year-old hat-maker who lives in the village. She makes the most wonderful Easter bonnets. The old girl's as friendly as they come but totally mute. Lost her voice at the age of twelve when she was scared by a rabid pig down by the salt mines. The Mute Milliner Woman. That's what everyone calls her. Before her scare the Mute Milliner Woman used to sing in the church choir. Like I did. But, unlike me, the Mute Milliner Woman had the voice of an angel apparently . . . Looks almost human, don't you think? The ostrich. A thin-legged human with a bloody long neck, I admit, but . . . well, there's something about the skin. When you kiss it – a dead person feels just the same, you know. Well, perhaps you don't. I do. Mum and Dad felt exactly like that . . . Okay, okay, enough reminiscing. Where's the chainsaw? Best cover your ears. This is one hell of a noisy fucker. Get it started and – There! What did I tell you? Now . . . dismemberment. Slice through the neck here . . . Yesss! Head and neck fall. Like a pink python or something, ain't it. Ha! Slice off the legs . . . Slice off the wings – All these bits I'm cutting off now are useful. Oh, yes. Burgers. Sausages. Mince. Not one bit of the bird goes to waste. Even the beak makes a very decorative soap dish – Oh, fuck this blood!

Dripping all over the joint. I'm drenched. Look at me. Jesus! Now . . . cut down the middle of the body – Giblets! Splosh! Makes the most gorgeous gravy. Just add some fresh cranberries and a dash of Tabasco sauce. Delicious – Hang on! What's that? Something's coming out the body. Turn chainsaw off . . . There! You see? Coming out of that hole . . . It's shiny and smooth like . . . like something shiny and – Mother of pearl! It's getting bigger. The size of a beach ball. It falls. Catch! Fuck! An egg – What's that? Shhh!

Slight pause.

I'm in the cottage now. It's late. Night. There's a log fire burning. I'm sipping a cup of warm milk and nibbling a digestive biscuit. They're home-made. Not by me. Oh, no. Ostrich rissole and two veg is about my culinary limit. A young man from the dairy farm across the way makes them. He was blinded by a rare tropical virus a few years ago. The infection was carried on the wings of some insect that came over in a crate of coconuts apparently. Several people went down with the virus. But our young man was the only one who lost his sight. Made him famous for a while. Oh, yes. It was in the papers and everything. One tabloid paid him to tell his story. Not a fortune, I grant you, but enough for him to set up his own home-made biscuit business. Blind Biscuit Maker Man. That's what everyone calls him – Mmm, and very delicious they are too. Some things are worth going blind for, don't you think? I've put the ostrich egg in front of the fire, as you can see. And, before you ask, no, I don't usually keep eggs here to hibernate in the cottage. But I was so drenched with blood after the abattoir I wanted to get back for a deep-pore cleansing bubble-bath soak pronto. Ostrich blood turns sticky as raspberry jam after a while. Mind you, it's very good for the complexion. See? I haven't had a troublesome spot or blemish since I started the slaughter. Perhaps there's a lucrative sideline to be had from Ostrich Blood Face Masks – It moved! The egg! You see that? . . . It did it again. A definite wobble. I can hear something tapping. Listen! A crack in the shell! It's hatching. The tip of a beak. The whole beak. The head! Neck. Body. My God! I've never seen a chick like it. Its feathers are the purest, purest white. Its eyes are bright pink. And . . . oh, the way it's looking up at me. 'Hello, little chick.' It's walking up to me. It's nuzzling against my leg like a cat. 'What do you want, then, eh?' It opens its beak. I know what it wants. Seaweed, saffron and par-boiled terrapin! – What's that? Shhh!

Slight pause.

'Ex-World Champion Surfer! What a surprise! How are you?' He often pops round to see me when the nights are drawing in. He likes to talk about his glory days. How he once surfed a wave for seven hours along the coast of Honolulu and how they made him King of some Island in the South Pacific and gave him many gifts including a gold toothpick that, unfortunately, he had to sell in order to purchase a state of the art prosthetic leg. 'Let me introduce you to my new pet, Ex-World Champion Surfer – Here, Vesper! Here, Vesper! . . . Aha! Here it is! . . . I know, I know, so cute . . . Two weeks old now. It does tricks. Watch . . . Vesper – Beg! Ha! Watch, watch – Gimme your claw! Ha, ha! Oh, it's such a good companion, Ex-World Champion Surfer. So affectionate. Yes, yes, of course it's safe to stroke it. A baby ostrich can't hurt you . . . – What's wrong, Ex-World Champion Surfer? . . . Your stump? What about your stump? Itching? . . . Well, of course, you can scratch it . . . Take your trousers off? Well, if you must but – What's wrong, Ex-World Champion Surfer? . . . Your stump is getting worse? Your stump is throbbing. You need to take your false let off – Here, here, give it to me! My God, Ex-World Champion Surfer! Your stump seems to be – A toe! A toe has started growing! Two toes. Three. A foot. It's getting longer. Longer. You're growing a new leg, Ex-World Champion Surfer! Look at it! It's fully grown now. It's so suntanned and healthy you could've just surfed a wave for seven hours off the coast of Honolulu. Can you stand up? . . . You can! How does it feel? Good as new? Well, it *is* new, Ex-World Champion Surfer. How could something like that happen? . . . Well, yes, I suppose it must be. There's no other explanation. Vesper! – What's that? Shhh!

Slight pause.

'Hello, Blind Biscuit Maker Man . . . You heard about the miracle that my pet baby ostrich performed on the Ex-World Champion Surfer, did you. Good Lord, news travels fast in these backward backwaters, doesn't it . . . No, no, I don't mind at all. Vesper! Vesper! . . . Here it is. Let the Blind Biscuit Maker Man stroke your feathers, Vesper . . . – What's that, Blind Biscuit Maker Man? Your eyes are itching . . . Your eyes are throbbing . . . Why are you looking at me like that! . . . Because you're not blind anymore!? How many fingers am I holding up? . . . Correct!' The local television news crew turns up. They want to see Vesper. They've brought along The Mute Milliner Woman. They want to see Vesper perform a miracle on her. Before I can say anything Vesper rushes between my legs and up to the Mute Milliner Woman. One of the news crew tells the Mute Milliner Woman to reach down and stroke it. She reaches. She strokes. The Mute Miller Woman starts scratching her throat. I see it throb. And then – Singing! The Mute Milliner Woman's singing at the top of her voice. And what a voice! It echoes from hillside to hillside. 'Jesu Joy of Man's Desiring'. She starts crying. The news crew start crying. I start crying. Next day there are hundreds of film crews camped outside my farm. From all over the world. And there's crowds of villagers. Not just from the local village. From every village in the county. And there's coaches of new people arriving all the time. Tourists. Paparazzi. And they're all chanting 'Vesper! Vesper!' They're hysterical. This could turn nasty at any moment. They could storm my cottage. If they all try to grab Vesper at once they could tear the bird to bits. I bolt the door and lock all the windows. I want to pray but the chanting outside is distracting me. The phone rings. 'Hello, Ostrich Paradise.' 'I saw you on television,' says a voice. 'Your beard and tweeds don't fool me.' It's him! The nasty man who peeled a boy's head and stomped on it till it was flat as a pancake. I say, 'I'm sorry for what I did but – ' 'Shut up!' he says. 'I know where you live now. And I'm gonna do to you what I did to that kid.' He's hung up. I've got to get out of here. I'm not safe. Nor is Vesper. I phone the police. They send a helicopter to rescue me. It lands in the ostrich pen. I grab Vesper and run out the back door. The press and paparazzi see me. They chase after me. I climb over the fence and into the ostrich pen. The ostrich are flocking everywhere in panic. A snowstorm of feathers. I run towards the helicopter. Press and paparazzi are clambering over the fence behind. Cameras flashing. Journalists shouting. A man in a solder's uniform is hanging out the side of the helicopter. He yells at me, 'Faster, man, faster!' I can feel little Vesper's heart pounding against my chest. I duck under the swirling blades of the helicopter. The soldier points at Vesper. 'No livestock allowed on board, sir!' 'I'm not leaving without my Vesper.' The press and paparazzi are almost on us. The soldier takes a gun from his pocket and fires it above their heads. 'Stay back!' Then he grabs me by the scruff of the neck and hauls me into the helicopter. It takes off. I kiss Vesper's beak. 'We're safe now, Vesper!' I'm given a new identity. I'm an antique dealer in the Outer Hebrides. I dye my hair red and wear glasses. Business is poor but I adore the smell of the ocean and the sound of fishermen singing their quant old sea shanties. I dye Vesper's feathers black. I put a lead round its neck and call it a new breed of dog. No one would ever recognise it as the snow-feathered, miracle-working chick on television. Me and Vesper play Frisbee on the beach and search for fossils in the shingle. We meet a war veteran down by the pier. He was burnt to a crisp by a petrol bomb in a country whose name I can't pronounce. Before I can stop him he's stroking Vesper. His skin starts to itch. Throb. His scars heal. Word spreads. Press. Paparazzi. A phone call. 'Antiques Paradise.' 'Your red hair and glasses can't fool me.' Helicopter. Grab Vesper. Run. Press and paparazzi. 'I'm not leaving without my Vesper!' Gun! Bang! Take off. 'We're safe now, Vesper.' New life. Cinema manager. Bleached hair. Moustache. Child crippled with arthritis. Stroke. Itch. Tingle. Child running a marathon. Word spreads. Press. 'Cinema Paradise.' 'Your bleached hair and moustache can't – ' Helicopter. 'I'm not leaving without – ' Bang. Take off. 'Safe now.' New life. Miner. Soot. Someone's got lung disease. Stroke. Itch. Throb. Cured. Paparazzi. Helicopter. Bang!

Take off. New life. I wear T-shirt. Jeans. Trainers. I look like this. I have no job. I live here. I keep Vesper outside in the garden shed. I feed Vesper a mixture of seaweed, saffron and par-boiled terrapin. Vesper thrives on it. Vesper's the size of small child now. Phone call. 'Your T-shirt and jeans don't fool me.' 'Help!' No helicopter. 'Help!' No one's coming. I'm alone now. Abandoned – What's that? Shhh! Splintering wood! It's the garden shed. The door's being ripped off. It's him. The nasty man. I can hear Vesper screaming and screaming. 'Oh, Vesper! Nooo!' The nasty man's eating Vesper. Eating every sinew and feather. I can hear Vesper's beak being crunched to bits. Blood is trickling down the nasty man's chin. Feathers are stroking against his lips – No! The nasty man is itching. The nasty man is throbbing. Look! Vesper's last miracle! The nasty man is growing. Bigger and bigger. He's bursting out of his clothes. He's huge. He's towering above the house. He's looking down at me. At us! Oh, yes! Don't imagine you're not part of this. Don't think you can just sit the staring like . . . like staring things – Zombies! Haven't you got feelings, for fuck's sake? Haven't you got a conscience? The nasty man is ripping the roof of the house. There's no escape for any of us now. We're all going to have our skulls peeled like tangerines and stomped flat as pancakes – Look. Up there. It's him! It's him! Him!

Blackout.

Sarah Kane: Interview with Dan Rebellato

This is an edited transcript of the Brief Encounter Platform, a public event during which Sarah Kane was interviewed by Dan Rebellato at Royal Holloway, University of London, on 3 November 1998.[1]

Dan Rebellato   I can't think of any playwright who has got quite such personal, vitriolic or hostile reviews from critics that you have. Why do you think that is?

Sarah Kane   Because they don't know what else to say. I honestly think that's true. If they don't know what to say about the work, they go for the writer, or the director, or the actors. [. . .] [The press night of *Blasted*] was a bit strange; the Court had programmed the play into a dead spot; they didn't really know what to do with it. A lot of people in the building didn't want to do it. They were a bit embarrassed about it, so they put it into a spot just after Christmas when no one was going to the theatre anyway and hopefully no one would notice.

And it was in the Theatre Upstairs, and what usually happens in the Theatre Upstairs is that they have two press nights because if you have one then every seat is full of press and it's completely unbearable. So you have two and you have a slightly mixed audience for both nights. Because everyone was a bit haphazard at the Court at that time, they failed to notice there was a major press night at another theatre, the Almeida in London [of Strindberg's *Dance of Death*], on one of those press nights so they were all coming on the same night anyway. So I was sitting at the back and I looked around and realised that the director [James Macdonald] was somewhere near the front and everyone else was a critic. I think there were about three other women in the audience. Everyone else was a middle-aged, white, middle-class man – and most of them had sort-of plaid jackets on. (*Laughter.*)

And it was literally only at that point that I realised that the main character of my play was a middle-aged male journalist (*laughter*) who not only raped his young girlfriend but that is then raped and mutilated himself. And it suddenly occurred to me that they wouldn't like it. (*More laughter.*) It genuinely hadn't – I really thought they were going to like it. I thought this is really good, they'll love it. And then the next morning, there was just complete chaos. My agent couldn't get off the phone to call me. There were apparently tabloid journalists running around the Royal Court going: 'Where is she?' She's at home in bed! You know, it's ten o'clock in the morning. And a lot of it passed me by at the time. My father is a tabloid journalist and very kindly didn't give my address to any other tabloid journalist. And they never caught up with me.

But I think largely what happened was that what I attempted to do, and it seemed I think probably succeeded, was to create a form for which I couldn't think of an obvious direct precedent so it wasn't possible to say: 'This form is exactly like the form in a play written twenty years ago.' I wanted to create a form that hadn't happened before. And because the form hadn't happened before no one knew what to say. [*Guardian* critic] Michael Billington couldn't say: 'Ah, this is a nice bit of social realism, I can talk about this.' He couldn't say: 'It's surrealism and I don't like that therefore don't go and see it.' So what he could say was that this writer is clearly mentally ill and she should be locked away. And the *Daily Mail* did actually suggest that the money spent on the play should be spent on getting me some therapy. (*Laughter.*) And I agree (*laughs*), but that's really not the point. But I genuinely think it's because if they don't have a clear framework within which to locate the play then they can't talk about it. So they have to talk about other things, such as the writer's personal life, their mental health, whatever it might be.

DR In all the reviews there is a list paragraph [of the play's atrocious acts] . . .

SK Yes, it drives me mad . . . Rape, masturbation . . . The thing is that the list is always wrong. It always includes 'an under-aged mentally retarded girl being crapped on by a doll' or something (*laughter*) that actually didn't happen. And a lot of the time it happened because once the story was picked up as a news story it was no longer the people who had seen it that were actually writing about it – it was people like my father, tabloid hacks, who if they don't know the facts make them up because that's what their job is. So, yeah, there's always the list. It's usually inaccurate. And a list of contents is not a review. But it doesn't only happen to me; I think it happens to most new plays. What you get is a brief synopsis, and you get a list of things that happen and then a little note at the end saying whether or not this particular middle-aged male journalist likes this play, and whether or not you should go and see it. And it tells you nothing. It tells you possibly what's in the play, but if you list the contents of any play, it really doesn't tell you whether it's any good or not.

[. . .]

DR   How do you write? [. . .]

SK   It's different for each thing that I write. And it often depends on what stage I'm at. At first draft stage, I tend to write an awful lot of rubbish very quickly and it has no form at all. *Blasted* was a very particular journey and I think because it was a first play, I wasn't really aware of what I was doing formally. I mean, I knew what I was doing but I wasn't consciously aware in the way I am now; I mean, within two pages when I started to write *Crave* I thought, 'Ah, I can see what form this is going to be, how interesting.' With *Blasted*, it wasn't until six months after it had closed that I went, 'Oh, that's what I was doing.'

And I think with *Blasted* it was a direct response to the material as it began to happen. I mean, I knew I wanted to write a play about a man and a woman in a hotel room, and that there was a complete power imbalance, which resulted in a rape. And I started writing that and I was, you know, writing away and had been doing it for a few days, and I switched on the news one night while I was having a break from writing, and there was a very old woman's face, a woman from Srebrenica [in Bosnia], just weeping and weeping and looking into the camera, and saying: 'Please, please, somebody help us. We need the UN to come here and help us. We need someone to do something.' And I was sitting there watching and I thought, 'No one's going to do anything. How many times have I seen another old woman crying from another town in Bosnia under siege and no one does anything?' And I thought, 'This is absolutely terrible, and I'm writing this ridiculous play about two people in a room – what does it matter? What's the point of carrying on [writing that play]?' So [Bosnia] is what I want to write about and yet somehow this story about this man and woman was still attracting me. And I thought, 'So what could possibly be the connection between a common rape in a Leeds hotel room and what's happening in Bosnia?' And then suddenly this penny dropped and I thought, 'Of course, it's obvious. One is, you know, the seed and the other is the tree.' And I do think that the seeds of full-scale war can always be found in peacetime civilisation, and I think the wall between so-called civilisation and what happened in central Europe is very, very thin and it can get torn down at any time.

And then I had to find a way of formally making that link, thinking: 'How do I say that what's happening in this country between two people in a room could lead to that or is emotionally linked to that?' And then at some point I think I actually had a conversation with [playwright] David Greig about this, about Aristotle's unities – time, place and action (David is the perfect man to talk to about this). And I thought, 'Okay, what I have to do is keep the same place but alter the time and action.' Or you can actually reverse it and look at it the other way around: that the time and the action stay the same, but the place changes. It depends actually how you look at the play; you can look at it either way.

And at that point I began to think: 'Is there a precedent?' If there's a precedent, I don't want to do it, I'm not interested. And after a day spent looking at plays, I couldn't think of one, and then I needed an event. I think in the first draft, the soldier literally began to appear at different points – it was like Ian was hallucinating and I just thought, 'This is awful, kind of American Expressionism.' And then I thought, 'What it needs is what happens in war – suddenly, violently, without any warning whatsoever, people's lives are completely ripped to pieces.' So I literally just picked a moment in the play; I thought, 'I'll plant a bomb, just blow the whole fucking thing up.' And I loved the idea of it as well: that you have a nice little box set in the studio theatre somewhere and you blow it up – because it's what I've always wanted to do, (*laughter*) just blow it up. It's that thing, you know, you go to the Bush [Theatre] and you go in and you see the set and you go, 'Oh no', and I was just longing for it to blow up and so it was such a joy for me to be able to do that. But for me the form did exactly mirror the content. And for me the form is the meaning of the play, which is that people's lives are thrown into complete chaos with absolutely no warning whatsoever.

Physically how I write (I haven't answered the question properly) physically how I write, half the time I can't remember. I seriously have a finished script and I think: 'God, when did I do that?' I seem to have been hanging around drinking coffee for six months and here's a play. It happens very haphazardly and brokenly and sometimes I write masses and sometimes . . . the thing I'm writing at the moment, I'm literally like writing a line in a notebook with no idea where it belongs in the play, but I know it's in there somewhere. I think probably these days . . . It was different with *Blasted* . . . but I tend to amass material before I start.

[. . .]

Now *Cleansed* is another story altogether. No one ever believes this, but it's totally true: I was having a particular sort-of fit about all this naturalistic rubbish that was being produced and I decided I wanted to write a play that could never ever be turned into a film, that could never ever be shot for television, that could never be turned into a novel. The only thing that could ever be done with it was it could be staged. And believe it or not (*laughs*) that play is *Cleansed*. That play can only be staged. Now you may say: 'It can't be staged', but it can't be anything else either, that's fine, it can only be done in the theatre. Of course, I knew they were impossible stage directions, but I also genuinely believe you can do anything on stage, both in terms of, you know, causing offence but pragmatically you can do anything; there's absolutely nothing you can't represent one way or another. It may not be represented naturalistically – it's completely impossible to do *Cleansed* naturalistically because half the audience would die just from sheer grief if you did that.

[. . .]

Audience question   Who do you write for?

SK   Me. Fuck everyone else. (*Laughter.*) I've only ever written for myself. In fact, the truth is that I've only ever written in order to escape from hell. And it's never worked. But, at the other end of it, when you sit there and watch something and think: 'Well, that's the most perfect expression of the hell that I've felt', then maybe it was worth it. I've never written anything for anyone else. Apart from a little comedy play for my dad once. But that's very hidden.

AQ How did you expect audiences to react?

SK Oh dear. Like I say, with *Blasted*, I expected them to like it, naively enough. Since then, I've always expected them to hate it and it's never been as bad as I thought. But for me, expecting something from the audience only ever comes after it's written and I've been through rehearsals. You can't ever anticipate, I mean particularly with what happened with *Blasted*, you can never anticipate that – and if you do anticipate that sort of response you don't get it. I mean, I know a lot of people who've written things in order to get that kind of response and it doesn't work. But you can't second-guess audiences and you can't make them behave in certain ways. I mean, I'm sure everyone in the room knows . . . everyone in the room must have been in a relationship where you think: 'I'm going to make the other person do this', and it completely backfires. And that's one person that you know really well, so imagine trying to make five hundred people [you don't know] behave in a particular way – it's just not possible. So I suppose what I think about when I'm writing is how I want a particular moment or idea to affect me, and what the best way of eliciting that response from myself is. And if it can make me respond in that way, then the chances are there'll be at least one other person who'll respond in the same way. And even if they don't, then it's satisfied me, which was the initial intention anyway.

    [. . .]

When I was writing *Blasted*, there was some point at which I realised there was a connection with *King Lear*. And I thought, 'I'm writing about fatherhood. There's this scene where he goes mad; and there's this Dover scene with Cate when she unloads the gun – is she going to give him the gun or is she not?' And I thought the only thing that I don't have in this play is blindness, which is really odd. At the time, God knows why, I was reading Bill Buford's *Among the Thugs*, about football violence.[2] You've all read *Blasted*, but when people hear it's real they get even more horrified. It's absolutely appalling. There was an undercover policeman who I think was pretending to be a Manchester United supporter [*side one of tape ends*] . . . he then sucked out one of his eyes, bit it off – you see, you've all read the play and yet you're all reacting like this – bit it off, spat it out on the floor and threw this guy down and left him there. And I just couldn't fucking believe what I'd read; I couldn't believe that a human being could do this to another person, could actually do this, but they had. I put it in the play and everyone was shocked. Then in the rehearsal room I'd say, 'Well, actually where this comes from is . . .' and I'd tell them and they'd go, 'Urgh', and they'd read the play – what, do you think I make this stuff up? (*Laughter.*)

A similar thing is true of Robin in *Cleansed*. Robin is based on a young black man who was on Robben Island with Nelson Mandela. He was eighteen years old; he was put in Robben Island and told he would be there for forty-five years. [It] didn't mean anything to him, he was illiterate, didn't mean a thing. Nelson Mandela and some of the other prisoners taught him to read and write. He learnt to count, realised what forty-five years was and hung himself. When I tell people that . . . you know, I told the actor playing Robin that story; he was really upset and shocked. I said, 'But you've read the play. It's in there.' I really don't invent very much. I take a look around and . . . I mean, I hate the idea of drama as journalism and I would never say that I'm a journalist, but when it comes to the acts of violence in my plays, my imagination isn't that fucking sick, do you know what I mean? – I just read the newspapers, it's not like there's something wrong with me. And all you have to do is look at the world around you and there it is. And I agree with you, *Blasted* is pretty devastating. But the only reason it's any more devastating than reading a newspaper is that it's got all the boring bits cut out.

DR   *Blasted* seems extraordinarily raw [. . .] but there's no sense that you believe Ian is a monster.

SK   The thing is I don't. (*Laughter.*) I really like Ian; I think he's funny. I can see that other people think that Ian is a bastard. And I knew that they would. But I think he's extremely funny. And the reason I wrote that character was this terrible moral dilemma that was thrown up at me when a man I knew who was dying of lung cancer was terribly, terribly ill, who was extremely funny, started telling me the most appalling racist jokes I've ever heard in my life. And I was completely torn: a) because they were very funny, and very good jokes, and I'd not heard them before; b) because I wanted to tell him I thought he was awful and I was glad he was dying of lung cancer; and c) because he was dying of lung cancer, I thought, 'This poor man is going to be dead and he probably wouldn't be saying this if he wasn't sick.' And it set up all kinds of turmoil in me, but in the end, yes, I liked him. And no, I think when I wrote *Blasted* I just thought, 'Well, I'll just show these people as they are.' I don't really know what I think of them. Yes, of course I think he's a monster; I also think he's great. All I knew is that I wanted the soldier to be worse. And I knew that, having created Ian, it was going to be a real problem having someone come through that door who made Ian look like a pussycat. So that was very difficult – actually, writing the soldier was probably the most difficult thing I've ever done.

But no, I don't really know what I think of any of them. And yes, I think Cate's very fucking stupid [in the sense of naive], and, of course, what's she doing in a hotel room in the first place? Of course she's going to get raped! But yes, isn't it utterly tragic that this happens to her? And I did actually have nights during rehearsals for *Blasted* when I would go home and cry and say to myself, 'How could I create that beautiful woman in order for her to be so abused?' And I really did feel a bit sick and depraved. A part of that was to do with the fact that there was no sort-of overwhelming sense that in the end Cate came out on top. Had there been that, I'm sure I would have felt completely exonerated.

But I didn't; but then I don't think that in the end those people do come out on top.

[. . .]

AQ I've been haunted by the image in *Cleansed* of sticking a pole up someone's arse and it coming out of their shoulder. Is it true?

SK (*Laughter.*) Yes, it is true. Okay, where that comes from . . . prepare to feel very guilty about laughing. It's a form of crucifixion which Serbian soldiers used against Muslims in Bosnia. And they would do it to hundreds and hundreds of Muslims and hang them all up and leave them there and it would take about five days for them to die. It's possible and unfortunately it happens. And I tend to think actually that anything that has been imagined, there's someone somewhere who's done it. I had this thought about (*laughs, laughter*) no forget that, yes, I'm afraid it's true.

[. . .]

My plays, I hope, certainly exist within a theatrical tradition. Not many people would agree with that, and they are at a rather extreme end of theatrical tradition; but they are not about other plays, they are not about methods of representation; on the whole, they are about love. And about survival and about hope. And to me that's an extremely different thing. So when I go and see a production of *Blasted* in which all the characters are complete shits, you don't care about them, and in the second scene of *Blasted* in that production – in the space between the first and second scenes Cate's been raped during the night – the lights came up and she's lying there completely naked with her legs apart, covered in blood, mouthing off at Ian. And I thought this is so . . . oh God, I just wanted to die in despair. And I said to the director, 'You know, she *has* been raped in the night, do you think it's either believable, interesting, feasible, theatrically valid, that she's lying there completely naked in front of the man who's raped her? Do you not think that she might cover herself up, for example?' And evidently that's not to do with my own feelings about nudity on stage – I've been naked on stage myself and I've no problem with that – It's simply about what is the truth of any given moment. And if the truth of a moment is that it refers to another film and the way in which someone's head's been blown off in that film, for me that's completely fucking meaningless. And I'm just not interested in it. Which is why I've only ever seen one [Quentin] Tarantino film, I'm afraid. I'm talking with great authority here. I've only seen *Reservoir Dogs*. But I thought I've given quite enough of my life to seeing that stuff and I'm not giving another second. Never mind three hours or whatever *Pulp Fiction* was.

[. . .]

DR   What are you working on now?

SK   I'm writing a play called *4.48 Psychosis*. It's got similarities with *Crave*, but it's different. It's about a psychotic breakdown. And what happens to a person's mind when the barriers which distinguish between reality and different forms of imagination completely disappear. So that you no longer know the difference between your waking life and your dream life. And also, you no longer – which is very interesting in psychosis – you no longer know where you stop and the world starts. So, for example, if I was a psychotic, I would literally not know the difference between myself, this table and Dan. They would all somehow be part of a continuum. And various boundaries begin to collapse. Formally, I'm trying to collapse a few boundaries as well, to carry on with making the form and content one. That's proving extremely difficult, and I'm not going to tell anybody how I'm doing it, because if any of you got there first I'd be furious. Whatever it is that I began with *Crave*, is going one step further. And for me there's a very clear line from *Blasted* through *Phaedra's Love* to *Cleansed* to *Crave* and this one. Where it goes after that I'm not quite sure.

Anthony Neilson: In His Own Words

The following quotations from Anthony Neilson are extracts from a diverse number of key sources.

- *Neilson's memory of being aged eleven and seeing his mother acting in Donald Campbell's* The Widows of Clyth *in 1978:[1]*
  At the end of the first half, the character played by my mother was told that her husband had died. She let out a scream of pain that left me chilled. Obviously it was doubly relevant to me, because she was my mum.

  In my work, I think I'm always trying to re-create the emotional shadow of that moment. I've always thought to put personal connections into my stuff, my life and the lives of the actors involved – and not shy away from difficult emotional subjects, from grief and pain and death. It was in the Traverse that night, in the pitch of my mother's scream, that I suddenly realised what theatre was about.

- *About* Penetrator, *Neilson talking to James Christopher in January 1994:[2]*
  'It's actually based on a true story,' Neilson says as he curls a cigarette into his fist. 'A soldier who's gone AWOL turns up at the seedy flat of two old school friends with a terrifying tale of intimidation and abuse. The "penetrators" are a group of guys in the army who exist solely to sodomise people with various instruments. The play relates how Tadge (the AWOL soldier) finds out about them while examining the discrepancy between what he was like and the ultra macho environment which subsequently shaped him. Like Peter Kurten [in *Normal*], Tadge begins to equate relationships and feelings with brutality and violence. It all explodes into unpleasantness, you'll be surprised to hear. Needless to say, some critics were virulently disgusted [. . .] Like almost everything I've done there's a fairly large amount of ugliness in *Penetrator*. But there's also something tender in my plays and I hope people see that. In *Normal* a lot of people told me that they wanted to go on

stage and stop it. That's really exciting to me; it's one of the great strengths of theatre. Of course every performance of every play on every night is different but I think with *Penetrator* this is even more so. Some critics felt that the tone wasn't consistent because it lurches from comedy to threat to violence. But I like that because that's exactly what it's like being in a room with someone who's completely mad.'

- *About* Heredity, *Neilson talking to Al Senter in April 1995:*[3]
'I can no longer draw a distinction between the writing and the directing of a piece, and I am trying to explore the areas where the text ends and the lighting and the sound begins,' he explains. 'I've always liked the ephemerality of the theatre, and I enjoy being flexible and more interactive, adding sections to be improvised and leaving more space for the actors and the audience. But for much of the time I am just trying things out and, quite frankly, groping in the dark.'

- *Sarah Hemming interviewing Neilson in November 1995:*[4]
For many writers now, violence not only expresses anger, but is the expression of it. The young Scottish playwright Anthony Neilson caused controversy with his brutal plays *Normal* and *Penetrator*. *Normal*, a play about the Düsseldorf Ripper, performed at the Edinburgh Festival in 1991, remains etched on the memory because of a ghastly scene in which the murderer clubbed a woman to death. Neilson argues that this is violence used morally, rather than for effect – designed to expose gratuitous brutality. 'You're meant to feel appalled. I don't think that is offensive; I think it's offensive when you don't feel appalled by violence.'

Neilson feels that his anger and that of his peers – who have only known a Conservative government – has largely to do with a sense of impotence. Now, however, he detects a shift among young writers away from numb despair, and he regards *Blasted* as a significant move forward.

'I think *Blasted* spoke for a generation which has a dulled, numb feeling – not apathy, but a feeling that nothing you do will make any difference. It expressed the feeling that horror coming into your living room is the only way you can feel something and get yourself going. I think that in-yer-face theatre is coming back – and that is good.'

- *Kate Stratton interviewing Neilson in June 1997:*[5]
  'I've realised that there's no point in being too shocking,' he says. 'It simply diverts attention from the wider picture – the ideas behind a piece. The challenge in *The Censor* was to take stuff that people might be repelled by and show them why they are that way; to get people to see beyond the detail; to look at *how* they react to things. [. . .] It's partly about how stunted so much of our debate about sex has become,' explains Neilson, who claims to have dashed off the play in under two weeks. 'I'm with [film director] David Cronenberg on the issue of censorship – it's a non-argument – but when you are sitting with your grandparents watching a hideously steamy shagging scene you can be quite glad of it. I was trying to get away from the political debate to look at some of the more emotional reasons for censorship – the ways we censor ourselves to control the messier aspects of our lives and our futures.'

- *From Neilson's 'Foreword' to his plays,* The Wonderful World of Dissocia/Realism:[6]
  I will presume that you know about the 'in-yer-face' school of theatre, of which I was allegedly a proponent. I suppose it's better to be known for something than for nothing but I've never liked the term because it implies an attempt to repel an audience, which was never my aim. In fact, the use of morally contentious elements was always intended to do the very opposite. Given that one's genuine morality (as distinct from the morality that we choose for ourselves) tends to be instinctive rather than cerebral, engaging a receptive audience with such issues is a useful way of scrambling the intellectual responses that inhibit/protect us from full involvement with what we are watching. Engage the morality of an audience and they are driven into themselves. They become, in

some small way, participants rather than voyeurs. That's why I prefer the term 'experiential' theatre. If I make anything, let it be that.

• *From Neilson's 'Don't Be So Boring', a 2007 newspaper article:*[7]
I was part of a theatrical movement once. As with most movements, no one who was a part of it noticed anything moving at the time. I still wouldn't know if a journalist hadn't told me. 'In-yer-face', it was called, which offended the more famous of my fellow movementarians, but I was just glad someone had noticed I was alive. As far as I can tell, in-yer-face was all about being horrid and writing about shit and buggery. I thought I was writing love stories.

Fifteen years on, there doesn't seem to have been another movement, so I thought I'd try to start one. Unfortunately, despite being pretty sure the next movement will be absurdist in nature, I couldn't think of a snappy name for it so I gave up on that. Then I thought I'd write a provocative Dogme-style manifesto, but I only came up with four rules, and I've already broken two of them in my new show. Then I thought I'd write Ten Commandments for young writers but a) that's a little pompous, and b) there's only one commandment worth a damn, and it's this: THOU SHALT NOT BORE.

Boring an audience is the one true sin in theatre. We've been boring audiences for decades now, and they've responded by slowly withdrawing their patronage. I don't care that the recent production of *The Seagull* at the Royal Court was sold out. To 95 per cent of the population, the theatre (musicals aside for now) is an irrelevance. Of that 95 per cent, we have managed to lure in maybe 10 per cent at some point in their lives, and we've so swiftly and thoroughly bored them that they've never returned. They're not the ones who broke the contract. They paid their money and expected entertainment; we sent them back into the night feeling bored, bullied and baffled. So what are we doing wrong?

The most depressing response I encounter when I'm chatting someone up and I ask them if they ever go to the theatre is this: 'I should go but I don't.' That emphatic 'should' tells you all you need to know. Imagine it in other contexts: 'I should play *Grand Theft Auto*'; 'I should watch *Strictly Come Dancing*.' That 'should' tells you that people see theatregoing not as entertainment but as self-improvement, and the critical/academic establishment have to take some blame for that.

Many critics still believe theatre has a quasi-educational/political role; that a play posits an argument that the playwright then proves or disproves. It is in a critic's interest to propagate this idea because it makes criticism easier; one can agree or disagree with what they perceive to be the author's conclusion. It is not that a play cannot be quasi-educational, or even overtly political – just that debate should organically arise out of narrative. But this reductive notion persists and has infected playwriting root and branch.

I can't tell you how often I've asked an aspiring writer what they're working on, and they reply with something like: 'I'm writing a play about racism.' On further investigation, you find that this play has no story and they've been stuck on page 10 for the past year; yet they're still hell-bent on writing it. You can be fairly sure the play, should it ever be finished, will conclude that racism is a bad thing. The writer is not interested in exploring the traces of racism that may lie dormant within their psyche, nor in making the case for selective racism (just to be 'provocative'). This is the writer using the play to project their preferred image of themselves; the ego intruding on art; the kind of literary posing that is fed by the idea of debate-led theatre. And if you think that example sounds naive, substitute the word 'racism' with 'George Bush' or 'Iraq' or 'New Labour'. Sound familiar?

Newspapers, or news programmes, are the places for debates, not the theatre. The general public don't think: 'Should I go to the theatre Friday, or that sociopolitical theory class?' Further education is not the competition. The pub is the competition, the cinema, a night in with a curry and a DVD. We are entertainers. What we do is not as important to society as brain surgery, or even refuse collection. But when the brain surgeon and the refuse collector finish work, they come to us and it is our job to entertain them – not necessarily just to distract them, but to stimulate, to refresh, to engage them. That's our place in the scheme of things, and it's a responsibility we should take seriously. To let our egos intrude is like the brain surgeon writing 'Jake was Here' on your frontal lobe before he puts your scalp back.

The way to circumvent ego (and thus reduce the risk of boring) is to make story your god. Find a story that interests you and tell it. Don't ask yourself why a story interests you; we can no more choose this than who we fall in love with. You may not be what you think you are – not as kind, as liberal, as original as you ought to be – and yes, the story (if you are true to it) will find that out. But while your attention is taken up with its mechanics, some truth may seep out, and that is the lifeblood of good, exciting art.

Mark Ravenhill: 'A Tear in the Fabric'

On 5 May 2004, playwright Mark Ravenhill gave the Marjorie Francis Lecture at Goldsmiths College, University of London. The title was 'A Tear in the Fabric: the James Bulger Murder and New Theatre Writing in the Nineties', and it offers a compelling account of the playwright's gradual understanding of how his own work, and that of his peers, was affected by a brutal public tragedy.[1] The following extracts tell the story, which begins in 2002 with Ravenhill being asked by a young film producer to make a film adaptation of Mark Fyfe's Asher, *a novel which the playwright describes as 'Oedipus with sex and drugs'.[2] Ravenhill was intrigued:*

I asked if I could meet the writer. We fixed a date in a tapas bar in Camden [north London]. I reread the novel several times. I was anxious to be meeting a real writer. I've always thought of myself as someone who makes plays – not a writer as such. I never wrote teenage poetry, novels, short stories. I don't even write letters. I don't consider myself to be particularly literary – beyond enjoying reading a good book.

The writer turned up at the Bar Ganza – himself looking nervous, no doubt with his own worries about meeting a dramatist. Pleasantries were exchanged. Then I breathed deep and started to talk about the book.

The central character I said was very alluring, attractive.

'Yes,' the novelist said, 'lots of people said that.' But he didn't agree.

'No? [. . .] But he's full of life.'

'Maybe. But he's evil.'

Ravenhill: 'Evil? Really?'

I still come over with a liberal flush when I hear that word. For my mum and dad it's the other four-letter words that get them reaching for the off button – but for me it's that particular four-letter word that leaves me a little short of air. A carefully laid-out set of liberal platitudes start to topple once the 'E' word enters the conversation. Because I still can't really deny that it never ever exists but I'd like to think that – what? – 75 per cent, 90 per cent, 99 per cent, that we could call evil isn't evil – that it's society and all that jazz. But still I leave a little window open for the occasional event when, yes, evil might be the only cause. It's almost certainly a cowardly stance – like hedging your bets about whether there is a God or not. And now here was the novelist dragging me into the whole evil thing.

[. . .]

I decided to push him a little further.

Ravenhill: 'Was there one thing that got you started writing the book?'

'How do you mean?'

Ravenhill: 'Well normally with me I can have all sorts of very general and often rather grand ideas about what I'd like to write, or could write or – worst of all – should write. But there's normally one concrete thing – an image, a word, a moment – that actually gets me started.'

'I can't remember.'

Ravenhill: 'It's just that I've got a hunch that that key image or word or whatever would be a good way in for me to adapting your book.'

But Mark Fyfe can't remember. They continue to talk, to get to know each other better, until finally it comes:

'I suppose there was one thing that started me writing.'

Ravenhill: 'Yes?'

I was nervous in that moment, but also rather titillated. I assumed – maybe hoped – that he was going to tell me something very personal now. Childhood abuse, beating his wife, methadone and rehab. Once before, directing a strange fable-like play, the writer had told me in the final week of rehearsals that he wrote the play because he'd hit his girlfriend – just once – and the fear of what he'd done had driven him to write this rather oblique play. It was a bit late but it was useful – without telling the actors – to try to feed that private moment into the production of the play. And now I was expecting something similar.

'I suppose the thing that really started me writing the book was the murder of Jamie Bulger.'

It was the key I wanted. Not that concrete images or details of the murder of Jamie Bulger are in the novel. The narrative is entirely different. But it was an emotional starting point, a way in that was simpler than a debate about the values of the Enlightenment. The murder of Jamie Bulger.

And I could understand very easily why that particular event – beyond the bigger social or political events of the preceding decade, beyond the very personal events of one's own life – might push someone who'd never written a novel before or since to sit down and write. The murder of Jamie Bulger.

It instantly made sense to me of the discussion we'd had about evil and of the novel's deep, corrosive sense that the three hundred-odd years of the Enlightenment might be drawing to a close.

[. . .]

Ravenhill finds it difficult to remember details of the case, in which toddler Jamie Bulger was abducted and then killed by two ten-year-old boys, Robert Thompson and Jon Venables, in Bootle in February 1993. At the time, media images of CCTV footage of the boys taking the toddler from a shopping mall imprinted themselves on the national consciousness. But he does some research and then decides to forget about the murder. Until:

It is a week after meeting the novelist that I realise something. A penny drops. I made my first attempt at writing a play shortly after the murder of Jamie Bulger. And it was a very direct – too direct – attempt to write about the murder. In the play – a one-act play which I directed for a few performances at the pub theatre the Man in the Moon – a young girl snatches a child from a shopping centre and murders it. The mother of the murdered child is driven to looping over and over the events of the day to try to work out if she is in any way culpable for the murder of her child. It wasn't a particularly good play – it was a pretty terrible play – but it was a play. The first thing I sat down and wrote and finished and put on. It was the winter of 1993 that I took my first faltering step as a playwright. It was the time of the trial of Venables and Thompson.

And suddenly I see my own personal narrative very clearly, in a way that I never did before – not even as I was talking to the novelist and he was telling me that it was the James Bulger murder that made him write.

How could I have never spotted before that I was someone who had never written a play until the murder of James? And it was the Bulger murder that prompted me to write? And that I've been writing ever since the murder. This now seems textbook clear and yet it's never struck me in nearly ten years.

This fascinates me. The way we often fail to spot even the most obvious links in our own narratives until way after the event. And presumably there are plenty that we miss altogether – stuff that's obvious to anyone else piecing together our story. And now here I was almost ten years later spotting a very obvious link: before the murder of James Bulger I was someone who thought about writing, who liked the idea of writing, who always meant to get around to writing some-thing – but who never actually wrote. And it was feeling the need to write about the murder – not the actual murder event, but the child who takes a child, the mother who loses a child – that finally made me sit down and write. And since I was dissatisfied with that piece then I had to keep on writing – circling around a prey that I couldn't quite identify. A prey that wasn't quite the murder of James Bulger but more like the feeling inside me – and the people around me – that the murder engendered.

I wonder if I was alone? I doubt it. I wonder how many other people there were who started to write with that [CCTV] picture of the boy led away somewhere in their head?

This one terrible event somewhere in a shopping centre in Bootle suddenly making it necessary to write. I know there was me. I know there was the novelist. How many others?

How many of the young British playwrights of the nineties – the so-called in-yer-face playwrights – were driven, consciously or unconsciously, by that moment?

It would be disingenuous not to include here another part of my personal narrative. In June 1993, between the murder of Bulger and the trial of Venables and Thompson, my boyfriend [Tim] died of a whole host of infections and diseases related to AIDS. A lot of 1993 for me was visits to and from hospitals, to hospices, brief spells when he was back in his flat and then some new infection that would send him back into hospital. The dying are shuttled around pretty mercilessly within our healthcare system. 1993: I experienced a lot of anxiety, a lot of tears, a fair bit of boredom. And then death: but not really one big death – I guess in life but not in the movies there are lots of little deaths, wave after wave of them creeping up the shore, chipping away at the person you know, until finally the tide goes out and there's nothing there. Just a blank, flat expanse of sand. Desolation.

[. . .]

I think something fundamental happened in Britain the day James Bulger died. I'm sure everybody changed in their own way – but I think most of us changed.

[. . .]

I can see now, it was the murder of James Bulger – and I would guess the projection of my own grief for Tim into that murder – pushed me into writing. Somehow now I felt that the existing plays just weren't right, that they wouldn't *do* any more. Not so much that they weren't any good – there were plenty of older writers' work that I admired. But that something had shifted, that a tear in the fabric had happened when Venables and Thompson took hold of Bulger's hand. It wasn't that I suddenly felt that I could write better than a previous generation. It was that I wanted to, suddenly felt the need to, try to write differently, write within the fracture that happened to me – and I think to the society around me – in 1993. And I would guess – having learnt that none of my experiences in life are unique – that this must be something that previous generations of writers have experienced. There's a kind of continuum of great plays that you love, that you wish you'd written, that you know you can never write – and then something happens, you hear a tear – and suddenly it seems necessary to write new plays – and find out later how good or bad they are.

[. . .]

Ravenhill then discusses the other playwrights that emerged in the 1990s, such as Sarah Kane, Joe Penhall, Patrick Marber and Martin McDonagh, and wonders what provoked them to write. Likewise, he mentions the influence of Martin Crimp and David Mamet, and of Brad Fraser and the blank generation of American novelists.

Piecing together the narrative now I see how much my first three plays were influenced by the murder of James Bulger. I could feel something of it at the time I was writing them – knew I was picking and picking away at the same scab, not knowing what it was but worried that I was repeating myself.

In *Shopping and Fucking* fourteen-year-old Gary finds himself with the twentysomethings Mark, Robbie and Lulu, and a game – part storytelling, part sexual, part financial – plays itself out and out until Gary is murdered by anal penetration with a knife.

In *Faust is Dead* the teenager Donnie comes to a motel room and cuts and cuts himself until he dies while an older teenager Pete and the French philosopher Alain video him.

In *Handbag* the young junkie Phil and the low-paid nanny Lorraine snatch a baby from the home of Lorraine's middle-class lesbian employers. Unable to care for the baby, and not really understanding what he is doing, Phil burns the baby with cigarettes until it stops breathing.

Lulu in *Shopping and Fucking* watches a stabbing of a shopkeeper one night – only later to discover a man masturbating to the security

219

camera video of the attack. In *Handbag* Phil snatches a handbag from a woman in a shopping centre beneath the watching eyes of the cameras and later Phil and Lorraine have to arrange the kidnapping of the baby beneath the eyes of cameras that Mauretta and Suzanne have now installed inside their home to keep an eye on their nanny.

Nobody in these plays is fully adult. They are all needy, greedy, wounded, only fleetingly able to connect with the world around them. Consumerism, late capitalism – whatever we call it – has created an environment of the infant 'me', where it is difficult to grow into the adult 'us'.

Gary in *Shopping*, Donny in *Faust*, the baby in *Handbag*. They are the youngest characters in each of these plays. And each of them is led away by a pair – or in the case of *Shopping* a trio – of these adult-children. And each one of the characters dies because of that.

Shops, videos, children killed by children. It wasn't a project I set out to write. But it became one.

[. . .]

Ravenhill then comments on the absent or abusive father figures in his plays, and then explains the shift in his later plays away from the 'set of obsessions' that characterise the earlier work.

Again with the benefit of hindsight, this maybe explains why my next play, *Some Explicit Polaroids* in 1999, was the hardest play of all to write. Blocked and blocked for months with rehearsals and then opening night looming. The other plays had come pretty easy – they were being drawn somehow from the same source. This one had to come from somewhere again. Five years on and I didn't feel the need to pick any more at the image of the boy on the video screen being led away.

Not that *Polaroids* is a clean break with what went before. Tim, Victor and Nadia, the adult-children of *Polaroids*, are the mirror images of Mark, Robbie and Lulu in *Shopping*. And *Polaroids* has Jonathan, the bad capitalism father who is the upmarket twin of Brian in *Shopping*. But this cast are joined by two new characters – Nick and Helen – genuinely adult people who can remember the political commitment of a lost age. And I think most importantly there's no lost child, no little boy destroyed as Gary and Donny and the baby are. Instead, Tim dies of AIDS. The experience that had been personal to me, and had somehow found itself filtered through the feelings of the Bulger case, now stands simply there without the filter. Tim dies of AIDS. My writing has broken free of a pattern.

And in *Mother Clap's Molly House* – set in the gay subculture of early eighteenth-century London – the two apprentice boys Martin and Thomas, watched over by the matriarch Mother Clap, are first married and then go through a mock birth inside the molly house. Martin. Thomas. The baby. I guess the imprint of Venables, Thompson and Bulger – the video pictures – are still there. But it's a game. The baby's a doll. And Martin looks after it. And at the end of the play, leaving for the country, Mother Clap decides to leave the baby behind, the game finished.

Very few of us write with a game-plan. We become obsessed with something – an image, a moment. We don't know why. We're not quite sure where they come from. But all we know is that it won't go away. And so we have to write – not really quite sure whether it's any good, not quite sure what it is we're saying, but just compelled to write. The experience of writing my plays has felt nothing like the narrative that I've just put together for you. That narrative only came later – started to fall into place after that conversation with the author of *Asher* two years ago. It's only really come into focus putting together this speech for you. Should a writer do this? Go back? Try to make sense? Make conscious what was unconscious? Isn't this killing the golden goose? Maybe it is. But it's something I can't help doing. Going back. Spotting a narrative where there only seemed muddle at the time.

Ravenhill concludes by acknowledging that there might be something real about evil, and then reads a passage from The Cut, *a play he was working on at the time. It's about a student who visits his imprisoned father, once part of an unspecified 'old regime' and responsible for systematic torture – by now, due to global events, a familiar kind of daily evil. So although in the end Ravenhill didn't write a film version of* Asher, *he has continued to write more plays.*

AFTERWORD

> – It's theatre – that's right – for a world in which theatre itself
> has died. Instead of the outmoded conventions of dialogue and
> so-called characters lumbering towards the embarrassing
> dénouements of the *theatre*, Anne is offering us a pure dialogue
> of objects.
>
> – Martin Crimp, *Attempts on Her Life*, 1997

The new young playwrights who emerged in the 1990s found that, by
1995, there was a real buzz about British theatre. The furore caused
by Sarah Kane's *Blasted* in January of that year slowly dissipated over
the following years, turning into a widespread critical appreciation of
a whole host of talented new playwrights. Inevitably this sense of
cultural excitement couldn't last, and indeed it didn't last. By the new
millennium, the moment of in-yer-face theatre was past and a new
theatre landscape began to open up. A key event was Kane's suicide on
20 February 1999. This meant that reception of new stagings of her
work in the 2000s was often coloured by the knowledge of her death.
And, although her plays were not put on in the UK as often as they
were, for example, in Germany and Continental Europe, some significant productions did gradually begin to alter public perception of her
talent.

In the immediate aftermath of Kane's death, however, the posthu-
mous staging of *4.48 Psychosis* provoked predictable reactions. Because
the play is concerned with psychotic breakdown, and suicidal
thoughts, many critics and journalists assumed that it was autobiographical, an expression of her personal angst. It was difficult to view
the play in a more detached way, as an experiment in theatrical form
which mirrored not so much Kane's personal depression as the medical
condition of psychosis, in which the boundaries between the subjective and objective worlds are broken down. At the same time, there is a

distinctly autobiographical flavour to the elegiac ending of the play, with its injunction to 'watch me vanish' and request to 'please open the curtains'.[1] Following this production, Ian Rickson, artistic director of the Royal Court, led his theatre in celebrating Kane's achievements by programming a season of her work in March–April 2001, a unique tribute to such a young writer. The season included readings of *Phaedra's Love* and *Cleansed*, plus the return of previous productions of *Crave* and *4.48 Psychosis*. But the most important gesture was to stage *Blasted* on the main stage, directed once again by James Macdonald, her most loyal and most modernistic interpreter. What had seemed, in its original low-budget studio-theatre production, to be a slice of dirty realism gone wrong, now came across as an ambitious state-of-Europe play, thrillingly alive not only as an account of personal politics, but also as an ageless vision of human survival in troubled times.

But the Royal Court was not the sole advocate of Kane's work. Other theatres contributed, including the Glasgow Citizens (*Blasted* directed by Kenny Miller in 2002) and Bristol Old Vic (*Phaedra's Love* directed by Anne Tipton in 2005, transferring to the Barbican as part of the *Young Genius* season). In London, Matt Peavor directed *Crave* in a production full of movement at BAC in 2004, while Graeae, the company that works with disabled actors, toured a fascinating version of *Blasted* in 2006–7, with a cast whose physical disabilities emphasised the bodily fragility which is such a strong undercurrent in the play. A visit to London's Barbican in November 2006 from the Berlin Schaubühne am Lehniner Platz theatre with a large-scale production of *Zerbombt* (*Blasted*), under the direction of wunderkind Thomas Ostermeier, and starring the late Ulrich Mühe as Ian, also showed how, despite changing political circumstances, the play remained relevant: here, the onstage television showed news from Iraq. Then in 2008 a young company, 19;29, performed a site-specific version of *Blasted* in a suite of the Queen's Hotel in Leeds. One critic wrote, 'Few contemporary plays have been prodded, poked and reassessed as much as Sarah Kane's play, which has gone from notoriety to respectability in slightly more than a decade.'[2] Sean Holmes directed a spare but intense *Cleansed* in 2005 for the Oxford Stage Company at the Arcola Theatre and *Blasted* in 2010 at the Lyric Hammersmith, in a determinedly naturalistic and meticulous version. The result of these revivals has been a much more complex picture of the playwright's work, and an open invitation to new interpretations. *Cleansed*, for example, can be staged as a modernistic extravaganza, with video projections and a mirrored ceiling, as James Macdonald did in 1998, or as a bare-stage example of poor theatre, in Holmes's hands.

The effect of this exploration of her work meant that Kane – who had once seemed to be a quintessential in-yer-face playwright of the mid-1990s – was gradually beginning to look less like a typical British young writer, and more like an anomaly. She can now clearly be seen as the exception to the rule that British playwrights are wedded to naturalism and social realism, and her work is best appreciated as part of an ongoing conversation between two distinct traditions: English naturalism and Continental modernism. In this context, not only is every play distinct in its form, but each also carries forward this conversation between naturalism and modernism. So *Blasted*, with its explosion midway through, uses this rupture of theatre form to illustrate the shock of war, and at the same time it welds a naturalistic first half with a symbolist, expressionistic or absurdist second half. *Phaedra's Love* inverts the classical Greek convention of not showing violence on stage and challenges directors to obey, and audiences to observe, some wryly amusing stage directions, including the final '*A vulture descends and begins to eat [Hippolytus's] body*'.[3] *Cleansed* continues the project of abandoning naturalism by radically stripping down the plot to show only the most necessary elements, with the result that the play feels like a contemporary version of Büchner's *Woyzeck* (which Kane directed at the Gate in 1997). With *Crave*, there is an abandonment of stage directions, character names and plot (all so important to naturalism) and a much more Continental sense of a play being just the voices inside a person's head. Finally, Kane parts company definitively with most English traditions in *4.48 Psychosis* (although many of the exchanges in the play remain in the form of everyday dialogues, as distinct from the *Sprachflächen* or 'language surfaces' so characteristic of postdramatic theatre).[4] But the point is that, because of her ceaseless desire to experiment in form and interrogate British theatre traditions, Kane fits comfortably into the modernist avant-garde of Bond, Barker, Churchill and Crimp. As time passes, her work becomes increasingly less similar to that of her 1990s contemporaries.

Likewise, Kane's influence has changed over the decade or so since her death. Soon after 1999, as books and articles about her work began to proliferate, she quickly became part of the canon of post-war British playwriting. Numerous playwrights, especially her contemporaries, testified to having been inspired by her exemplary rigour and by her rawness and directness of expression. Her later plays, especially *Crave* and *4.48 Psychosis*, opened up exciting possibilities by virtue of their innovative attitude to theatre form. But the legacy of Kane could be more ambiguous. As Graham Saunders remarks, the widespread canonisation or lionisation of the playwright – especially by young students – 'contains its own inherent dangers', namely an uncritical attitude to all aspects of her work.[5] Such an unquestioning approach does her work no favours – you can only take a playwright seriously if your approach is nuanced. Likewise, some playwrights responded to the legacy of Kane's writing not by copying it, but by reacting against it. In November 2010, at a public platform during the run of Holmes's revival of *Blasted* at the Lyric Hammersmith, playwright Laura Wade said that when she first heard about the play it was 'very distant from what I was doing'.[6] In a similar vein, playwright Simon Stephens, who was tutor of the Royal Court Young Writers group 2001–5, has commented that many of newly emerging playwrights of the 2000s consciously wrote against the influence of Kane.[7]

Philip Ridley and Anthony Neilson, the two outsiders of the London theatre scene, both went on to develop their careers in the first decade or so of the new millennium. Ridley continued his prolific output of novels, films and works for young people. But he also developed his interest in playwriting. *Vincent River*, an intense two-hander about the mother of a thirtysomething victim of gay bashing and his schoolboy lover, opened at the Hampstead Theatre in 2000, directed by Matthew Lloyd, one his most sympathetic directors. The play is more intensely naturalistic than his 1990s work, but with its acting out of the narratives about the past by its two characters it exemplifies

Ridley's fascination with the uses of storytelling. He then staged, at various venues and with the support of Paines Plough and the Soho Theatre, a trilogy of plays on the subject of brotherly love. These were *Mercury Fur* (2005), *Leaves of Glass* (2007) and *Piranha Heights* (2008). Likewise, his play *Moonfleece* (2004) also revisited the relationship of two brothers. But although his interest in the dynamics between two brothers draws sustenance from his own relationship with his brother, his playwriting style developed considerably in the 2000s. In general, in *Leaves of Glass* and *Piranha Heights* the gothic and science-fiction elements of his writing have been muffled. There are mentions of terrible deaths, UFOs and nuclear apocalypse, of angels, time machines, and being born in the belly of a whale, of a radioactive donkey and even of a snake roasted on an electric heater, but these remain in the background.

But in one play in mid-decade Ridley triumphantly resuscitated a sci-fi world and showed how his ability to provoke remained undiminished – *Mercury Fur* is a dystopic story about a future in which the government is controlling the population by feeding them hallucinogenic butterflies, bombing cities, and where rich men buy perverted sex acts from impoverished child-gangs. Although the action concerns the touching relationship between the brothers Elliot and Darren, there are plenty of narratives of horrific actions (some as shocking as those of *Blasted*) and the climatic scene of child abuse feels almost unbearable, even though it takes place offstage. The shock reactions that greeted *Mercury Fur* were reminiscent of the uproar over *Blasted*, and just as short-lived. Ridley's publisher, Faber, refused to publish the playtext because of its explicit language, and some critics were vitriolic in their condemnation of the playwright. One claimed that 'he is actually turned on by his own sick fantasies', another said that many scenes were 'shallow, meretricious, self-regarding and – in some cases – downright vile', while yet another condemned the play as full of 'reactionary despair'.[8] In fact, the play actually represents a thrillingly imagined and coherent world where the mind-corroding effects of the butterflies allude to the loss of historical memory in contemporary culture and where the ability of the rich to buy forbidden pleasures is clearly a critique of social inequality. Although the language that the characters speak is peppered with expletives, these are often delightfully baroque, and the narratives of ghastly atrocity are a clear condemnation of state terrorism and war-mongering, as well as acting as a visionary warning of social collapse. Not only is the play an excitingly imaginative piece but it is also rigorously moral at the same time. It demonstrates the power of the in-yer-face sensibility, and shows how effective experiential theatre can be (it's a 120-minute piece that unfolds in real time).

Mercury Fur, along with *Leaves of Glass* and *Piranha Heights*, suggests the possibility of new sexual and emotional relationships, and explores the emotionally devastating effects of an absent father. Although different in tone to *Mercury Fur*, the other two plays show how the different memories of two siblings explode in the present. Both illustrate how narratives can be used to twist meaning and both stage a complex web of relationships, which now include wives, mothers and lovers. As well as his adult plays, Ridley also created the *Storyteller Sequence* for the National Theatre's *Connections* festival of youth theatre: *Sparkleshark* (1997), *Fairytaleheart* (1998), *Brokenville* (2003), *Moonfleece* (2004) and *Karamazoo* (2004). These plays all feature the acting out of narratives, and range in form from a monologue (*Karamazoo*) to a large-cast play (*Moonfleece*). The latter was revived in 2010, and features Ridley's characteristic themes – identity, memory, storytelling, racism and homophobia. In 2011, his new play, *Tender Napalm* (2011) marked a departure, being a two-hander about a love affair and the death of a child presented in a completely fractured form. At the same time, during the 2000s, numerous revivals of Ridley's plays – on the fringe, Off-West End and West End – have led to a much wider appreciation of his particular gifts. There can be few playwrights who deserved this as much as he does.

Similarly, Neilson continued to write and direct experiential drama, such as the shocking *Stitching* (2002), which portrayed the psychological hell of one young couple, whose child is killed in an accident, by means of a fragmented theatre form and taboo-breaking content (the woman finally sews up her vagina, and the man claims he had his first orgasm while looking a pictures of naked women waiting to go to the gas chambers at Auschwitz). On stage, there was an unforgettable scene when the actors rolled around the floor in the grip of sexual passion while the soundtrack played Iggy Pop's 'I Wanna Be Your Dog'. This play is recognisably one of those where Neilson uses the form of experiential theatre to stage a battle between inner and outer realities, in which inner realities are privileged. But, in the 2000s, there were also signs of this playwright taking a new direction, a turn towards more surrealistic, unrealistic or absurdist ways of staging subjective reality. As Neilson himself wrote, in 2007, he was 'groping in the dark for new forms, better forms' and he even suggested that 'the next movement in British theatre would be (for want of a better word) absurdist in nature', citing Churchill, Crimp and David Greig as playwrights with a similar interest 'in this style'.[9] As early as 2002, his *Edward Gant's Amazing Feats of Loneliness!* took the form of a Victorian entertainment, a freak show in which stories are told, gross acts are represented and Gant faces down a mutiny by one of his actors. If *The Lying Kind* (Royal Court, 2002), a serious farce that showed the disastrous effects of the attempts by two policemen to be kind to a woman whose daughter had apparently been killed, received a critical pasting, Neilson bounced back with two superb plays, *The Wonderful World of Dissocia* (2004) and *Realism* (2006). Whether you call this style absurdist or surreal matters less than appreciating how well the form of these plays fitted their subject matter. They all show his characteristic interest in the subjective, sometimes extreme, states of mind.

In keeping with the increased interest in devised and site-specific theatre in the 2000s, Neilson then found himself, in the words of David Lane, 'expanding the role of the writer away from just a provider of text and into that of a hands-on theatre-maker'.[10] In 2007, the RSC allowed Neilson access to a large company of actors, who devised and workshopped *God in Ruins*. The resulting play took a hammer to that seasonal classic, Dickens's *A Christmas Carol*. Starting with a dramatic reversal of the original story, in which Scrooge appears as a generous old codger and Bob Cratchit as an embittered employee, Neilson's retelling of the story is a wonderfully freewheeling version that jumps from real life to dream to digital Second Life. Crossing between reality, memory, nightmare, with its share of ghosts and fantasies, it also demonstrated a serious engagement with the way in which new media has affected our sense of storytelling. And it was fun too. His next play, the chilling *Relocated* (2008), was another experiment in form, which centred on a woman dreamily remembering her guilty involvement with a child killer. This evoked deep cultural memories about murderous men (Ian Huntley) and men who keep girls secretly locked up in order to abuse them (Joseph Fritzl).[11] After this experiment in darkness, Neilson returned, with the humorous *Get Santa!* (Royal Court, 2010), to one of his favourite terrains, the season of Christmas. Previously, he'd set his plays *Year of the Family* (1994), *Dirty Laundry* (1994) and *The Night Before Christmas* (1995) as well as *The Lying Kind* and *God in Ruins* during this public holiday. This time, fart jokes alternate with magical enchantment, and warm desires heat up the chilly depths of young depression. With its psychological insights and onstage talking teddy, *Get Santa!* is both a critique of Christmas clichés and a celebration of the soothing power of song and laughter. The agony of the separation of a daughter from her father is overcome by the wild wanderings of a vivid imagination.

In 2000, photographer Lisa Fleming took some portraits of writers at the Royal Court, focusing on their hands instead of their faces. Neilson's photograph shows a hand crushing a raw egg, which drips through his fingers. When it came to Ravenhill's turn, he emptied his pockets and the picture shows him offering up a petty cash voucher and some medication. It's a characteristically wry image for a writer whose career developed successfully in the 2000s. With his arrival at the National, where *Mother Clap's Molly House* was directed by the flagship's newly appointed artistic director Nicholas Hytner, he soon became an associate of the theatre and an outspoken advocate of new writing, penning provocative journalistic pieces as well as generously helping younger writers. On one occasion in May 2004, when he shared a public platform at the Theatre Museum with playwright Richard Bean, the latter reminded him that he'd been the consultant director on Bean's first work, the libretto for Stephen McNeff's *Paradise of Fools* at the Unicorn.[12] For the National's *Connections* festival of youth theatre, Ravenhill wrote *Totally Over You* (2003) and *Citizenship* (2005), two plays which engage well with teenage

concerns, painting vivid pictures of celebrity culture and sexual inse-
curity. *Citizenship* was especially successful and was soon revived with
a professional cast. At the same time, he developed his media profile,
writing cultural commentaries for the *Guardian* and appearing on
countless platforms, radio and television programmes. Very soon, it
was clear that he was – along with Kane – 'the most well-known and
controversial of the new generation of young writers in British
theatre'.[13]

Mother Clap's Molly House at first seemed to be the last of
Ravenhill's adult plays to have an overtly queer theme. By the middle
of the decade, he was busy expanding his output by penning short
plays, pantomimes and adaptations. He wrote three shorts: *North
Greenwich* (2000), *Moscow* (2004) and *Education* (2004), translated
Luis Enrique Gutiérrez Ortiz Monasterio's *The Girls of the 3.5 Floppies*
in 2004, and then made his acting debut in his own *Product* (2005), a
satirical monologue about how Hollywood movies create images of an
alien Other, in this case 'a tall dusky fellow' who is an Islamist
extremist.[14] He then worked with Frantic Assembly on *pool (no water)*
in 2006, where the text, as in Crimp's *Attempts on Her Life* and Kane's
4.48 Psychosis, has no character names. The play told the story of an
artist who suffers a terrible accident, and showed how the desire for
celebrity seduces her friends into exploiting her misfortunes. Frantic's
Scott Graham and Steven Hoggett directed with exquisite attention to
movement and short but thrilling dance sequences. As far as single
plays are concerned, Ravenhill's most impressive was *The Cut* (2006),
whose Donmar production was directed by Michael Grandage, the
venue's artistic director, and whose cast included Sir Ian McKellen.
This was about a torturer and his fate after regime change puts him
out of work. Written with a profoundly imaginative understanding of
the ambiguous relationship between the master and servant, it was
also a play that didn't take itself too seriously, as when the sadist
comments, 'I'm a piece of shit. I'm a speck of shit on a lump of shit on
a piece of shit. I'm nothing.'[15] The contrast between humour and seriousness is typical of Ravenhill at his best.

In December 2006, his version of *Dick Whittington and His Cat*
played at the Barbican, a pantomime which he says was indirectly

inspired by his own *Mother Clap's Molly House*: 'When I looked back over it, I realised that the play – with its songs, cross-dressing and spectacle – did have a great deal in common with the pantomimes I had loved as a child.'[16] Gradually, however, his work became more and more influenced by that of Crimp, especially his amazingly ambitious epic play cycle, *Shoot/Get Treasure/Repeat* (Paines Plough, 2008). Ravenhill calls this an exploration 'of our contemporary urge to bring our own values and definitions of freedom and democracy to the whole planet', and the cycle comprises sixteen twenty-minute plays. [17] His next play, on the subject of Germany, was the seventy-minute *Over There* (Royal Court, 2009). And he ended the first decade of the new millennium with a flurry of activity, returning to a gay theme by collaborating with seventy-year-old drag icon Bette Bourne on the biographical *A Life in Three Acts*, which Ravenhill co-scripted, directed and co-performed with Bourne in Edinburgh, London and on a world tour. Next, his adaptation of Terry Pratchett's novel *Nation* at the National Theatre, directed by Melly Still, opened to mixed reviews in 2009. In 2010, he worked on *Ten Plagues*, a musical with composer Conor Mitchell for singer Marc Almond, part of Rough Cuts experimental mini-season at the Royal Court, and he directed a live broadcast of his forty-minute television drama *Ghost Story* for the Sky Arts channel on 16 June 2010.

Contemporary history is notoriously tricky. In Alan Bennett's award-winning play *The History Boys* (2004), the history teacher Irwin argues that his pupils should step back from the present: 'Distance yourselves. Our perspective on the past alters. Looking back, immediately in front of us is dead ground. We don't see it and because we don't see it this means that there is no period so remote as the recent past and one of the historian's jobs is to anticipate what our perspective of that period will be.'[18] If *In-Yer-Face Theatre* tried to 'anticipate' a perspective on the 1990s in 2000, when it was written, today it is essential to alter that perspective by looking at the past through a different optic. In conclusion, here are five ways of applying a different focus on the 1990s.

1) *Art schools not theatres*. Most narratives of new writing tend to

foreground theatres, but what if you look elsewhere, at different cultural institutions? In the 1980s and 1990s, in a broader cultural perspective, perhaps art schools are the institutions where the action begins. So, for example, at Goldsmiths College, you have the emergence of artists such as Damien Hirst, with his 1988 exhibition *Freeze*. Clearly the Young British Artists were the in-yer-face provocateurs of the art scene and their 1997 *Sensation* exhibition was an immensely influential example of that 1990s sensibility. But, for theatre history, the most important art student of the 1980s was, of course, Ridley. He went to St Martin's and his unusually original debut, *The Pitchfork Disney* in 1991, is the place where all narrative histories of new writing in the 1990s should begin. Certainly, his career of provocation anticipates that of Kane, and was reasonably well publicised: in April 1994, one critic attacked his *Ghost from a Perfect Place* for its 'degrading and quasi-pornographic' violence, while the play's director and the theatre's chief defended him robustly.[19]

2) *Euro-modernism not in-yer-face.* In the mid- to late 1990s, a whole gang of in-yer-face playwrights emerged: they were young, and their work was raw and explicit, both provocative and controversial. From a distance, however, these plays now look less original than they seemed at the time – indeed, you might say that they have merely refreshed the traditions of British naturalism and dirty realism. By contrast, the real avant-garde was composed of those playwrights who were deliberately unnaturalistic, constantly questioning theatre form, and innovating in this area. So, in the broader cultural perspective, Kane's work represents the incursion of a kind of Continental modernism into the normally placid world of British naturalism. Her true contemporaries are thus older playwrights such as Churchill, Barker and Crimp, and newer talents such as Greig and Ravenhill, as well as David Harrower, Phyllis Nagy or new arrivals such as debbie tucker green and and Dennis Kelly. In the long run, in-yer-face theatre reinforced elements of the British tradition; the innovators were those writers who drank most deeply of Continental modernistic influences.

3) *Older and darker, not younger.* Most accounts of new writing in the 1990s stress the cult of youth, and the contribution of white

playwrights. In many reviews, the age of the new playwrights is given and their precocity is stressed. And this is typical of a wider culture in which youth is valued more than age, but in reality the most influential playwrights of the 1990s were older hands: Harold Pinter, Edward Bond, Churchill, Steven Berkoff and Crimp. Doug Lucie and Terry Johnson produced better work than most of the highly hyped Royal Court brat-pack. Crimp's 1993 play *The Treatment* anticipated and influenced the work of the in-yer-face generation. In the following decade, two of the most important playwrights were Richard Bean and Simon Stephens, who both came to playwriting comparatively late in life. By the same token, during the 1990s black and Asian companies such as Talawa, Tara and Tamasha did good work in developing writers, and thus prepared the ground for the explosion of black and Asian plays in the 2000s: beneficiaries included Roy Williams and Tanika Gupta. The huge success of Ayub Khan Din's *East is East* is a potent reminder of this strand in contemporary theatre.

4) *Scotland not England.* The story of new writing in the 1990s is frequently told as a metropolitan tale. You can plot it all on a tube map: there's Sloane Square, there's Shepherd's Bush, there's Swiss Cottage, and there's Waterloo and Oxford Circus. Okay, let's take a trip to Stratford, or Kilburn, or Highbury and Islington; oh, don't forget to pop down to Hammersmith or Earl's Court. But you could just as easily upend this cultural perspective and tell it from the point of view of Edinburgh. From the north, looking south, the key figure is Ian Brown at the Traverse Theatre: he seeks out and finds new writers from Canada and the USA, namely Brad Fraser and Tracy Letts in the late 1980s. He supports Neilson, who pioneers experiential theatre. But the Scottish influence runs deeper still. *Trainspotting* is an Edinburgh story. Kane was crucially influenced by Jeremy Weller, whose work she saw in Edinburgh. The new writing boom of the 1990s began in Scotland, and continued to develop there: just think of Greig and Harrower. As far as London is concerned, the revival of new writing was due to a Scottish invasion.

5) Finally, the last example is not about writers or playwrights, but concerns the effects of *an unpredictable real-life tragedy*: the murder of toddler Jamie Bulger. In any account of 1990s culture, including

theatre culture, this is a key event. When in November 1993 the judge in the trial of the perpetrators explained the murder by speculating that the boys had been exposed to a violent video, *Child's Play 3*, this created a media storm which is the cultural context for British arts in the crucial time of the mid-1990s. The Bulger murder resulted in calls for the censorship of films, television and art works, and this lasted long enough to be the immediate background to the media uproar over *Blasted*. It was part of the same phenomenon. On a different level, Ravenhill has written eloquently about how the Bulger murder affected his own sensibility and imagination. So it's possible to conclude that without this killing, there might have been no fuss about *Blasted* and maybe no *Shopping and Fucking*. Without this unpredictable event, the theatre history of the 1990s might have been very different. The exceptional and the odd often have more influence than the usual accounts given in standard histories.

NOTES

Introduction: Living in the 1990s

1. Jonathan Coe, *The Rotters' Club* (London: Viking, 2001), p. 4.
2. 'Terms of the 90s', 'Slang of the Nineties', www.inthe90s.com/generated/terms.shtml.
   David Rowan, *A Glossary for the Nineties* (London: Prion Books, 1998). Andrew Marr,
   A History of Modern Britain (London: Pan, 2008). Ken Roberts, *Class in Modern
   Britain* (Basingstoke: Palgrave Macmillan, 2001). Arthur Marwick, *British Society
   Since 1945* (London: Penguin, 2003). A. N. Wilson, *Our Times: The Age of Elizabeth*
   (London: Arrow, 2009). 'Great Britain – Family Roles: Men's Work, Women's Work',
   http://family.jrank.org/pages/738/Great-Britain-Family-Roles-Men-s-Work-Women-
   s-Work.html. Trends in UK Statistics since 1900, p. 22; Communities and Local
   Government website, Housing: Simple Averages, Table 504, www.communities.gov.
   uk/housing/housingresearch/housingstatistics/housingstatisticsby/housingmarket/
   livetables/housepricestables/simpleaveragestables/. Office of National Statistics; The
   Nature of Family Change in Great Britain, http://family.jrank.org/pages/737/Great-
   Britain-Nature-Family-Change-in-Great-Britain.html. A Century of Change: Trends
   in UK Statistics since 1900, House of Commons Research paper 99/111 (December
   1999), http://docs.google.com/viewer?a=v&q=cache:c0VLygbgsVIJ:www.parliament.
   uk/commons/lib/research/rp99/rp99–111.pdf+britain%2B1990s%2Bstatistics&hl=e
   n&gl=uk&pid=bl&srcid=ADGEESiSCYlZhKwtx7poWU7dse27Jvb16C-U3cNKCq
   mQSKWolMS84zUQJJbeVuHyQL9oMjYnR3rUyZgjBsDQlwNp_dT68ivB47RftW
   UqF4HJevnLXj2VpWtSBI-gJZ7bKBl_fyBaLIp3&sig=AHIEtbSGAoammyevuO
   uLpR-ENn4H1lbxCA. 'World City: 1950s – Today', permanent exhibition, Museum
   of London, Barbican, London.
3. Marwick, *British Society Since 1945*.
4. Jane Stokes and Anna Reading (eds), *The Media in Britain: Current Debates and
   Developments* (London: Macmillan, 1999). Hewison, *Culture and Consensus: England,
   Art and Politics Since 1940*, rev. edn (London: Methuen, 1997).
5. John Harris, *Britpop: Cool Britannia and the Spectacular Demise of English Rock*
   (Cambridge, MA: Da Capa, 2004). Hewison, *Culture and Consensus*. Elizabeth Young
   and Graham Caveney, *Shopping in Space: Essays on American 'Blank Generation' Fiction*
   (London: Serpent's Tail, 1992). Rachelle Thackray, 'The 50 Best Selling Books of the
   1990s', *Independent*, 26 September 1998. 'Historical & Cultural Sources for
   20th-Century Fashion', V&A website, www.vam.ac.uk/collections/fashion/features/
   sources_20th_century/index.html.

6. Marr, *A History of Modern Britain*. Marwick, *British Society Since 1945*.
7. Michael Howard and William Roger Louis, *The Oxford History of the Twentieth Century* (Oxford: Oxford University Press, 1998).

1 Theatre in the 1990s

1. Mark Ravenhill, *Plays One: Shopping and Fucking; Faust is Dead; Handbag; Some Explicit Polaroids* (London: Methuen Drama, 2001), p. 138.
2. James Naughtie, 'Bookclub: Douglas Coupland', BBC Radio 4, 7 March 2010.
3. Michael Billington, *One Night Stands: A Critic's View of Modern British Theatre* (London: Nick Hern, 1993), p. 328.
4. Robert Hewison, *Culture and Consensus: England, Art and Politics Since 1940* (London: Methuen, 1997), p. 262.
5. Ibid., p. 257.
6. Ibid., p. 258.
7. Dominic Shellard, *British Theatre Since the War* (New Haven, CT: Yale University Press, 1999), p. 189.
8. Stephen Lacey, 'British Theatre and Commerce, 1979–2000', in Baz Kershaw (ed.), *The Cambridge History of British Theatre: Volume 3, since 1895* (Cambridge: Cambridge University Press, 2004), p. 431.
9. Hewison, op. cit., p. 303.
10. Jen Harvie, *Staging the UK* (Manchester: Manchester University Press, 2005), p. 22.
11. Baz Kershaw, 'British Theatre, 1940–2002: An Introduction', in Baz Kershaw (ed.), op. cit., pp. 313–14.
12. Michael Billington, *State of the Nation: British Theatre Since 1945* (London: Faber, 2007), p. 348.
13. *Country Life*, 24 October 1996, p. 46.
14. Benedict Nightingale, *The Future of Theatre* (London: Phoenix, 1998), p. 3.
15. Society of London Theatre, photocopied statistical abstract (London: SOLT, nd [1996]); London Arts Board, *The Arts and Cultural Industries in London: Key Facts* (London: London Arts Board, nd [April 1996]), p. 8.
16. Ibid.; National Campaign for the Arts, *Facts About the Arts*, 3rd edn (London: NCA, 1995), pp. 15–17; and John Elsom, 'United Kingdom', in Dom Rubin (ed.), *The World Encyclopedia of Contemporary Theatre. Vol. 1 Europe* (London: Routledge, 1994), pp. 906–8.
17. Mimi Kramer, review of *The Phantom of the Opera*, New Yorker, 8 February 1988. See also Aleks Sierz, 'British Theatre in the 1990s: A Brief Political Economy', *Media, Culture and Society*, Vol. 19, No. 3 (1997), pp. 461–9.
18. Billington, *One Night Stands*, p. 350, see also p. 375.
19. Royal National Theatre, *An Inspector Calls*, programme, London, 1992. See Aleks Sierz, 'A Postmodernist Calls: Class, Conscience and the British Theatre', in Jane Stokes and Anna Reading (eds), *The Media in Britain: Current Debates and Developments* (London: Macmillan, 1999), pp. 236–45.

20. The name was changed to the Royal National Theatre in 1988, but most people continued to call it the National.
21. Shellard, op. cit., p. 208.
22. Colin Chambers, 'National Theatre (London)', in his *Continuum Companion to Twentieth Century Theatre* (London: Continuum, 2002), p. 532.
23. See John Bull, *Stage Right: Crisis and Recovery in British Contemporary Mainstream Theatre* (Basingstoke: Macmillan, 1994), pp. 207–19.
24. David Hare, *Asking Around: Background to the David Hare Trilogy* (London: Faber, 1993), p. 5.
25. Richard Eyre and Nicholas Wright, *Changing Stages: A View of British Theatre in the Twentieth Century* (London: Bloomsbury, 2000), p. 292. See also Richard Boon, *About Hare: The Playwright and the Work* (London: Faber, 2003), pp. 44–8.
26. David Hare, 'Introduction', *Plays Three: Skylight; Amy's View; The Judas Kiss; My Zinc Bed* (London: Faber, 2008), p. ix.
27. Martin Crimp, *Plays Two: No One Sees the Video; The Misanthrope; Attempts on Her Life; The Country* (London: Faber, 2005), p. 122.
28. Hare, *Plays Three*, p. 180.
29. Tom Stoppard, *Plays Five: Arcadia; The Real Thing; Night & Day; Indian Ink; Hapgood* (London: Faber, 1999), p. 8.
30. John Fleming, *Tom Stoppard's Arcadia* (London: Continuum, 2008), p. 71.
31. Charles Spencer, *Daily Telegraph*, 3 October 1997, *Theatre Record*, Vol. XVII, No. 20 (1997), p. 1259.
32. Nesta Jones, *Brian Friel* (London: Faber, 2000), pp. 156, 179–81. See also Patrick Lonergan, *Theatre and Globalization: Irish Drama in the Celtic Tiger Era* (Basingstoke: Palgrave Macmillan, 2010), pp. 31–55.
33. Shellard, op. cit., p. 211.
34. Michael Frayn, *Copenhagen*, Student edn (London: Methuen Drama, 2003), p. 73.
35. Billington, *One Night Stands*, p. 330.
36. Robert Butler, 'It'll be All Right on the Night', *Independent on Sunday*, 27 March 1994.
37. Michael Coveney, *The Aisle is Full of Noises: A Vivisection of the Live Theatre* (London: Nick Hern, 1994), pp. 68, 67.
38. Andrew Canham, 'Campaign for "Coriolanus"', Letter, *Independent*, 12 August 1995.
39. Paul Taylor, *Independent*, 7 June 1995, *Theatre Record*, Vol. XV, No. 12 (1995), p. 752. David Edgar, *Pentecost* (London: Nick Hern, 1995), p. 104.
40. Edgar, *Pentecost*, p. 98.
41. Billington, *State of the Nation*, p. 340.
42. Colin Chambers, *Inside the Royal Shakespeare Company: Creativity and the Institution* (London: Routledge, 2004), p. 96.
43. Billington, *State of the Nation*, p. 343.
44. Paul Taylor, *Independent*, 7 September 1995, *Theatre Record*, Vol. XV, No. 18 (1995), p. 1206.
45. Charles Spencer, *Daily Telegraph*, 23 September 1998, *Theatre Record*, Vol. XVIII, No. 19 (1998), p. 1234.

46. Quoted in Matt Wolf, *Sam Mendes at the Donmar: Stepping into Freedom* (London: Nick Hern, 2002), p. 67.
47. Richard Norton-Taylor, *The Colour of Justice* (London: Oberon, 1999), p. 143.
48. Quoted in Aleks Sierz, 'On a Platform of Change', *The Stage*, 2 December 2004.
49. Winsome Pinnock, 'Breaking Down the Door', in Vera Gottlieb and Colin Chambers (eds), *Theatre in a Cool Climate* (Oxford: Amber Lane, 1999), p. 35.
50. Simon Trussler, *The Cambridge Illustrated History of British Theatre* (Cambridge: Cambridge University Press, 1994), p. 370.
51. Charles Spencer, *Daily Telegraph*, 19 March 1992, *Theatre Record*, Vol. XII, No. 5 (1992), p. 289.
52. Jatinder Verma, 'Cultural Transformations', in Ted Shank (ed.), *Contemporary British Theatre* (Basingstoke: Macmillan, 1994), pp. 59–60.
53. David Edgar, *State of Play: Playwrights on Playwriting* (London: Faber, 1999), p. 19.
54. Kate Harwood, 'Introduction', in Kate Harwood (ed.), *First Run: New Plays by New Writers* (London: Nick Hern, 1989), no page number.
55. Billington, *One Night Stands*, p. 360.
56. Dominic Dromgoole, *The Full Room: An A–Z of Contemporary Playwriting*, 2nd edn (London: Methuen Drama, 2002), p. 241.
57. Dan Rebellato, 'Commentary', Ravenhill, *Shopping and Fucking; Faust is Dead; Handbag; Some Explicit Polaroids*, Student edn (London: Methuen, 2001), p. xii.
58. Graham Saunders, *About Kane: The Playwright and the Work* (London: Faber, 2009), p. xxi.
59. Ravenhill, *Shopping and Fucking*, p. 66.
60. See Aleks Sierz, *In-Yer-Face Theatre: British Drama Today* (London: Faber, 2001).
61. Paul Taylor, *Independent*, 14 April 1994, *Theatre Record*, Vol. XIV, No. 8 (1994), p. 440; Jeremy Kingston, *The Times*, 19 December 1995, *Theatre Record*, Vol. XV, No. 25–6 (1995), p. 1717.
62. Quoted in Sarah Hemming, 'Look Forward in Anger', *Financial Times*, 18 November 1995. See also Sierz, *In-Yer-Face Theatre*, p. 66.
63. Simon Napier-Bell, *Black Vinyl White Powder* (London: Ebury, 2002), p. 390.
64. David Pattie, 'Theatre Since 1968', in Mary Luckhurst (ed.), *A Companion to Modern British and Irish Drama 1880–2005* (Oxford: Blackwell, 2006), pp. 394–5.
65. Mike Bradwell, *The Reluctant Escapologist: Adventures in Alternative Theatre* (London: Nick Hern, 2010), p. 257.
66. See Philip Roberts, *The Royal Court Theatre and the Modern Stage* (Cambridge: Cambridge University Press, 1999), pp. 209–18.
67. Ben Payne, interview with Aleks Sierz, London, 16 April 2002.
68. Adrienne Scullion, 'Theatre in Scotland in the 1990s and Beyond', in Baz Kershaw (ed.), op. cit., p. 471; see also Lyn Gardner, 'The Bold, the Old and the Obsolete', *Guardian*, 27 April 2009.
69. Rebecca D'Monté and Graham Saunders, *Cool Britannia? British Political Drama in the 1990s* (Basingstoke: Palgrave Macmillan, 2008), p. 2.
70. Theatre Worker, 'Encore Revivals', *Encore Theatre Magazine*, 6 June 2003, http://encoretheatremagazine.blogspot.com/Revivals.html#Blue (accessed 21 January 2010).

71. Dromgoole, *The Full Room*, p. 189. See also Martin Middeke and Peter Paul Schnierer, 'Introduction', *The Methuen Drama Guide to Contemporary Irish Playwrights* (London: Methuen Drama, 2010).

72. Kate Kellaway, *Observer*, 9 April 1995, *Theatre Record*, Vol. XV, No. 7 (1995), p. 411.

73. Clare Wallace, *Suspect Cultures: Narrative, Identity and Citation in 1990s New Drama* (Prague: Litteraria Pragensia, 2006), p. 237.

74. Lonergan, *Theatre and Globalization*, p. 109.

75. Middeke and Schnierer, 'Introduction', p. xi.

76. Elaine Aston, *Feminist Views on the English Stage: Women Playwrights, 1990–2000* (Cambridge: Cambridge University Press, 2003), p. 30.

77. Philip Roberts, *About Churchill: The Playwright and the Work* (London: Faber, 2008), p. 142.

78. Alan Sinfield, in Mireia Aragay et al. (eds), *British Theatre of the 1990s: Interviews with Directors, Playwrights, Critics and Academics* (Basingstoke: Palgrave Macmillan, 2007), p. 189.

79. Nicholas de Jongh, in Aragay et al., op. cit., p. 127.

80. Quoted in Aleks Sierz, 'Curtain Up for Act Two', *Independent*, 12 February 2003.

81. Quoted in Heidi Stephenson and Natasha Langridge, *Rage and Reason: Women Playwrights on Playwriting* (London: Methuen Drama, 1997), pp. 28, 137.

82. Elaine Aston and Janelle Reinelt, *The Cambridge Companion to Modern British Women Playwrights, 1990–2000* (Cambridge: Cambridge University Press, 2000), p. 16. See also Aston, *Feminist Views*, p. 5.

83. Nick Curtis, *Evening Standard*, 30 May 1997, *Theatre Record*, Vol. XVII, No. 11 (1997), p. 677; Patrick Marber, *Plays One: Dealer's Choice; After Miss Julie; Closer* (London: Methuen Drama, 2004), p. 272.

84. Amelia Howe Kritzer, *Political Theatre in Post-Thatcher Britain: New Writing 1995–2005* (Basingstoke: Palgrave Macmillan, 2008), p. 83.

85. See Aleks Sierz, *The Theatre of Martin Crimp* (London: Methuen Drama, 2006), p. 91.

86. Quoted in Ruth Little and Emily McLaughlin, *The Royal Court Theatre Inside Out* (London: Oberon, 2007), p. 287.

87. Quoted in Aleks Sierz, 'The Write Stuff', *Independent*, 9 April 1997.

88. Philip Roberts and Max Stafford-Clark, *Taking Stock: The Theatre of Max Stafford-Clark* (London: Nick Hern Books, 2007), p. xviii.

89. Pattie, 'Theatre Since 1968', pp. 393–4. See also Edgar, *State of the Nation*, pp. 27–8, 29.

90. Quoted in Gabriella Giannachi and Mary Luckhurst, *On Directing: Interviews with Directors* (London: Faber, 1999), p. 74.

91. Lloyd Newson, programme note, DV8, *Enter Achilles*, 1995.

92. Scott Graham and Steven Hoggett, *The Frantic Assembly Book of Devising Theatre* (Abingdon: Routledge, 2009), p. 177.

93. Baz Kershaw, *The Politics of Performance: Radical Theatre as Cultural Intervention* (London: Routledge, 1992), pp. 238, 239.

94. Quoted in Mark Berninger, 'Variations of a Genre: The British History Play in the Nineties', in Bernhard Reitz and Mark Berninger (eds), *British Drama of the 1990s* (Heidelberg: Universitätsverlag C Winter, 2002), p. 52.

95. David Ian Rabey, *English Drama Since 1940* (Harlow: Longman, 2003), p. 85.

96. Rupert Christiansen, 'Abuzz in Battersea', *Daily Telegraph*, 3 May 2003.

97. Dominic Dromgoole, interviewed by Aleks Sierz, London, 29 March 2001.

98. Baz Kershaw, 'Alternative Theatres, 1946–2000', in Baz Kershaw (ed.), op. cit., p. 371.

99. See Dan Rebellato, '"Because It Feels Fucking Amazing": Recent British Drama and Bodily Mutilation', in Rebecca D'Monté and Graham Saunders (eds), *Cool Britannia? British Political Drama in the 1990s* (Basingstoke: Palgrave Macmillan, 2008).

100. Bull, *Stage Right*, p. 209.

101. Ibid., p. 212; National Campaign for the Arts quoted in Billington, *State of the Nation*, pp. 364–5.

102. Olivia Turnbull, *Bringing Down the House: The Crisis in Britain's Regional Theatres* (Bristol: Intellect, 2008), p. 13.

103. Fiachra Gibbons, 'Curtains for Debt-Laden Theatres?', *Guardian*, 28 January 2000; Turnbull, op. cit., p. 203.

104. Edgar, *State of Play*, p. 19.

105. Kate Dorney and Ros Merkin, 'Introduction' to their *The Glory of the Garden: English Regional Theatre and the Arts Council 1984–2009* (Newcastle upon Tyne: Cambridge Scholars, 2010), p. 1.

106. Claire Cochrane, *The Birmingham Rep: A City's Theatre 1962–2002*, p. 166.

107. Ibid., p. 179.

108. John Godber was not only a playwright but also artistic director of Hull Truck Theatre from 1984.

109. See Sierz, 'A Postmodernist Calls'.

110. Shellard, op. cit., p. 217.

111. Adrienne Scullion, 'Theatre in Scotland in the 1990s and Beyond', in Baz Kershaw (ed.), op. cit., pp. 470–1.

112. Dan Rebellato, 'Introduction', David Greig, *Plays One: Europe; The Architect; The Cosmonaut's Last Message to the Woman He Once Loved in the Former Soviet Union* (London: Methuen Drama, 2002), p. xii.

113. David Greig, 'Bard's Poor Scottish Relation', *Herald*, 14 November 1995; also quoted in *Theatre Record*, Vol. XV, No. 24 (1995), p. 1599.

114. David Pattie, '"Mapping the Territory": Modern Scottish Drama', in D'Monté and Saunders (eds), op. cit., p. 156.

115. Roger Owen, 'Theatre in Wales in the 1990s and Beyond', in Baz Kershaw (ed.), op. cit., pp. 491–2.

2 Playwrights and Plays: Philip Ridley

1. Royal Court mission statement, Mark Ravenhill, *Shopping and Fucking* (London: Methuen Drama, 1996), no page number.
2. Philip Ridley, 'My Best Teacher', *Times Educational Supplement*, 13 March 1998, p. 38.
3. Ibid.
4. Philip Ridley, quoted in Aleks Sierz, 'Putting a New Lens on the World: The Art of Theatrical Alchemy', *New Theatre Quarterly*, Vol. 25, No. 2 (2009), p. 110. Three of his poems are in Mike Bradwell, *The Bush Theatre Book* (London: Methuen Drama, 1997), pp. 75–8, and five more in his *Tender Napalm* playtext (London: Methuen Drama, 2011), pp. 61–9.
5. Aleks Sierz, *In-Yer-Face Theatre: British Drama Today* (London: Faber, 2001), p. 42.
6. Dominic Dromgoole, *The Full Room: An A–Z of Contemporary Playwriting*, 2nd edn (London: Methuen Drama, 2002), p. 241.
7. See Baz Kershaw, *The Cambridge History of British Theatre. Volume 3, Since 1895* (Cambridge: Cambridge University Press, 2004).
8. David Ian Rabey, *English Drama Since 1940* (Harlow: Longman, 2003), p. 196.
9. See Andrew Wyllie, *Sex on Stage: Gender and Sexuality in Post-War British Theatre* (Bristol: Intellect, 2009), pp. 77–80, and Rabey, op. cit., pp. 196–7.
10. Ken Urban, 'Ghosts from an Imperfect Place: Philip Ridley's Nostalgia', p. 326.
11. Ibid.
12. Dan Rebellato, 'Philip Ridley', Martin Middeke, Peter Paul Schnierer and Aleks Sierz (eds), *The Methuen Drama Guide to Contemporary British Playwrights* (London: Methuen Drama, 2011), pp. 426, 441.
13. Dromgoole, op. cit., p. 240.
14. Quoted in Sierz, 'Putting a New Lens on the World', p. 111.
15. Philip Ridley, *Plays One: The Pitchfork Disney; The Fastest Clock in the Universe; Ghost from a Perfect Place* (London: Faber, 2002), p. 5. Page references to plays are to this edition. Malcolm de Chazal (1902–81) was a Mauritian polymath.
16. Maureen Paton, *Daily Express*, 8 January 1991; Nicholas de Jongh, *Guardian*, 8 January 1991, *Theatre Record*, Vol. XI, No. 1 (1991), pp. 11, 12.
17. Paul Taylor, *Independent*, 7 January 1991, *Theatre Record*, Vol. XI, No. 1 (1991), p. 13.
18. This image of a cloud might be an unconscious echo of the sinister cloud in one of Ridley's favourite sci-fi books, Christopher Priest's *The Glamour* (Orion, 2005; orig. pub. 1984), p. 55.
19. John Walliss, 'Apocalypse at the Millennium', in John Walliss and Kenneth G. C. Newport, *The End All Around Us: Apocalyptic Texts and Popular Culture* (London: Equinox, 2009), p. 76.
20. James Berger, *After the End: Representations of Post-Apocalypse* (Minneapolis: University of Minnesota Press, 1999), p. 11.

21. Urban, op. cit., p. 328.
22. Ibid.
23. Ibid., p. 331.
24. Ibid., p. 326.
25. Frank Kermode, *The Sense of an Ending: Studies in the Theory of Fiction*, 2nd edn (New York: Oxford University Press, 2000), p. 182.
26. Robert Bloch quoted in David Stevens, *The Gothic Tradition*, p. 32. See Sierz, 'Putting a New Lens on the World', p. 117.
27. Quoted in Sierz, *In-Yer-Face Theatre*, p. 43.
28. Charles Osborne, *Daily Telegraph*, 10 January 1991, *Theatre Record*, Vol. XI, No. 1 (1991), p. 12.
29. Alastair Macaulay, *Financial Times*, 7 January 1991, *Theatre Record*, Vol. XI, No. 1 (1991), p. 13.
30. In the early 1970s, Peter Cook terrorised women in Cambridge, wearing a leather mask; he was convicted in 1975.
31. Mary Douglas, *Purity and Danger: An Analysis of the Concepts of Pollution and Taboo* (London: Routledge & Kegan Paul, 1978), p. 40.
32. Quoted in Andrew Smith, *Gothic Literature* (Edinburgh: Edinburgh University Press, 2007), p. 15.
33. Charles Osborne, *Daily Telegraph*, 10 January 1991; Jane Edwardes, *Time Out*, 9 January 1991, *Theatre Record*, Vol. XI, No. 1 (1991), pp. 12, 14.
34. Bloom quoted in Stevens, op. cit., p. 6.
35. Stevens, op. cit., pp. 25, 32.
36. Quoted in Adam Roberts, *Science Fiction (New Critical Idiom)*, 2nd edn (London: Routledge, 2006), p. 18.
37. Rabey, op. cit., p. 196.
38. John Gross, *Sunday Telegraph*, 24 May 1992, *Theatre Record*, Vol. XII, No. 10 (1992), p. 612.
39. Urban, op. cit., p. 331.
40. Lee Levitt, *Jewish Chronicle*, 29 May 1992, *Theatre Record*, Vol. XII, No. 10 (1992), p. 612.
41. Dick Pountain and David Robins, *Cool Rules: Anatomy of an Attitude* (London: Reaktion, 2000), pp. 23, 165.
42. Nicholas de Jongh, *Evening Standard*, 20 May 1992, *Theatre Record*, Vol. XII, No. 10 (1992), p. 612.
43. Kate Kellaway, *Observer*, 24 May 1992, *Theatre Record*, Vol. XII, No. 10, (1992), p. 611.
44. Rebellato, 'Philip Ridley'. See Wolfgang Kayser, *The Grotesque in Art and Literature*, trans. Ulrich Weisstein (Bloomington: Indiana University Press, 1963), pp. 184–5.
45. Ian Shuttleworth, *City Limits*, 28 May 1992, *Theatre Record*, Vol. XII, No. 10, (1992), p. 611.
46. Philip Ridley, *The Fastest Clock in the Universe*, rev. edn (London: Methuen Drama, 2009), p. 95.

47. Clive Bloom, *Gothic Histories: The Taste for Terror, 1764 to the Present* (London: Continuum, 2010), p. 3.

48. Urban, op. cit., p. 336.

49. Berger, op. cit., p. 19.

50. Urban, op. cit., pp. 333, 335. See also Roberts, op. cit., p. 26.

51. Maureen Paton, *Daily Express*, 15 April 1994, *Theatre Record*, Vol. XIV, No. 8 (1994), p. 444.

52. Jeremy Kingston, *The Times*, 14 April 1994, *Theatre Record*, Vol. XIV, No. 8 (1994), p. 439. Urban, op. cit., p. 340.

53. See Hirst's *Mother and Child, Divided* and *The Physical Impossibility of Death in the Mind of Someone Living*.

54. Paul Taylor, *Independent*, 14 April 1994, *Theatre Record*, Vol. XIV, No. 8 (1994), p. 440.

55. Rebellato, 'Philip Ridley', p. 428.

56. Rabey, op. cit., p. 196.

57. Jeremy Kingston, *The Times*, 14 April 1994, *Theatre Record*, Vol. XIV, No. 8 (1994), p. 439.

58. Wyllie, op. cit., p. 80.

59. Berger, op. cit., p 26.

60. Fred Botting, *Gothic (New Critical Idiom)* (London: Routledge, 1995), p. 157.

61. Urban, op. cit., p. 341.

62. Ibid.

63. James Christopher, *Time Out*, 20 April 1994, *Theatre Record*, Vol. XIV, No. 8 (1994), p. 444.

64. Quoted in Sierz, *In-Yer-Face Theatre*, p. 45.

65. Mark Gatiss, *A History of Horror with Mark Gatiss*, Part One, BBC4 TV, 11 October 2010.

66. Quoted in Sierz, 'Putting a New Lens on the World', p. 111.

67. Wyllie, op. cit., p. 78.

68. Steven Connor, *Postmodernist Culture: An Introduction to Theories of the Contemporary* (Oxford: Blackwell, 1989), p. 90.

69. Botting, op. cit., p. 157.

70. Smith, op. cit., pp. 141, 163.

71. Kenneth Hurren, *Mail on Sunday*, 6 January 1991; Charles Spencer, *Daily Telegraph*, 21 May 1996, *Theatre Record*, Vol. XI, No. 1 (1991), p. 11 and Vol. XVI, No. 11 (1996), p. 653.

72. John A. Walker, *Art and Outrage: Provocation, Controversy and the Visual Arts* (London: Pluto, 1999), pp. 149–64. The Pitchfork Disney puts Mickey Mouse figures on the bodies of his victims (pp. 83–4) and one of Miss Sulphur's lipstick colours is called 'Crushed Foetus' (270).

73. Quoted in Sierz, 'Putting a New Lens on the World', p. 111 and in Sierz, *In-Yer-Face Theatre*, p. 47.

74. Thanks to Cath Badham for this information, and for copies of the programmes.

75. Bloom, op. cit., p. 4.

76. See Dan Rebellato, 'Introduction', Mark Ravenhill, *Plays One: Shopping and Fucking; Faust is Dead; Handbag; Some Explicit Polaroids* (London: Methuen Drama, 2001), pp xiv–xvi.
77. Smith, op. cit., p. 15.

2 Playwrights and Plays: Sarah Kane

1. David Greig, 'Introduction', Kane, *Complete Plays* (London: Methuen Drama, 2001), p. xviii. Page references to plays are to this edition.
2. Quoted in Graham Saunders, *About Kane: The Playwright and the Work* (London: Faber, 2009), p. 124.
3. Mary Luckhurst, 'Infamy and Dying Young: Sarah Kane, 1971–1999', in Mary Luckhurst and Jane Moody (eds), *Theatre and Celebrity in Britain, 1600–2000* (Basingstoke: Palgrave, 2005), p. 120.
4. Aleks Sierz, '"We All Need Stories": The Politics of In-Yer-Face Theatre', in Rebecca D'Monté and Graham Saunders (eds), *Cool Britannia? British Political Drama in the 1990s* (Basingstoke: Palgrave, 2008), p. 32.
5. Aleks Sierz, *In-Yer-Face Theatre: British Drama Today* (London: Faber, 2001), pp. xiii and 5.
6. Lauren De Vos and Graham Saunders, 'Introduction', *Sarah Kane in Context* (Manchester: Manchester University Press, 2010), p. 1.
7. Christopher Innes, *Modern British Drama: The Twentieth Century* (Cambridge: Cambridge University Press, 2002), p. 529; Billington quoted in Sierz, *In-Yer-Face Theatre*, p. 96. See also *Theatre Record*, Vol. XV, No. 1/2 (1995), pp. 38–43.
8. Eckart Voigts-Virchow, '"We are Anathema": Sarah Kane's Plays as Postdramatic Theatre versus the "Dreary and Repugnant Tale of the Sense"', in De Vos and Saunders (eds), op. cit. (Manchester: Manchester University Press, 2010), p. 198.
9. Sierz, *In-Yer-Face Theatre*, p. 93.
10. Aleks Sierz, '"We're All Bloody Hungry": Images of Hunger and the Construction of the Gendered Self in Sarah Kane's *Blasted*', in Elisabeth Angel-Perez and Alexandra Poulain (eds), *Hunger on the Stage* (Newcastle: Cambridge Scholars, 2008), p. 274.
11. Innes, op. cit., p. 532.
12. Luckhurst, op. cit., p. 107; quoted in Heidi Stephenson and Natasha Langridge, *Rage and Reason: Women Playwrights on Playwriting* (London: Methuen Drama, 1997), p. 132.
13. Steve Waters, 'Sarah Kane: From Terror to Trauma', in Mary Luckhurst (ed.), *A Companion to Modern British ans Irish Drama* (Oxford: Blackwell, 2006), p. 377.
14. Quoted in Saunders, *About Kane*, p. 90.
15. Quoted in Sierz, *In-Yer-Face Theatre*, p. 101.
16. Michael Billington, *State of the Nation: British Theatre Since 1945* (London: Faber, 2007), p. 356.
17. Quoted in Stephenson and Langridge, op. cit., p. 134.

18. Elaine Aston, 'Reviewing the Fabric of *Blasted*', in De Vos and Saunders (eds), op. cit., p. 14.
19. Quoted in Stephenson and Langridge, op. cit., p. 133.
20. David Ian Rabey, *English Drama Since 1940* (Harlow: Longman, 2003), p. 195.
21. Elaine Aston, *Feminist Views on the English Stage*, p. 84.
22. Aston, 'Reviewing the Fabric of *Blasted*', pp. 22, 25.
23. Sierz, *In-Yer-Face Theatre*, p. 30.
24. See Aston, *Feminist Views*; Christopher Wixson, '"In Better Places": Space, Identity, and Alienation in Sarah Kane's *Blasted*', *Comparative Drama*, Vol. 39, No. 1 (2005), pp. 75–91; and Annabelle Singer, 'Don't Want to be This: The Elusive Sarah Kane', Drama Review, Vol. 48, No. 2 (2004), pp. 139–71.
25. Elaine Scarry, *The Body in Pain: The Making and Unmaking of the World* (Oxford: Oxford University Press, 1985), pp. 28, 27.
26. Ibid., p. 41.
27. Ibid., p. 38.
28. Ibid., p. 54.
29. Ibid., p. 36.
30. Peter Buse, *Drama + Theory: Critical Approaches to Modern British Drama* (Manchester: Manchester University Press, 2001), p. 178.
31. Ibid., p. 180.
32. Ibid., p. 182.
33. Scarry, op. cit., pp. 4, 5 and 6.
34. Ken Urban, 'An Ethics of Catastrophe: The Theatre of Sarah Kane', *A Journal of Performance and Art*, Vol. 23, No. 3 (2001), p. 45.
35. Aleks Sierz, '"Looks Like There's a War On": Sarah Kane's *Blasted*, Political Theatre and the Muslim Other', in De Vos and Saunders (eds), op. cit. (Manchester: Manchester University Press, 2010), p. 56.
36. Saunders, op. cit., p. 74.
37. Quoted in Saunders, op. cit., p. 93.
38. Urban, op. cit., p. 42.
39. Quoted in Urban, op. cit., p. 39.
40. Mark Ravenhill, *Plays One: Shopping and Fucking; Faust is Dead; Handbag; Some Explicit Polaroids* (London: Methuen Drama, 2001), p. 66.
41. Scarry, op. cit., p. 49.
42. Scarry, op. cit., p. 42.
43. Michel Foucault, *Discipline and Punish: The Birth of the Prison*, trans. Alan Sheridan (Harmondsworth: Penguin, 1991), p. 12.
44. Ibid., pp. 202–3.
45. Ibid., p. 175.
46. Ibid., p. 200.
47. Ibid., p. 25.
48. Judith Butler, *Precarious Life: The Powers of Mourning and Violence* (London: Verso, 2004), p. 26.
49. Ibid., p. 22.

50. Sanja Nikcevic, 'British Brutalism, the "New European Drama", and the Role of the Director', *New Theatre Quarterly*, Vol. 21, No. 3 (2005), p. 264.

51. Hillary Chute, '"Victim. Perpetrator. Bystander": Critical Distance in Sarah Kane's Theatre of Cruelty', in De Vos and Saunders (eds), op. cit. (Manchester: Manchester University Press, 2010), p. 171.

52. Hans-Thies Lehmann, *Postdramatic Theatre*, trans. Karen Jürs-Munby (London: Routledge, 2006), p. 178.

53. Ibid., p. 187.

54. Quoted in Stephenson and Langridge, op. cit., p. 130.

55. Michael Billington, *Guardian*, 30 June 2000, *Theatre Record*, Vol. XX, No. 13 (2000), p. 829.

56. Sarah Gorman, 'The Mythology of Sarah Kane: How to Avoid Reading *4.48 Psychosis* as a Suicide Note', Anglophiles: Journal of English Teaching, No. 126 (2002), p. 37.

57. Ibid., p. 36.

58. See, for example, ibid., p. 35, Ken Urban, op. cit., p. 36, and Sierz quoted in Saunders, op. cit., p. 125.

59. Ehran Fordyce, 'The Voice of Kane' , in De Vos and Saunders (eds), op. cit., p. 112.

60. Alicia Tycer, '"Victim. Perpetrator. Bystander": Melancholic Witnessing of Sarah Kane's *4.48 Psychosis*', *Theatre Journal*, Vol. 60 (2008), p. 31.

61. Elizabeth Kuti, 'Tragic Plots from Bootle to Baghdad', *Contemporary Theatre Review*, Vol. 18, No. 4 (2008), p. 468.

62. Lehmann, op. cit., p. 55.

63. For example, Kuti, Gorman, Voigts-Virchow and Gritzner.

64. Lehmann, op. cit., p. 48.

65. Lehmann, op. cit., p. 163.

66. Urban, op. cit., p. 44

67. David Barnett, 'When is a Play Not a Drama? Two Examples of Postdramatic Theatre Texts', *New Theatre Quarterly*, Vol. 24, No. 1 (2008), p. 16.

68. Voigts-Virchow, op. cit., p. 203 and Karoline Gritzner, '(Post)Modern Subjectivity and the New Expressionism: Howard Barker, Sarah Kane, and Forced Entertainment', *Contemporary Theatre Review*, Vol. 18, No. 3 (2008), p. 340.

69. Quoted in Saunders, op. cit., p. 95.

70. Quoted in Saunders, op. cit., p. 128.

71. Aleks Sierz, 'Still In-Yer- Face? Towards a Critique and a Summation', *New Theatre Quarterly*, Vol. 18, No. 1 (2002), pp. 19–20.

72. Voigts-Virchow, op. cit., p. 195, and Saunders, op. cit., p. 38.

73. Saunders, op. cit., p. 66.

74. Rabey, op. cit., p. 175.

75. Rabey, op. cit., p. 233.

76. Quoted in Saunders, op. cit., p. 129.

77. Quoted in Saunders, op. cit., p. 62.

78. Billington, *State of the Nation*, p. 355. See also *Theatre Record*, Vol. XXI, No. 7 (2001), pp. 418–23.

79. Kuti, op. cit., p. 458.

2 Playwrights and Plays: Anthony Neilson

1. Adrienne Scullion, 'Theatre in Scotland in the 1990s and Beyond', in Baz Kershaw (ed.), *The Cambridge History of British Theatre: Volume 3. Since 1895* (Cambridge: Cambridge University Press, 2004), p. 484.

2. Ibid.

3. For reference to Neilson as a specifically Scottish artist see Adrienne Scullion, 'Devolution and Drama: Imagining the Possible', in Berthold Schoene (ed.), *The Edinburgh Companion to Contemporary Scottish Literature* (Edinburgh: Edinburgh University Press, 2007), p. 74; Ian Brown, 'Alternative Sensibilities: Devolutionary Comedy and Scottish Camp', Schoene (ed.), op. cit. (Edinburgh: Edinburgh University Press, 2007), pp. 323–4 and Trish Reid, '"Deformities of the Frame": The Theatre of Anthony Neilson', in *Contemporary Theatre Review*, Vol. 17, No. 4 (2007), pp. 487–98.

4. Aleks Sierz, *In-Yer-Face Theatre: British Drama Today* (London: Faber, 2001), p. 4.

5. Stephen Daldry, in Mireia Aragay et al., *British Theatre of the 1990s: Interviews with Directors, Playwrights, Critics and Academics* (Basingstoke: Palgrave Macmillan, 2007), p. 9.

6. Rebecca D'Monté and Graham Saunders, *Cool Britannia? British Political Drama in the 1990s* (Basingstoke: Palgrave Macmillan, 2008), p. 12.

7. David Lane, *Contemporary British Drama* (Edinburgh: Edinburgh University Press, 2010), p. 25.

8. Aleks Sierz, 'Blasted and After: New Writing in British Theatre Today', 'New Writing Special', *Theatrevoice* website, 16 February 2010, www.theatrevoice.com/listen_now/player/?audioID=819.

9. Anthony Neilson, personal interview. The moment in *The Censor* is the onstage defecation scene.

10. See Scullion, 'Devolution and Drama', Schoene (ed.), op. cit., p. 74; Brown, 'Alternative Sensibilities', Schoene (ed.), op. cit., pp. 323–4, Reid, '"Deformities of the Frame"' and Kathleen Starck, 'Battlefield "Body": Gregory Burke's *Gagarin Way* and Anthony Neilson's *Stitching*', in Hans-Ulrich Mohr and Kerstin Mächler (eds), *Extending the Code: New Forms of Dramatic and Theatrical Expression* (Trier: Wissenschaftlicher Verlag Trier, 2004).

11. Patrick Marmion, *What's On in London*, 13 October 1993, *Theatre Record*, Vol. XIII, No. 21 (1993), p. 1151.

12. Alastair Galbraith, personal interview.

13. David Harrower and David Greig, 'Why a New Scotland Must Have a Properly Funded Theatre', *Scotsman*, 25 November 1997.

14. Anthony Neilson, 'Introduction', *Plays Two: Edward Gant's Amazing Feats of Loneliness!; The Lying Kind; The Wonderful World of Dissocia; Realism* (London: Methuen Drama, 2008), p. x.

15. Charles Spencer, *Daily Telegraph*, 16 June 2008; Paul Taylor, *Independent*, 17 June 2008, *Theatre Record*, Vol. XXVIII, No. 12 (1993), p. 689.

16. Neilson, personal interview.
17. Page references to plays are to *Plays One: Normal; Penetrator; Year of the Family; The Night Before Christmas; The Censor* (London: Methuen Drama, 1998).
18. Neilson, personal interview.
19. Joyce McMillan, *Guardian*, 13 August 1991, *Theatre Record*, Vol. XI, No. 20 (1991), p. 1222.
20. Quoted in Sierz, *In-Yer-Face Theatre*, p. 72.
21. Omer Ali, *Scotsman*, 12 August 1991, *Theatre Record*, Vol. XI, No. 20 (1991), p. 1222.
22. Sierz, *In-Yer-Face Theatre*, p. 69.
23. McMillan, op. cit. See Reid, '"Deformities of the Frame"', p. 495.
24. Ian Shuttleworth, *City Limits*, 3 October 1991, *Theatre Record*, Vol. XI, No. 20 (1991), p. 1222.
25. See also Jeremy Kingston, *The Times*, 4 October 1991, and Jo Graham, *What's On in London*, 9 October 1991, *Theatre Record*, Vol. XI, No. 20 (1991), p. 1222.
26. Sierz, *In-Yer-Face Theatre*, p. 71.
27. Ernst Toller, 'My Works', trans. Marketa Goetze, *Tulane Drama Review*, No. 3 (March 1959), p. 100.
28. Peggy Phelan, *Unmarked: The Politics of Performance* (London: Routledge, 1993), p. 4.
29. Marmion, op. cit.
30. Robert Shore identified the play's theme, in reference to a 2003 revival, as 'the big 1990s theme of masculinity in crisis'. *Time Out*, 3 December 2003, *Theatre Record*, Vol. XXIII, No. 24 (2003), p. 1601.
31. Bethan Benwell, 'Is There Anything New About These Lads', in Lia Litosseliti and Jane Sutherland (eds), *Gender Identity and Discourse Analysis* (Amsterdam: John Benjamins, 2002), p. 151.
32. Elaine Aston, *Feminist Views on the English Stage: Women Playwrights, 1990–2000* (Cambridge: Cambridge University Press, 2003), p. 5.
33. Ibid., p. 80. Similarly, Patrick Marmion recalls feeling 'nauseated by the experience' (Marmion, op. cit.).
34. Benedict Nightingale, *The Times*, 17 August 1993, *Theatre Record*, Vol. XIII, No. 21 (1993), p. 1151.
35. Caroline Donald, *Scotsman*, 16 August 1993. Both Claire Armitstead in the *Guardian* and Nicholas de Jongh in the *Evening Standard* expressed concerns about the play's homophobia, *Theatre Record*, Vol. XIII, No. 21 (1993), p. 1151 and Vol. XIV, No. 1 (1994), p. 38.
36. See Brown, 'Alternative Sensibilities' for a fuller discussion of the subversive potential of shifting linguistic registers in contemporary Scottish drama.
37. Specifically, this construction recalls Spanky Farrell's reference to 'Kris Kris-fuckin-stoffersen' in John Byrne's *Still Life* (1982) (*The Slab Boys Trilogy* (Harmondsworth: Penguin, 1987), p. 114).
38. *Still Game* was produced by the Comedy Unit with the BBC, 2002–7. It won the BAFTA Scotland award for best entertainment programme in 2004 and 2005.
39. See Sierz, *In-Yer-Face-Theatre*, pp. 76–7.

40. Dan Rebellato, '"Because It Feels Fucking Amazing": Recent British Drama and Bodily Mutilation', in Rebecca D'Monté and Graham Saunders (eds), *Cool Britannia? British Political Drama in the 1990s* (Basingstoke: Palgrave Macmillan, 2008), p. 204.

41. Galbraith, op. cit.

42. 'The Censor', Ebb and Flow Theatre website, 2010, http://thecensorchicago.com.

43. See 'Press', 'News/Events', Patrick Jones website, 2008–9, www.patrick-jones.net.

44. Quoted in Matt Thomas, 'Faction Collective Bring The Censor to Cardiff', *WalesOnline.co.uk*, 11 September 2009, www.walesonline.co.uk/showbiz-and-life-style/2009/09/11/faction-collective-bring-the-censor-to-cardiff-91466-24658089/.

45. Neilson quoted in Sierz, *In-Yer-Face Theatre*, p. 84.

46. Charles Spencer, *Daily Telegraph*, 10 June 1997, *Theatre Record*, Vol. XVII, No. 12 (1997), p. 712.

47. Galbraith, op. cit.

48. Christopher Innes, *Avant-Garde Theatre, 1892–1992* (London: Routledge, 1993), p. 37.

49. Neilson, personal interview.

50. For Peter Marks, the actors in the first New York production struggled 'valiantly to make something true out of their sick seduction' but were 'defeated by a playwright who can't keep his mind out of the toilet' (*New York Times*, 29 April 1999).

51. Erin Hurley, *Theatre & Feeling* (Basingstoke: Palgrave Macmillan, 2010), p. 13.

52. Galbraith, op. cit.

53. Dominic Dromgoole, *The Full Room: An A–Z of Contemporary Playwriting*, 2nd edn (London: Methuen Drama, 2002), p. 216.

54. Michael Coveney, *Daily Mail*, 13 June 1997, *Theatre Record*, Vol. XVII, No. 12 (1997), p. 713.

55. Charles Taylor, *Sources of the Self: The Making of the Modern Identity* (Cambridge, MA: Harvard University Press, 1989), p. 157.

56. Ruth Little and Emily McLaughlin, *The Royal Court Theatre Inside Out* (London: Oberon, 2007), p. 360.

57. Neil Smith, *What's On in London*, 11 June 1997; Caroline Donald, *Scotsman*, 16 August 1993, *Theatre Record*, Vol. XVII, No. 12 (1997), p. 712.

58. Margaret Thatcher, *Woman's Own*, 31 October 1987.

59. Amelia Howe Krizter, *Political Theatre in Post-Thatcher Britain: New Writing 1995–2005* (Basingstoke: Palgrave Macmillan, 2008), p. 30.

60. Vera Gottlieb, '1979 and After: A View', in Kershaw (ed.), op. cit., p. 413.

61. See David Pattie, '"Mapping the Territory": Modern Scottish Drama', in D'Monté and Saunders (eds), op. cit. (Basingstoke: Palgrave Macmillan, 2008).

62. Adrienne Scullion, 'Self and Nation: Issues of Identity in Modern Scottish Drama by Women', *New Theatre Quarterly*, Vol. 17, No. 4 (2001), p. 374.

63. Quoted in Brown, 'Alternative Sensibilities', in Schoene (ed.), op. cit., pp. 322–3 and Sierz, *In-Yer-Face Theatre*, p. 65.

2 Playwrights and Plays: Mark Ravenhill

1. Stephen Daldry, no title, *Evening Standard*, 20 February 1997.
2. See Aleks Sierz, *In-Yer-Face Theatre: British Drama Today* (London: Faber, 2001), pp. 122–52.
3. Dan Rebellato, 'Introduction', Mark Ravenhill, *Plays One: Shopping and Fucking; Faust is Dead; Handbag; Some Explicit Polaroids* (London: Methuen Drama, 2001), p. x. Page references to the plays are to this edition, unless otherwise stated, and to its companion, *Plays Two*.
4. Jean-François Lyotard, *The Postmodern Condition: A Report on Knowledge* (Manchester: Manchester University Press, 1979), pp. xxiv, 37.
5. Michael Billington, 'Events Following', *Guardian*, 27 February 1976.
6. Dominic Dromgoole, *The Full Room: An A–Z of Contemporary Playwriting* (London: Methuen Drama, 2002), p. 237
7. Clare Wallace, *Suspect Cultures: Narrative, Identity and Citation in 1990s New Drama* (Prague: Litteraria Pragensia, 2006), p. 129; Vera Gottlieb, 'Lukewarm Britannia', in Vera Gottlieb and Colin Chambers (eds), *Theatre in a Cool Climate* (Oxford: Amber Lane, 1999), pp. 210–12.
8. See Peter Ansorge, *From Liverpool to Los Angeles: On Writing for Theatre, Film and Television* (London: Faber, 1997); Wallace, op. cit., pp. 85–130; Gottlieb, 'Lukewarm Britannia', op. cit., and Vera Gottlieb 'Theatre Today: the "New Realism"', *Contemporary Theatre Review*, Vol. 13, No. 1 (2003), pp. 5–14.
9. Christopher Shinn, 'Introduction', *Plays One: Other People; The Coming World; Where Do We Live: Dying City* (London: Methuen Drama, 2007), p. vii.
10. Rebellato, op. cit., p. x.
11. Sierz, *In-Yer-Face Theatre*, pp. 125–6.
12. Mark Ravenhill, *Shopping and Fucking; Faust is Dead; Handbag; Some Explicit Polaroids* (1996 edition) (London: Methuen Drama, 2001), pp. 73–4.
13. Dominic Shellard, *British Theatre Since the War* (New Haven: Yale University Press, 1999), p. 198; Philip Roberts and Max Stafford-Clark, *Taking Stock: The Theatre of Max Stafford-Clark* (London: Nick Hern Books, 2007), p. 197.
14. Rebellato, op. cit., p. x.
15. Ruth Little and Emily McLaughlin, *The Royal Court Theatre Inside Out* (London: Oberon, 2007), p. 352.
16. Ibid., p. 354.
17. Ibid., p. 353.
18. Ibid., p. 355.
19. Rebellato, op. cit., p. xii.
20. Little and McLaughlin, op. cit., p. 355; David Edgar, *State of Play: Playwrights on Playwriting* (London: Faber, 1999), p. 29.
21. Edward Bond, letter to Graham Saunders, 23 February 2001.
22. Sierz, *In-Yer-Face Theatre*, p. 125.

23. Ibid., p. 151.
24. Nicholas de Jongh, *Not in Front of the Audience: Homosexuality on Stage* (London: Routledge, 1992), p. 2.
25. Dan Rebellato, op. cit., pp. xii–xiii.
26. Mireia Aragay et al., *British Theatre of the Nineties: Interviews with Directors, Playwrights, Critics and Academics* (Basingstoke: Palgrave Macmillan, 2007), p. 95.
27. Wallace, *Suspect Cultures*, p. 114.
28. Mark Ravenhill, 'A Tear in the Fabric: the James Bulger Murder and New Theatre Writing in the Nineties', *New Theatre Quarterly*, Vol. 20, No. 4 (2004), p. 312.
29. See David Ian Rabey, *English Drama Since 1940* (Harlow: Longman, 2003), p. 203; Aleks Sierz, 'In-Yer-Face Theatre: Mark Ravenhill in the 1990s', in Bernhard Reitz and Mark Berninger (eds), *British Drama of the 1990s* (Heidelberg: Universitätsverlag C Winter, 2002), pp. 123–35.
30. Roberts and Stafford-Clark, *Taking Stock*, p. 209. Sierz also observes that the play was the first 'that really connects to a deep and painfully emotional core' (*In-Yer-Face Theatre*, p. 147).
31. For a detailed account of the production history see Roberts and Stafford-Clark, *Taking Stock*, pp. 196–216.
32. Rebellato, op. cit., p. x.
33. Steve Blandford, *Film, Drama and the Break-Up of Britain* (Bristol: Intellect, 2007), p. 120.
34. See Mark Ravenhill, 'A Touch of Evil', *Guardian*, 22 March 2003.
35. Blandford, op. cit., p.119.
36. Ibid.
37. Rebellato, op. cit., p. ix.
38. Rabey, op. cit., p. 201.
39. Rebellato, op. cit., p. xii.
40. Aragay et al, op. cit., p. 102.
41. Jarrod Hayes, 'Queer Resistance to (Neo-)Colonialism in Algeria', in J. C. Hawley (ed.), *Post-colonial, Queer: Theoretical Intersections* (Albany, NY: State University of New York Press, 2001), p. 94.
42. Roberts and Stafford-Clark, op. cit., p. 216.
43. See Graham Saunders, *About Kane: The Playwright and the Work* (London: Faber, 2009), pp. 47–8; Ravenhill in 'Reputations: Edward Bond', *theatreVOICE* website, 11 March 2005, www.theatrevoice.com/listen_now/player/?audioID=283.
44. Aragay et al., op. cit., p. 99.
45. Aragay et al., op. cit., p. 101.
46. Aragay et al., op. cit., pp. 91–2.
47. Aragay et al., op. cit., p. 125.
48. Ibid.
49. Alan Sinfield, *Gay and After* (London: Serpent's Tail, 1998), p. 192.
50. Judith Butler, 'Critically Queer', in Shane Phelan (ed.), *Playing with Fire: Queer Politics, Queer Theories* (London: Routledge, 1997), p. 21.

51. Butler, op. cit., p, 23.
52. Michael Warner, 'Introduction: Fear of a Queer Planet', *Sexual Text*, No. 29 (1991), pp. 3–17.
53. Eve Kosofsky Sedgwick, 'Shame, Theatricality, and Queer Performativity: Henry James's *The Art of the Novel*', in David M. Halperin and Valerie Traub (eds), *Gay Shame* (Chicago, IL: University of Chicago Press, 2009), p. 61.
54. Sierz, 'In-Yer Face Theatre: Mark Ravenhill in the 1990s', p. 117.
55. Leo Bersani, 'Homos', in Donald Morton (ed.), *The Material Queer: a LesBiGay Cultural Studies Reader* (Boulder, CO: Westview Press, 1996), p. 227.
56. Aragay et al., op. cit., p. 125.
57. Shellard, op. cit., p. 197; Sarah Jane Dickenson, 'Fear of the Queer Citizen: From Canonisation to Curriculum in the Plays of Mark Ravenhill', in Dimple Godiwala (ed.), *Alternatives within the Mainstream II: Queer Theatres in Post-War Britain* (Cambridge: Cambridge Scholars Publishing, 2007), p. 124.
58. Kevin Elyot, *My Night with Reg* (London: Nick Hern, 1997), p. 5.
59. See Sierz, *In-Yer-Face Theatre*, p. 123.
60. Aragay et al., op. cit., p. 45.
61. Donald Morton, 'Changing the Terms: (Virtual) Desire and (Actual) Reality', in Morton (ed.), op. cit. (Boulder, CO: Westview Press, 1996), p. 14.
62. Wallace, op. cit., pp. 88, 93.
63. Jonathan Croall, *Inside the Molly House: The National Theatre at Work* (London: National Theatre Publications, 2001), p. 45.
64. Croall, op. cit., p. 71.
65. See Sierz, *In-Yer-Face Theatre*, p. 129; Peter Billingham, *At the Sharp End: Uncovering the Work of Five Leading Dramatists* (London: Methuen Drama, 2007), p. 126.
66. Patrice Pavis, 'Ravenhill and Durringer, the *Entente Cordiale* Misunderstood', trans. David Bradby, *Contemporary Theatre Review*, vol. 14, no. 2 (2004), p. 6.

3 Documents: Sarah Kane

1. A recording of this event is available (2010): www.rhul.ac.uk/dramaandtheatre/research/researchgroups/politicalcurrentsinrecentbritishtheatre/sarahkane.aspx
2. Bill Buford, *Among the Thugs* (London: Arrow, 1992).

3 Documents: Anthony Neilson

1. Anthony Neilson, 'Dramatic Moments', *Guardian*, 11 September 1996.
2. James Christopher, 'Inside Story', *Time Out*, 5–12 January 1994.
3. Al Senter, 'Curtain Call: On Anthony Neilson', *What's On in London*, 26 April 1995.

4. Sarah Hemming, 'Look Forward in Anger', *Financial Times*, 18 November 1995, reprinted in *Theatre Record*, Vol. XV, Issue 22 (1995), p. 1471.
5. Kate Stratton, 'Censor Sensibility', *Time Out*, 4–11 June 1997.
6. Anthony Neilson, 'Foreword', *The Wonderful World of Dissocia/Realism* (Methuen Drama, 2007).
7. Anthony Neilson, 'Don't be So Boring', *Guardian*, 21 March 2007.

3 Documents: Mark Ravenhill

1. A full transcript of 'A Tear in the Fabric' is published in *New Theatre Quarterly*, Vol. 20, No. 4 (November 2004), pp. 305–14. For a report on the Goldsmiths lecture see Aleks Sierz, 'Hearts of Darkness', *Financial Times Magazine*, 10 July 2004.
2. Mark Fyfe, *Asher: A Novel* (Marion Boyars, 1997).

Afterword

1. Sarah Kane, *Complete Plays: Blasted; Phaedra's Love; Cleansed; Crave; 4.48 Psychosis; Skin* (London: Methuen Drama, 2001), pp. 244–5.
2. Lyn Gardner, *Guardian*, 20 February 2008, *Theatre Record*, Vol. XXVIII, No. 4 (2008), p. 193.
3. Kane, *Complete Plays*, p. 103.
4. Hans-Thies Lehmann, *Postdramatic Theatre*, trans. Karen Jürs-Munby (London: Routledge, 2006), p. 18. This difference in practice surely casts doubt on the modish assimilation of Kane into the category of the postdramatic.
5. Graham Saunders, *About Kane: The Playwright and the Work* (London: Faber, 2009), p. 2; see also pp. 123–7.
6. 'Sarah Kane Special', theatreVOICE website, 8 November 2010, www.theatrevoice. com/listen_now/player/?audioID=923.
7. Simon Stephens, personal interview with Aleks Sierz, London, 11 June 2004.
8. Charles Spencer, *Daily Telegraph*, 4 March 2005; John Gross, *Sunday Telegraph*, 13 March 2005; Michael Billington, *Guardian*, 4 March 2005, *Theatre Record*, Vol. XXV, No. 5 (2005), pp. 279–81.
9. Anthony Neilson, 'Foreword', *The Wonderful World of Dissocia/Realism* (London: Methuen Drama, 2008), no page number.
10. David Lane, *Contemporary British Drama* (Edinburgh: Edinburgh University Press, 2010), p. 89.
11. Ibid., p. 90.

12. Richard Bean, 'Debate: New Writing (1/2)', theatreVOICE website, 28 May 2004, www.theatrevoice.com/listen_now/player/?audioID=169.

13. Peter Billingham, *At the Sharp End: Uncovering the Work of Five Leading Dramatists* (London: Methuen Drama, 2007), p. 134.

14. Mark Ravenhill, *Plays Two: Mother Clap's Molly House; Product; The Cut; Citizenship; pool (no water)* (London: Methuen Drama, 2008), p. 155.

15. Ibid., p. 199.

16. Mark Ravenhill, 'Confessions of a Panto-lover', *Guardian*, 28 November 2006.

17. Mark Ravenhill, 'Introduction', *Shoot/Get Treasure/Repeat* (London: Methuen, 2008), p. 5.

18. Alan Bennett, *The History Boys* (London: Faber, 2004), p. 74.

19. Michael Billington, 'A Little Blood Goes a Long Way', *Guardian*, 20 April 1994; Matthew Lloyd, 'The Cost of Cruelty', *Guardian*, 23 April 1994; Jenny Topper, 'Pushing the Barrier', *Guardian*, 23 April 1994.

SELECT BIBLIOGRAPHY

1. Books on the 1990s

Blandford, Steve, *Film, Drama and the Break-Up of Britain* (Bristol: Intellect, 2007). Wide-ranging study of the cultural politics of the second part of decade, the book looks at both theatre and film in the context of the election of a New Labour government in 1997, and subsequent devolution.

Garnett, Mark, *Anger to Apathy: The British Experience Since 1975* (London: Jonathan Cape, 2007). Contemporary political, economic and cultural history as seen through the eyes of a polemical historian who challenges received ideas about how Britain is a better place now than it was in the 1970s. Provocative chapter on the 1990s.

Marr, Andrew, *A History of Modern Britain* (London: Pan, 2008). BBC journalist offers a very readable account of Britain in the post-war era that is rich in detail, controversial opinion and anecdotes, with solid chapters about the governments of John Major and Tony Blair, plus reflections on the cultural history of the 1990s.

Marwick, Arthur, *British Society Since 1945* (London: Penguin, 2003). The most comprehensive social history of Britain in the post-war era, rich in detail, statistics and considered judgement, with comprehensive chapters on class, gender and race, plus fascinating information on national identity, social attitudes and cultural trends.

Wilson, A. N., *Our Times: The Age of Elizabeth II* (London: Arrow, 2009). An angry and opinionated look at British politics and culture during the reign of Elizabeth II, spanning the years between 1953 and 2009.

2. Key books on British theatre in the 1990s

The following books, most of them written in the immediate aftermath of the 1990s, focus in detail on British theatre of that decade and are very useful sources of first-hand information.

Ansorge, Peter, *From Liverpool to Los Angeles: On Writing for Theatre, Film and Television* (London: Faber, 1997).

Aragay, Mireia, Hildegard Klein, Enric Monforte and Pilar Zozaya (eds), *British Theatre of the 1990s: Interviews with Directors, Playwrights, Critics and Academics* (Basingstoke: Palgrave Macmillan, 2007).

Aston, Elaine, *Feminist Views on the English Stage: Women Playwrights, 1990–2000* (Cambridge: Cambridge University Press, 2003).

Bradwell, Mike, *The Reluctant Escapologist: Adventures in Alternative Theatre* (London: Nick Hern, 2010).

D'Monté, Rebecca, and Graham Saunders (eds), *Cool Britannia? British Political Drama in the 1990s* (Basingstoke: Palgrave Macmillan, 2008).

Dromgoole, Dominic, *The Full Room: An A–Z of Contemporary Playwriting*, 2nd edn (London: Methuen Drama, 2002).

Edgar, David (ed.), *State of Play: Playwrights on Playwriting* (London: Faber, 1999).

Gottlieb, Vera and Colin Chambers (eds), *Theatre in a Cool Climate* (Oxford: Amber Lane, 1999).

Knapp, Annelie, Erwin Otto, Gerd Stratmann and Merle Tönnies (eds), British Drama of the 1990s (Heidelberg: Universitätsverlag C Winter, 2002).

Little, Ruth, and Emily McLaughlin, *The Royal Court Theatre Inside Out* (London: Oberon, 2007).

Nightingale, Benedict, *The Future of Theatre* (London: Phoenix, 1998).

Sierz, Aleks, *In-Yer-Face Theatre: British Drama Today* (London: Faber, 2001).

Stephenson, Heidi, and Natasha Langridge, *Rage and Reason: Women Playwrights on Playwriting* (London: Methuen Drama, 1997).

Wallace, Clare, *Suspect Cultures: Narrative, Identity and Citation in 1990s New Drama* (Prague: Litteraria Pragensia, 2006).

Wolf, Matt, *Sam Mendes at the Donmar: Stepping into Freedom* (London: Nick Hern, 2002).

3. Recommended books on post-war British theatre

The following books offer broader coverage but include insightful material pertaining to 1990s theatre.

Aston, Elaine, and Janelle Reinelt (eds), *The Cambridge Companion to Modern British Women Playwrights* (Cambridge: Cambridge University Press, 2000).

Billington, Michael, *State of the Nation: British Theatre Since 1945* (London: Faber, 2007).

Boon, Richard, *About Hare: The Playwright and the Work* (London: Faber, 2003).

Brown, Mark (ed.), *Howard Barker Interviews 1980–2010: Conversations in Catastrophe* (London: Oberon, 2011).

Bull, John, *Stage Right: Crisis and Recovery in British Contemporary Mainstream Theatre* (Basingstoke: Macmillan, 1994).

Chambers, Colin (ed.), *The Continuum Companion to Twentieth Century Theatre* (London: Continuum, 2002).

——, *Inside the Royal Shakespeare Company: Creativity and the Institution* (London: Routledge, 2004).

——, *Black and Asian Theatre in Britain: A History* (London: Routledge, 2011).

Davis, Geoffrey V., and Anne Fuchs (eds), *Staging New Britain: Aspects of Black and South Asian British Theatre Practice* (Brussels: Presses Interuniversitaires Européennes, 2006).

Devine, Harriet (ed.), *Looking Back: Playwrights at the Royal Court 1956–2006* (London: Faber & Faber, 2006).

Dorney, Kate, *The Changing Language of Modern British Drama 1945–2005* (Basingstoke: Palgrave Macmillan, 2009).

Dorney, Kate, and Ros Merkin (eds), *The Glory of the Garden: English Regional Theatre and the Arts Council 1984–2009* (Newcastle upon Tyne: Cambridge Scholars, 2010).

Eyre, Richard, and Nicholas Wright, *Changing Stages: A View of British Theatre in the Twentieth Century* (London: Bloomsbury, 2000).

Graham, Scott, and Steven Hoggett, *The Frantic Assembly Book of Devising Theatre* (Abingdon: Routledge, 2009).

Griffin, Gabriele, *Contemporary Black and Asian Women Playwrights in Britain* (Cambridge: Cambridge University Press, 2003).

Hewison, Robert, *Culture and Consensus: England, Art and Politics Since 1940*, rev. edn (London: Methuen, 1997).

Howe Kritzer, Amelia, *Political Theatre in Post-Thatcher Britain: New Writing 1995–2005* (Basingstoke: Palgrave Macmillan, 2008).

Innes, Christopher, *Modern British Drama: The Twentieth Century* (Cambridge: Cambridge University Press, 2002).

Kershaw, Baz (ed.), *The Cambridge History of British Theatre*, Volume 3, *Since 1895* (Cambridge: Cambridge University Press, 2004), pp. 412–25.

Kustow, Michael, *theatre@risk* (London: Methuen, 2000).

Lane, David, *Contemporary British Drama* (Edinburgh: Edinburgh University Press, 2010).

Lonergan, Patrick, *Theatre and Globalization: Irish Drama in the Celtic Tiger Era* (Basingstoke: Palgrave Macmillan, 2009).

Middeke, Martin, Peter Paul Schnierer and Aleks Sierz (eds), *The Methuen Drama Guide to Contemporary British Playwrights* (London: Methuen Drama, 2011).

Rabey, David Ian, *English Drama Since 1940* (Harlow: Longman, 2003).

Rebellato, Dan, *Theatre & Globalization* (Basingstoke: Palgrave Macmillan, 2009).

Roberts, Philip, *The Royal Court Theatre and the Modern Stage* (Cambridge: Cambridge University Press, 1999).

Roberts, Philip and Max Stafford-Clark, *Taking Stock: The Theatre of Max Stafford-Clark* (London: Nick Hern Books, 2007).

Shellard, Dominic, *British Theatre Since the War* (New Haven, CT: Yale University Press, 1999).

Sierz, Aleks, *The Theatre of Martin Crimp* (London: Methuen Drama, 2006).

Sinfield, Alan, *Out on Stage: Lesbian and Gay Theatre in the Twentieth Century* (New Haven, CT and London: Yale University Press, 1999).

Stark, Kathleen, *'I Believe in the Power of Theatre': British Women's Drama of the 1980s and 1990s* (Trier: Wissenschafter Verlag Trier, 2005).

Wandor, Michelene, *Post-War British Drama: Looking Back in Gender* (London: Routledge, 2001).

Wyllie, Andrew, *Sex on Stage: Gender and Sexuality in Post-War British Theatre* (Bristol: Intellect, 2009).

4. The playwrights

For each of the four playwrights included in this volume, a key critical book is recommended along with selected further reading. The editions of plays are those cited in Chapter 2.

Philip Ridley

Plays

Ridley, Philip, *Plays One: The Pitchfork Disney; The Fastest Clock in the Universe; Ghost from a Perfect Place* (London: Faber, 2002).

Key book

Sierz, Aleks, *In-Yer-Face Theatre: British Drama Today* (London: Faber, 2001).

Recommended books

Middeke, Martin, Peter Paul Schnierer and Aleks Sierz (eds), *The Methuen Drama Guide to Contemporary British Playwrights* (London: Methuen Drama, 2011).

Sierz, Aleks, *Rewriting the Nation: British Theatre Today* (London: Methuen Drama, 2011).

Sarah Kane

Plays

Kane, Sarah, *Complete Plays: Blasted; Phaedra's Love; Cleansed; Crave; 4.48 Psychosis; Skin* (London: Methuen Drama, 2001).

Key book

Saunders, Graham, *About Kane: The Playwright and the Work* (London: Faber, 2009).

Recommended books

Aston, Elaine, *Feminist Views on the English Stage: Women Playwrights, 1990–2000* (Cambridge: Cambridge University Press, 2003).

De Vos, Laurens, and Graham Saunders (eds), *Sarah Kane in Context* (Manchester: Manchester University Press, 2010).

Howe Kritzer, Amelia, *Political Theatre in Post-Thatcher Britain: New Writing 1995–2005* (Basingstoke: Palgrave Macmillan, 2008).

Kane, Sarah, with 'Commentary' by Ken Urban, *Blasted* (London: Methuen Drama Student Edition, 2011).

Luckhurst, Mary (ed.), *A Companion to Modern British and Irish Drama* (Oxford: Blackwell, 2006).

Middeke, Martin, Peter Paul Schnierer and Aleks Sierz (eds), *The Methuen Drama Guide to Contemporary British Playwrights* (London: Methuen Drama, 2011).

Saunders, Graham, *'Love Me or Kill Me': Sarah Kane and the Theatre of Extremes* (Manchester: Manchester University Press, 2002).

Sierz, Aleks, *In-Yer-Face Theatre: British Drama Today* (London: Faber, 2001).

Wallace, Clare, *Suspect Cultures: Narrative, Identity and Citation in 1990s New Drama* (Prague: Litteraria Pragensia, 2006).

Anthony Neilson

Plays

Neilson, Anthony, *Plays One: Normal; Penetrator; Year of the Family; The Night Before Christmas; The Censor* (London: Methuen Drama, 1998).

———, *Plays Two: Edward Gant's Amazing Feats of Loneliness!; The Lying Kind; The Wonderful World of Dissocia; Realism* (London: Methuen Drama, 2008).

Key book

Sierz, Aleks, *In-Yer-Face Theatre: British Drama Today* (London: Faber, 2001).

Recommended books

Middeke, Martin, Peter Paul Schnierer and Aleks Sierz (eds), *The Methuen Drama Guide to Contemporary British Playwrights* (London: Methuen Drama, 2011).

Sierz, Aleks, *Rewriting the Nation: British Theatre Today* (London: Methuen Drama, 2011).

Mark Ravenhill

Plays

Ravenhill, Mark, *Plays One: Shopping and Fucking; Faust Is Dead; Handbag; Some Explicit Polaroids* (London: Methuen Drama, 2001).

—, *Plays Two: Mother Clap's Molly House; Product; The Cut; Citizenship; pool (no water)* (London: Methuen Drama, 2008).

Key book

Sierz, Aleks, *In-Yer-Face Theatre: British Drama Today* (London: Faber, 2001).

Recommended books

Aragay, Mireia, Hildegard Klein, Enric Monforte and Pilar Zozaya (eds), *British Theatre of the 1990s: Interviews with Directors, Playwrights, Critics and Academics* (Basingstoke: Palgrave Macmillan, 2007).

Billingham, Peter, *At the Sharp End: Uncovering the Work of Five Leading Dramatists* (London: Methuen Drama, 2007).

Croall, Jonathan, *Inside the Molly House: The National Theatre at Work* (London: National Theatre Publications, 2001).

Howe Kritzer, Amelia, *Political Theatre in Post-Thatcher Britain: New Writing 1995–2005* (Basingstoke: Palgrave Macmillan, 2008).

Middeke, Martin, Peter Paul Schnierer and Aleks Sierz (eds), *The Methuen Drama Guide to Contemporary British Playwrights* (London: Methuen Drama, 2011).

Ravenhill, Mark, with 'Commentary' by Dan Rebellato, *Shopping and Fucking* (Methuen Drama Student Edition, 2005).

Sierz, Aleks, *Rewriting the Nation: British Theatre Today* (London: Methuen Drama, 2011).

Wallace, Clare, *Suspect Cultures: Narrative, Identity and Citation in 1990s New Drama* (Prague: Litteraria Pragensia, 2006).

5. Web resources

TheatreVoice: www.theatrevoice.com/
A terrific resource for audio content relating to British theatre, featuring interviews with playwrights and other practitioners, round-table discussions and reviews of contemporary productions. It includes contributions from, and interviews with, a number of key theatre people featured in this book. The site was established in 2003 by founding editor Dominic Cavendish and is now managed by the Department of Theatre and Performance at the V&A and Rose Bruford College.

In-Yer-Face Theatre: www.inyerface-theatre.com
Although originally set up in 2000 by Aleks Sierz to offer resources to support his book *In-Yer-Face Theatre*, this website was subsequently expanded to cover all of new writing for the British theatre 1990–2010. The archive section includes several key articles and there is an abundance of useful information.

INDEX

Page references in bold type denote main references to topics.

NOTES ON CONTRIBUTORS

Catherine Rees is Lecturer in Drama at Loughborough University. Her research interests are in the area of contemporary British and Irish theatre, and she has published several articles on playwrights Martin McDonagh, Harold Pinter and Marie Jones.

Trish Reid is Deputy Head of the School of Performance and Screen Studies at Kingston University. She has published on Neilson, the National Theatre of Scotland and on post-devolutionary Scottish playwriting. She is currently completing the book *Theatre & Scotland* (Palgrave, forthcoming).

Graham Saunders is Reader in Theatre Studies at the University of Reading. He is author of *Love Me or Kill Me: Sarah Kane and the Theatre of Extremes* (Manchester University Press, 2002), *About Kane: The Playwright and the Work* (Faber, 2009) and *Patrick Marber's Closer* (Continuum, 2008), and co-editor of *Cool Britannia: Political Theatre in the 1990s* (Palgrave, 2008) and *Sarah Kane in Context* (Manchester University Press, 2010).